THE STATE OF FAMILIES, 3

LOSING DIRECTION

Families,
Human Resource Development,
and Economic Performance

THE STATE OF FAMILIES, 3

LOSING DIRECTION

Families,
Human Resource Development,
and Economic Performance

RAY MARSHALL

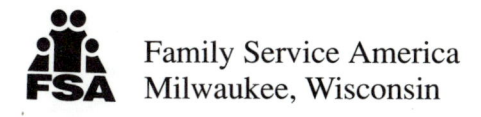

Family Service America
Milwaukee, Wisconsin

Copyright © 1991
Family Service America
11700 West Lake Park Drive
Milwaukee, Wisconsin 53224

ISBN 0-87304-249-2

All rights reserved. None of the content of this publication may be reproduced, stored in a retrieval system, or transmitted in any form or by any means (electronic, mechanical, photocopying, recording, or otherwise) without the prior written permission of the publisher.

Library of Congress Cataloging-in-Publication Data
(Revised for vol. 3)

The State of families.
    Includes bibliographical references.
    Contents: — v. 2. Work and family — v. 3. Losing direction / Ray Marshall.
    1. Work and family—United States. 2. United States—Social conditions—1980–
I. Marshall, Ray. II. Family Service America.
HD4904.25.S83 1987   306.8'5'0973   87-24374
ISBN 0-87304-226-3 (pbk. : v. 2)

Contents

Preface		vii
Acknowledgments		ix
1	Introduction	1
2	The Economic and Demographic Context	5
3	Changes in Family Structure	25
4	Family Employment, Income, and Wealth: Growing Inequalities	33
5	International Perspectives	53
6	Family Policy Issues	63
7	Summary and Recommendations	103
A	Appendix A: Tables 2.1 to 5.6	113
B	Appendix B: Related Family Service America Research Projects	145

Preface

This is the third in a series on the state of families. Since 1984, Family Service America (FSA) has commissioned these publications in order to illustrate with hard data the conditions facing American families. Initially, in the first volume, we examined the general trends of American family life and expectations for the future. The second report, *The State of Families, 2*, examined more closely the relationship between work and family, because we were observing problems that evolved from the growing immersion of families in work outside the home.

During the past several years, member agencies of FSA have been reporting an increase in economic factors intensifying or causing family problems. In particular, family service agencies have been struck by the economic disadvantages faced by single parents. This led to participation in a research project, the Adolescent Family Project, which studied the plight of young, pregnant, single women.

Another FSA study, American Families in Trouble, surveyed a broad cross section of the families using family service agencies. This, the largest survey of its kind, showed that these families were losing ground in the American economy. (For a summary of this study and the Adolescent Family Project, see Appendix B.) In addition, Family Service America's Committee on Government Relations, a board subcommittee, recommended that FSA attend to the plight of working families who remain in poverty or economically marginal circumstances, despite the employment of one or more family members.

All of these activities suggested that we needed to develop an overview of how families relate to the economy and particularly to consider why America is home to a growing number of disadvantaged and economically vulnerable families. We felt that our *The State of Families* series provided the appropriate vehicle with which to do this.

We found an extraordinary author for our current volume. Dr. Ray Marshall is both a distinguished scholar in economics and an influential leader in social policy. Currently he holds the Audre and Bernard Rapoport Centennial Chair in Economics and Public Affairs at the University of Texas at Austin. Previously he was Secretary of Labor of the United States between 1977 and 1981. He holds many distinguished offices in the worlds of foundations, technology, industry, research, and education. He is a prolific writer in many of these fields. Best of all, he is a humanitarian who cares deeply about how human beings fare in the larger society and the possibilities for the improvement of quality of life.

Dr. Marshall's observations reflect what we see as a service organization, that growing numbers of families find themselves at a serious disadvantage in the American economy. Dr. Marshall, however, projects the problem on a much wider screen, the growth of a world economy. He carefully links family life with economic facts. He sees the family as both the victim of problems within the economy and a potential resource with which to improve it. The reader of this publication will share Dr. Marshall's vision of a world-class American economy and how families can both benefit from it and contribute to it.

The conclusions reached herein detail what is new in American family life and how that has produced more families at risk. Dr. Marshall's recommendations are particularly directed to these families as well as to the need to prepare children for an education that helps them to compete in a new world economy. Although his policy recommendations are not officially those of Family Service America, we recommend their consideration as new family policies are forged under new world conditions.

Geneva B. Johnson
President and CEO
Family Service America

Acknowledgments

The material for this publication was developed over a number of years and owes much to many people. My earliest thinking about the importance of family naturally derives from my own childhood experience, in which my parents, especially my mother, taught me the importance of values and thinking skills as the surest guides to personal conduct. Later, as a child in the Mississippi Baptist Orphanage, I learned that caring institutions and individuals could compensate for the loss of natural parents. My wife, Pat, and our five children also have helped me to understand the importance of close family relations for the development of both children and parents.

As a labor economist and Secretary of Labor, I learned how important human resource development is for national and personal economic welfare and how important families are for human resource development. These experiences also convinced me that the American economic policymaking process is deficient because of its neglect and even denigration of family and human resource development matters. All too often these issues are considered to be "social" and therefore "soft" areas not appropriate for economic policy.

My understanding of these matters further deepened as a result of some of my activities during the 1980s, especially my work as a member of the steering committee of the Economic Policy Council of the United Nations Association of the U.S.A. (EPC-UNA) and as a trustee of the Carnegie Corporation of New York. The EPC-UNA Family Policy Panel, chaired by Alice Ilchman and John Sweeney, with staff assistance and direction from Sylvia Hewlett, synthesized a wealth of information about families and the economy. The work of the Family Policy Panel demonstrated that too many male business and economic specialists considered family subjects to be appropriate considerations mainly for women, despite the demonstrated importance of these matters for economic performance.

I have, in addition, benefited greatly from my association with the staff and trustees of the Carnegie Corporation, which has a deep and abiding interest in the development of and prevention of damage to children and families. David Hamburg, Carnegie's president, and Vivien Stewart, program officer in charge of matters related to education, families, and youth, have taught me a lot about the subjects covered in this book. I am especially grateful to David and Vivien for reading and commenting on an earlier draft of this manuscript. David Hamburg and his wife, Betty, have, in addition, taught me much about early childhood and adolescent development. I am also indebted to Ruby Takanishi, director of the Carnegie Council on Adolescent Development, for collecting and synthesizing material that helped me understand the serious problems faced by adolescents and their families in today's rapidly changing world. My fellow Carnegie trustee Jim Comer helped me understand the importance of parental involvement for school restructuring. Marc Tucker, Lewis Branscomb, Jim Hunt, Alden Dunham, and others associated with the Carnegie Task Force on Education and the Economy, as well as Ira Magaziner, Bill Brock, and the members of the Commission on the Skills of the American Workforce, helped me understand the relationships among economic performance, school restructuring, human resource development, and families.

In addition, Shirley McBay, Bernie Charles, and the members of the Action Council on Minority Education provided valuable information and ideas on the unique problems of disadvantaged minority families. My former student, Ernie Cortes, head of the Texas Industrial Areas Foundation (TIAF), helped me understand how important "mediating institutions" are for the development of families with little economic or political power; Ernie and his TIAF associates also demonstrated that hard work and effective organizing can empower these parents and strengthen families, community organizations, and democratic processes. Larry Mishel, at the Economic Policy Institute, has been an extremely valuable source of good data and analysis on the economy in general, but especially on the conditions of American workers and their families.

Several colleagues at the University of Texas helped me with this volume. I am grateful to David Warner and David Austin for comments on an early draft. Bob Glover, Luis Plascencia, Bob Nielsen, and the students in several policy research projects assisted me with material and discussions of the importance of early childhood development, school-based services, and parental education. I am grateful to my research assistant, Jon Wainwright, for invaluable bibliographical and statistical help. I owe a great debt to Cheryl McVay, not only for her invaluable help with manuscripts and scheduling, but also for her efficient work, helpful comments, and encouragement in the development of this manuscript. Finally, I owe Family Service America many thanks for providing me the opportunity to pull these materials and experiences together in this book.

It goes without saying, of course, that despite much help and many valuable suggestions, I alone am responsible for the judgments and recommendations in this monograph. I hope they will contribute to stronger families and therefore to a stronger America.

Ray Marshall
Austin, Texas
April 13, 1991

1

Introduction

The economy and the well-being of families are inextricably linked in a close, symbiotic relationship. Family financial security is derived mainly from paid work, and most adults organize their lives around their workday and identify themselves at least in part by the work they do. The earnings and working conditions of family members affect their economic and emotional welfare as well as their family relationships. Family relationships, in turn, strongly influence human resource development, which has become the most important factor in determining personal incomes and national economic performance.

The Family as a Learning System

It is vitally important for economic and social policymakers to recognize that the quality of a nation's human resources depends significantly on what happens to its families. The family is a major institution that preserves the physical and cultural linkages among people and their past, present, and future. It is also the institution within which most basic human development takes place. Families are critically important learning systems, a fact that we are increasingly coming to realize. The intensification of international business competition during the 1970s and 1980s made it very clear that a nation's economic strength depends heavily on the quality of learning within the family as well as in the schools. Mounting empirical evidence suggests that the nature of the relationship between parents and children from infancy on can have lasting effects on the children's cognitive, social, physical, and emotional development. Furthermore, children acquire the values that guide their personal conduct from their parents and extended family, peers, and community institutions.

The family as a learning system has been influenced significantly by the nature of parents' work. When the family was the main economic producing unit, as it was in preindustrial times, children could learn about work by observing their parents and actively participating in work themselves. Participation not only helped children learn but affected their emotional development as well, because they learned early on to enjoy the satisfaction and sense of personal accomplishment that come from contributing to the family's welfare. They also learned firsthand about the extent to which their parents sacrificed to care for them.

Changes in 20th-Century Family Life

The changes that have taken place in families during this century, especially since World War II, have aroused considerable concern among social policy analysts. Family relationships have been altered, and the kinds of values that are formed and types of nurturing and learning that occur within the family have changed. The traditional family of the post-World War II generation, in which the father's earnings were the sole source of income and the mother worked mainly at home, has become a much smaller proportion of all families today. Most mothers of small children now work at jobs outside the home. Not only has work for pay become much more important in the lives of women, but the increased employment of mothers has interacted with developments in technology and the economy in order to produce some very important changes in living arrangements for men, women, and children.

American Family Dilemmas

The family, like the surrounding economy and society, is much less stable than it was earlier in this century. Children no longer learn about their parents' work by firsthand observation and experience and no longer gain a sense of personal satisfaction from contributing to the family's material welfare. Parents also spend much less time with fewer children, and a greater number of fathers than ever before abandon or never care for their children. At the same time, however, the increased earnings of women have made it possible to improve the material welfare of some families and for parents to give higher priority to the development of their children if they wish to do so.

More children are nevertheless growing up in single-parent and unstable families. Single-parent families, especially those headed by women, are less likely to have the necessary physical and emotional resources to nurture their children. With some remarkable exceptions, many families are losing their effectiveness as positive learning systems at the very time that national and personal economic performance depend more heavily on higher-order thinking skills. Children from disadvantaged families are likely to start school with inadequate preparation to perform at grade level. And early disadvantages are likely to be cumulative, causing children to fall farther and farther behind the longer they stay in school. Many will drop out, greatly increasing the risks of debilitating activities that will shorten their lives and reduce their developmental chances. These trends imply a growing polarization between those families that are good development systems and those that are not.

These problems do not pertain only to families and individuals, however. In an increasingly interdependent and technologically sophisticated world, people will either be economic assets or liabilities. Healthy, educated, motivated people are virtually unlimited assets, but people without these characteristics are likely to become serious economic liabilities. At the same time, the growing polarization of family incomes and life experiences has serious implications for the nation's political, social, and economic health. Under modern conditions, inequalities in wealth and income make it very difficult for countries to achieve the internal unity needed to solve their problems. As the experience of the United States and various developing countries demonstrated during the 1980s, governments of countries that have

---

Many families are losing their effectiveness as positive learning systems at the very time that national and personal economic performance depend more heavily on higher-order thinking skills.

In a technologically sophisticated world, people will either be economic assets or liabilities. Healthy, educated, motivated people are virtually unlimited assets, but people without these characteristics are likely to be serious economic liabilities.

citizens with widely unequal distributions of income have trouble taxing high-income groups and must borrow to pay their bills. Large external debts then create further economic and social problems.

These interrelated changes in families and the economy have reduced the effectiveness of the principles that served both institutions very well during America's economic "golden era" between 1945 and 1970. Our public-policy challenge, therefore, is to develop ways to support families so they can function effectively in a more dynamic, globally interrelated, knowledge-intensive world.

From an economic perspective, the symbiotic relationships between families and the economy require that businesses, schools, labor organizations, religious institutions, community organizations, and governments all develop policies that will help families with diverse needs. The well-being of nations and individuals depends on how social institutions compensate for some of the child-care, learning, and other developmental services formerly performed by the family, even though it is highly unlikely that any of these social institutions can ever substitute very effectively for families.

Because of the changes that have occurred in families, the principles and values that guided past generations are less useful to the more fluid and diverse families of the 1990s and beyond. Family health and national welfare, therefore, depend on the ability of families to develop new principles to guide them in a more dangerous and uncertain world.

Similarly, economic and social changes also have reduced the effectiveness of the national policies that served past generations of Americans so well. New public policies must be formulated that reflect the requirements of a fundamentally different economic and social environment. It is the basic thesis of this monograph that the dependence of economic success upon human resources demands that we develop more comprehensive economic and social policies that will support the role of families.

My main objective is to clarify the symbiotic relationships between families and the economy in order to provide the factual and analytical bases for public and private family policies. Economic and social policies can be improved with a better understanding of the interrelationships between families and the economy. In order to achieve these objectives, this monograph outlines the economic, demographic, and labor-market contexts within which families function; examines changing family structures, especially those that have developed since World War II; considers family income and employment relationships in the United States; and compares the United States with other industrialized democratic countries. The last two sections analyze important issues brought about by changes in families and the economy and offer recommendations as to how our country might better support families.

Our public-policy challenge is to support families so they can function effectively in a more dynamic, globally interrelated, knowledge-intensive world.

2

The Economic and Demographic Context

The future of American families is not predetermined, but depends heavily on the choices made by families, employers, and especially public institutions. An important lesson that history has taught us in the United States and abroad is that family policy choices are closely related to, and have important implications for, other economic and social policies.

National economic performance depends significantly on the extent to which family policies are integrated with other policies. The need for high-performance production systems in a more competitive global economy causes families to be increasingly important to a nation's economic, political, and social health. At the same time, of course, a society's ability or willingness to support families depends not only on the economy's strength, but also on the extent to which family policies are compatible with general economic policies.

In order to help clarify the context within which family policy choices must be made, this chapter explores the following hypotheses:

1. Our basic economic and social policies are rooted in the mass production/ natural resource economy that made the United States the world's leading industrial nation during the first half of this century. These policies were reinforced by macroeconomic policies that were basically designed to sustain the mass-production system and make it more equitable.

2. Mass production and its supporting economic policies have become anachronisms because of changing technology and the globalization of economic activity. In a competitive global economy, economic viability requires greater attention to quality, productivity, and flexibility, all of which were a good deal less important to mass-production systems.

3. These changes require that companies or countries that wish to be high-income, world-class players adopt very different economic and human resource development policies.

4. The United States is losing its status as a high-performance country because its economic and human resource development systems and policies have been slow to adjust to this more competitive world. A failure to adapt implies economic decline, growing inequalities in wealth and income, and declining real wages.

The Changing Economy

Traditional family structures are deeply rooted in the economic policies and institutions that made the United States the world's strongest economy during the first half of this century. Besides our free institutions and a steady supply of highly motivated workers, the most important factors in America's economic success were abundant natural resources and the mass-production system, which made it possible to achieve relatively rapid improvements in productivity and total output through economies of scale and reinforcing developments among industries, whereby advances in one industry led to improvements in others. A high-quality work force resulted from the migration of highly motivated people from other countries and rural areas and a universal free public school system that produced a population with adequate levels of education to function well in the industrial economy.

The Mass-production System

The mass-production system organized work so that most thinking, planning, and decision making was done by managerial, professional, and technical elites. Line work was simplified so that it could be done by relatively unskilled workers. The assumption was that "one best way" existed to perform a task. It was management's responsibility to discover that method and impose it on the system through procedures that could be enforced by supervisors and inspectors. Management assumed that workers would loaf unless they were closely supervised. Therefore, work processes were standardized and ideas, skills, and knowledge were transferred to managers and machines. The monotonous and degrading working conditions that resulted were made more bearable by higher wages than could be earned on the farm or in the home countries of the immigrants who flocked to America's factories, mills, and mines during the early part of this century.

However, the system had some serious weaknesses, most of which were gradually worked out by the 1940s. A major problem for mass-production companies was controlling markets and prices in order to maximize profits and justify the large investments required for equipment and plants. These firms therefore avoided price competition and adjusted to change mainly by varying output and employment while holding prices relatively constant.

But once mass-production companies stabilized the prices of their products, they experienced cyclical instability because production (supply) tended to outrun demand at administered prices. In the democratic industrialized countries, this problem was fixed through so-called Keynesian monetary and fiscal policies, which manipulated government spending and interest rates to generate enough total demand to keep the system operating at relatively low levels of unemployment.

Welfare (or "income maintenance") and industrial relations policies reinforced price policies. Unions, collective bargaining, unemployment compensation, Social Security, and other family-support systems were justified as ways to sustain purchasing power and provide support for people who were not expected to work as well as to counteract the market system's natural tendency to produce inequities. During this period, it was assumed that almost all mass-production workers would be males. Women were heavily concentrated in service occupations, teaching, and health care. Originally, the welfare system was conceived mainly for the support of widows, orphans, the elderly, and the handicapped. Although many large companies were initially reluctant to accept such policies, by the time of the Great Depression of the 1930s, they could see the wisdom of providing purchasing power to people who could not work. Business support for the system grew when it became clear that these policies were not really going to challenge business control of the economy. The policies were merely intended to codify work-force practices, protect workers from some of the more arbitrary company practices, and provide income for people who were not able to work. The unemployment-compensation and welfare systems also helped companies maintain their work forces by providing income support during layoffs, thus, in effect, supplementing wages.

Policymakers in all industrialized democracies came to accept the theory that income supports not only sustained purchasing power and relieved human misery, but promoted economic efficiency as well. It was generally recognized that a function of public policy was to maximize the market-oriented mass-production system's obvious advantages by minimizing or compensating for its equally obvious weaknesses. Socioeconomic theorists, like the Webbs,[1] argued that removing labor from competition through collective bargaining, government regulations, and family-support systems increased efficiency by preventing companies from depressing labor standards, thus forcing them to compete by becoming more efficient. The Webbs reasoned that employers who paid less than the living wage were being subsidized either by workers and their families or by society. Such subsidies therefore generated inefficiencies and made it difficult for countries to develop their human resources. Income-support systems, by contrast, helped families preserve themselves and raise their children.

Both the mass-production system and its supporting policies were justified by the American economy's remarkable performance in World War II. After the war, the combination of economies of scale, abundant natural resources, strong global demand, and a backlog of technology ushered in the longest period of equitably shared prosperity in human history. In most democratic industrial countries, the system's enormous economic advantages made it possible to maintain a humane income-support system for those who, according to society, could not or should not work.

The American System Erodes

Toward the end of the 1960s, it gradually became clear that some of America's traditional economic policies and institutions were no longer working as well as they had in the past. Technological change and increased international competition rendered much of the traditional mass-production system and its supporting institutions much less effective. The conditions for economic viability were also dramatically altered. In a more competitive world dominated by knowledge-intensive technology, the key to economic success became human resources and a more effective organization of production systems, not natural resources and traditional economies of scale. Indeed, as the work of Theodore Schultz and other economists demonstrated, the process of substituting knowledge and skills for physical resources has been the main source of improved productivity at least since the 1920s.[2]

Technology not only contributed to the globalization of markets but also made the mass-production system and traditional economies of scale less important. Although assembly lines can be automated, automation is not the most efficient use of the new technology. Computerized technology allows many of the benefits of economies of scale to be achieved through flexible manufacturing systems, which have enormous advantages in a more dynamic and competitive global economy. The new technology provides economies of scope as well as scale because the same technology can be used to produce different products.

After World War II, the combination of economies of scale, abundant natural resources, strong global demand, and a backlog of technology ushered in the longest period of equitably shared prosperity in human history.

Toward the end of the 1960s, technological change and increased international competition rendered much of the traditional mass-production system and its supporting institutions much less effective.

Technology makes new organizations of production *possible*, but competition makes them *necessary*. A competitive, internationalized, information-oriented economy has very different requirements for national, organizational, and personal success than do largely national goods-producing systems. One of the more important economic developments in the past two decades, for public policy purposes, is that national governments have less control of their economies. It is no longer possible for a single country to maintain high wages and full employment through traditional combinations of monetary and fiscal policies, administered wages and prices, and fixed exchange rates. In the 1970s and '80s, internationalization weakened the link between domestic consumption, investment, and output that had formed the basic structure of the traditional Keynesian demand-management system. The weakening of these linkages became very clear when in the early 1980s tax cuts in the United States increased consumption but also greatly stimulated imports. The tax cuts thus produced much smaller increases in domestic investment than had earlier tax cuts in less globalized markets. The weakening of economic performance, symbolized by declining growth in productivity and total output, led to policy confusion in the United States and reduced support for programs to aid low-income people.

The High-Performance Workplace

Low Wages or Higher Quality and Productivity?

These new economic conditions do not just change the requirements for economic success—they fundamentally alter the necessary structures and policies. In the more competitive global information economy, success requires greater emphasis on factors that were much less important in traditional mass-production systems: quality, productivity, and flexibility. Because these new requirements apply to schools and social service organizations that serve families, they need to be understood by those concerned primarily with family policy. In other words, they apply to all organizations, not just businesses.

Quality, best defined in this context as meeting the needs of customers (or members, clients, students), becomes more important for two reasons. First, as the mass-production system matured and personal incomes rose, consumers became less satisfied with standardized products. Second, the more competitive environment of the 1990s is largely consumer driven. The mass-production system was more producer driven, especially after governments and large corporations "stabilized" prices. In the more competitive environment of the 1970s, administered prices became less tenable; flexible prices became essential to the viability of companies in global markets. Furthermore, the mass-production system depended heavily on controlling national markets; with internationalization, American companies have much less market control.

Productivity and flexibility are closely related to quality. The difference is that now productivity improvements are achieved through using all factors of production more efficiently, not, as in the mass-production system, mainly through economies of scale and reinforcing shifts of resources from less to more productive sectors. Indeed, in the 1970s and '80s, interindustry shifts lowered productivity growth because they were, on balance, away from more productive manufacturing activities to less productive services.

Flexibility enhances productivity by facilitating the shift of resources to more productive outputs and improves quality through the ability to respond quickly to diverse and changing consumer needs. Moreover, flexibility in the use of workers and technology improves productivity by reducing the waste of labor and physical capital.

Firms and economies can compete in more global, knowledge-intensive markets either by lowering wages or by becoming more productive. Since the early 1970s, American companies have been competing mainly through reducing wages and shifting production facilities to low-wage countries. This is one of the reasons real wages are lower in the United States in 1990 than they were in 1970, and why in 1989 American wages ranked about 10th among the major industrialized countries.[3]

Worker Participation and Learning Skills

How can production be organized in order to achieve quality, productivity, and flexibility? By restructuring production systems and developing and using leading-edge technologies. Productivity is improved by organizations that reduce waste of materials through better inventory control, promote the efficient use of labor, and develop more effective quality controls to prevent defects. High-performance systems have a high degree of employee involvement in what were once considered management functions in mass-production systems. Indeed, in more productive and flexible systems, the distinctions between managers and workers become blurred.

High-performance production systems encourage worker participation. Workers must have more knowledge and skill. And skilled, educated workers are less tolerant of monotonous, routine work and authoritarian management. In addition, quality, productivity, and flexibility are enhanced when production decisions are made as close to the point of production as possible. Mass-production managerial bureaucracies were designed to achieve quantity output, managerial control, and stability, not flexibility, quality, or productivity in the use of all factors of production. Mass-production systems were based on managerial information monopolies and worker controls; high-performance systems require that workers be free to make decisions. To accomplish this, information must be shared, not hoarded, because in high-performance systems machines do more of the routine, direct work and people do more indirect work. One of the most important skills required for indirect work is the ability to analyze the flood of data produced by information technology. Workers who can impose order on chaotic data can use information to add value to products, solve problems, and improve their company's productivity, quality, and technology.

Indirect work also is more likely to be group work, requiring more communication and interpersonal skills. Productivity, quality, and flexibility require close coordination among functional groupings that were formerly more discrete components of the production process (e.g., research and development, design, production, inspection, distribution, sales, services). In the mass-production system, relationships among these functional departments were more linear; in dynamic, customer-oriented production systems, the relations are more interactive.

In high-performance systems, workers must have the ability to learn. Learning is not only more important than it is in mass-production systems, it also is very different. The simplification of tasks and the standardization of technology and productivity in the mass-production system limited the amount of learning needed or achieved by workers. More learning is required in a dynamic, technology-intensive workplace and much of that learning must occur through the manipulation of abstract symbols. For line workers, mass-production systems stressed learning almost entirely by observation and doing.

High-performance systems have a high degree of employee involvement in what were once considered management functions. Indeed, in more productive and flexible systems, the distinctions between managers and workers become blurred.

More learning is required in a dynamic, technology-intensive workplace and much of that learning must occur through the manipulation of abstract symbols.

In more productive workplaces, learning is likely to be communal and cooperative. The mass-production system's adversarial relationships impede the sharing of information among workers, managers, and suppliers. A high-performance system, by contrast, encourages the sharing of information and cooperative efforts to achieve common objectives. Communal learning also becomes important in building the consensus needed to improve the performance of highly integrated production processes. High-performance workers are required not only to be self-managers but also to perform a greater array of tasks and adapt more readily to change. This requires a reduction of the mass-production system's detailed job classifications and work rules. Well-educated, well-trained, highly motivated workers are likely to be much more flexible and productive, especially in supportive systems that stress equity and internal cohesion. Indeed, humans are likely to be the most flexible components in a high-performance system.

Other features of high-performance workplaces also require greater worker participation. One feature is the need for constant improvements in technology—or what the Japanese call "giving wisdom to the machine." Technology is best defined as how things are done. The most important thing about technology is not machines or know-how, but the ideas, skills, and knowledge embodied in machines and structures. Technology becomes standardized when the rate at which ideas, skills, and knowledge can be transferred to a machine or structure becomes very small. Standardized technology requires fewer ideas and less skill and knowledge than leading-edge technology. High-performance organizations emphasize developing and using leading-edge technologies because standardized technologies can be moved and therefore are likely to be employed mainly by low-paid workers. In other words, it is unlikely that American workers earning $10.00 an hour can compete with equally skilled foreign workers earning $2.00 an hour if both are using the same technology. By contrast, leading-edge technology requires more highly skilled workers. Higher wages can be justified for these workers because the technology cannot be as readily exported to low-income, unskilled workers.

Some American companies have responded to these competitive pressures by attempting to combine high technology and low skills through automation. This effort has proved to be little, if any, more productive than the combination of standardized technology and low-skilled workers. The most productive systems have highly skilled workers who can develop and use leading-edge technology. And the shorter life cycle of products and technologies in the dynamic and competitive global economy makes continuing innovation and creativity absolutely essential. The more mobile technologies become, the more critical participation by highly skilled workers becomes to competitiveness in high-performance systems. In other words, high skills and leading-edge technology will give workers a competitive advantage over less skilled workers using either standardized or leading-edge technology.

Incentive Systems

Explicit or implicit incentives in any system are basic determinants of its outcomes. High-performance organizations stress positive incentive systems. Mass-production incentives tend to be negative—fear of discharge or punishment, for example. They also tend to be more individualistic and implicit. Process- and time-based compensation systems, which were commonly used by mass-production companies, tend to be unrelated to productivity or quality. They can even be perverse, as, for example, when workers fear they will lose their jobs if productivity improves. Similarly, incentives, especially for managers, that bear no relationship to objective performance or equity create disunity within the work group. During the 1980s, this was exemplified most conspicuously in the automotive industry. Managers in companies that were performing poorly increased their own salaries while asking workers to make wage and benefit concessions. Under these circumstances, it was difficult for management to convince the workers that "we are all in this together." Sometimes, although the expressed intent of incentives is to improve productivity, they actually foster stability and control or affect some component of the production process (e.g., reducing shipping costs or the cost of supplies) that has negative effects on the whole system. High-performance incentives, by contrast, are more likely to be communal, positive, explicit, based on measurable outcomes, and directly related to the enterprise's stated objectives.

It would be hard to overemphasize the importance of internal unity and positive incentives for high-performance, knowledge-intensive organizations. All parties must be willing to go "all out" to achieve common objectives. In traditional mass-production systems, workers are justifiably afraid to do this for fear that they will lose their jobs. For this reason, job security is one of the most important positive incentives a high-performance company can have. Similarly, the fragmentation of work within mass-production systems gives workers little incentive to control quality—quality is somebody else's responsibility. A high-performance system, by contrast, is customer driven and therefore makes quality control everybody's responsibility. Positive incentives are required, in addition, because the effective use of information technology tends to give workers greater discretion.[4] It is difficult to compel workers to think—they must be motivated and able to so do.

Human Resource Development: The Key to Economic Success

Firms, individuals, or countries can compete either by lowering wages or by improving productivity, quality, and flexibility. Competitive firms that wish to maintain and improve incomes must give high priority to participation systems and the recruitment and training of highly skilled workers. Clearly, the quality of human resources is the key to economic success.

How are we doing in this regard? Nobody knows, because we do not have good measures of labor-force quality. A reasonable hypothesis is that the top 25% to 30% of our work force is world class, because many of our colleges and universities are world class. Traditionally, we have also attracted many highly educated and skilled workers from other countries. Finally, some of our companies are world-class learning environments.

Unfortunately, for a number of reasons, we have very serious problems with the rest of our work force. Perhaps the most serious problem is that, almost alone among industrialized countries, the United States has no strategy to remain a high-wage country.[5] Very little has been done to develop the work skills of the non–college bound. Less than 10% of non–college-bound workers in America receive any formal training designed to prepare them for work. Every other major industrialized country has systems to facilitate the transition from school to work for those who are not going to college. In these countries, most non–college-bound youth enroll in apprenticeships or other technical training programs to prepare them for specific crafts or occupations. And because we have no overall wage strategy, we place no constraints on companies that pursue low-wage strategies. Other countries limit wage competition because they do not believe they can, or wish to, win wage-cutting contests with low-wage countries.

Internal unity and positive incentives are crucially important for high-performance, knowledge-intensive organizations. All parties must be willing to go "all out" to achieve common objectives.

Very little has been done to develop the work skills of the non–college bound. Every other major industrialized country has systems to facilitate the transition from school to work for those who are not going to college.

Our schools, like our national and corporate policies, are rooted in the national mass-production system. They turn out students who are literate but whose achievement, especially in math and science, is low.

A second major problem for the United States is that our schools, like our national and corporate policies, are rooted in the national mass-production system. They turn out students who are literate but whose achievement, especially in math and science, is low relative to that in other industrialized countries. Once again, the United States is almost alone among industrialized democracies in having no national standards for secondary school graduates.

Third, and most important, the absence of supportive family policies—another area where we are unique—creates serious human resource development problems. Families are our most basic human-development and learning institutions. But, as will be demonstrated in chapter 5, the United States does less than any other major industrial country to support children and their mothers. We consequently have a much larger proportion of children in poverty than does any other major industrialized country and we do less to support working mothers or to provide effective care for preschool children.

Demographic and Labor-Market Changes

Some powerful demographic and labor-market developments will affect families and other institutions, as well as our nation's ability to develop a competitive, high-income economy, in coming years. A nation's people are the fundamental determinant of its ability to maintain its international standing and quality of life. The United States has demographic strengths, weaknesses, and problems that need to be understood by those concerned with family policy and economic development.

Population

Although broad demographic trends are fairly easy to project during "normal" times, unpredictable events (like wars and epidemics) cause dramatic changes in total fertility rates.[6] Such shifts occurred, for example, between 1945 and 1965 in America, when high fertility rates produced the "baby boom," followed by the "baby bust" after 1965, when fertility rates fell from a peak of 3.7 births per woman to 1.8, which is well below the replacement rate of 2.1.[7] Neither the boom nor the bust was predicted by most demographers, though the bust was compatible with long-standing demographic trends.

The absence of supportive family policies creates serious social problems in the United States. Families are our most basic human-development and learning institutions. But the United States does less than any other major industrial country to support children and their mothers.

Given these developments, the prospect for the United States is for very slow population growth. In fact, this phenomenon is already occurring in other industrialized countries, where populations are aging because of low birth and death rates and restrictive immigration policies. However, both the size of the postwar baby-boom generation (some 77 million Americans are "boomers") and large inflows of immigrants will prevent American population growth from stagnating until well into the 21st century. Immigration will also accelerate the transformation of the ethnic composition of the American population. Furthermore, growing internationalization of world economies will cause developments in other countries (such as conflicts in Southeast Asia or Central America) to have important and often unpredictable effects on migration to the United States.

Viewed in a long-term global context, the world's population began to grow at a phenomenal rate approximately 200 years ago, when medical and technological developments associated with the Industrial Revolution reduced death rates while birth rates remained high. For thousands of years before the Industrial Revolution, high birth *and* death rates kept population growth low. Although population growth has generally stabilized in first-world countries, many developing nations are still at the population-explosion stage. Indeed, most developing countries, especially in Africa and Latin America, have not been able to prevent population explosions or the growth of working-age populations from creating strong pressures for migration to the developed countries, especially the United States.[8]

World population growth has slowed to 1.7% a year, down from 2% in the 1960s. Population growth in the United States is less than 1%; this rate is much slower than the world rate but is faster than that of some other industrial countries (e.g., Germany, Japan, and Denmark), which have older populations and less immigration. As a consequence, the American share of the world's population has shrunk from 6% after World War II to 4.6% in 1987.

Even though population growth in the United States has been faster than that of other industrial countries, the growth of the nation's work force is expected to decline to about 1% a year during the 1990s, after having reached a high of 2.9% during the 1970s because of immigration, the maturing of the baby boomers, and the accelerated labor-force participation of women. Labor-force growth slowed to 1.5% during the 1980s.

The aging of the United States population will be particularly pronounced after 2000, when the first of the baby boomers reach age 55. In 1985, 28.5 million Americans (or 12% of the population) were 65 years of age or older; the percentages in future years will be:

2000	13%
2010	14%
2020	17%
2030	21%

The aging of the American population represents a shift in the population structure from a pyramid with relatively few people in the higher-age groups on top, supported by a base of many younger persons below, to a "squaring," with many more older people and relatively fewer young ones.

Changing Racial and Ethnic Compositions of the Population and Work Force

Table 2.1 (page 115) presents details on the changes in the civilian labor force between 1976 and 1988 and shows projections to 2000 by age and race. Note that white men will constitute the slowest growing group—only 8.5% compared with 19.9% for white women. Blacks are projected to grow at a faster rate than are whites (24.6% versus 13.6%, respectively). Black men are expected to grow by 21.4%, whereas black women are projected to increase in the work force by 28%. Because Asians and Hispanics are heavily represented among immigrant groups and start from much smaller bases, they are projected to experience the fastest work-force growth. The entire work force is expected to grow by approximately 19.5 million between 1988 and 2000; of this, 14.2 million (73%) are expected to be white and 12.1 million (62%) are expected to be women. Thus, although minorities are expected to grow at a relatively rapid rate, most of the growth will be among whites and women.

Figure 2.1 presents another perspective on these changes. The statistics in Table 2.1 distribute Hispanics according to race. Hispanic is not a racial category: 93% of Hispanics are classified as white, 5% as black, and 2% Asian and others. If we compare Hispanics, blacks, and Asians and others with non-Hispanic whites, we get the distribution shown in Figure 2.1. Note that in contrast with Table 2.1, non-Hispanic whites will constitute less than half of the growth of the work force between 1989 and 2000. Between 1976 and 1988,

The prospect for the United States is for very slow population growth. However, the size of the postwar baby-boom generation and large inflows of immigrants will prevent American population growth from stagnating until well into the 21st century.

FIGURE 2.1

Percentage Distribution of the Civilian Labor Force by Race (top)
Percentage Distribution of the *Growth* in the Civilian Labor Force by Race (bottom)

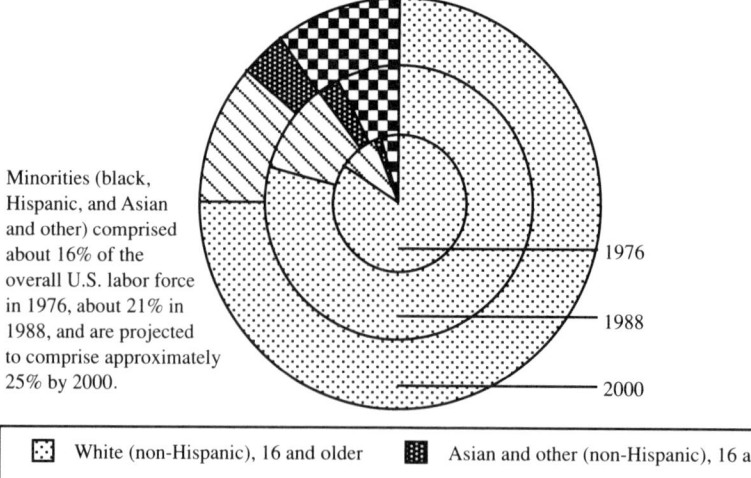

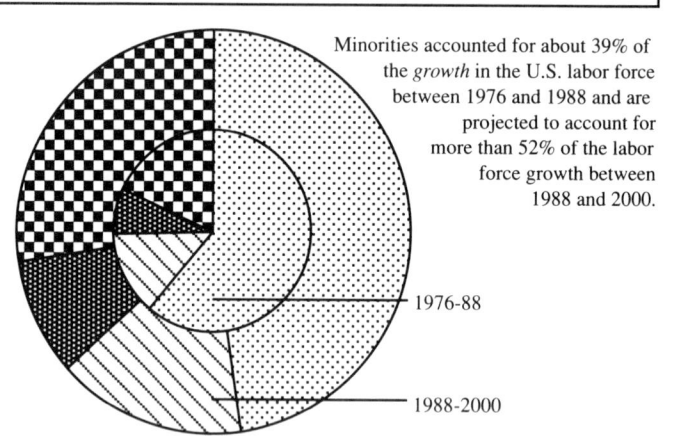

Minorities (black, Hispanic, and Asian and other) comprised about 16% of the overall U.S. labor force in 1976, about 21% in 1988, and are projected to comprise approximately 25% by 2000.

1976
1988
2000

| ⋮⋮ White (non-Hispanic), 16 and older | ▦ Asian and other (non-Hispanic), 16 and older |
| ⧅ Black (non-Hispanic), 16 and older | ▪ Hispanic, 16 and older |

Minorities accounted for about 39% of the *growth* in the U.S. labor force between 1976 and 1988 and are projected to account for more than 52% of the labor force growth between 1988 and 2000.

1976-88
1988-2000

Source: Howard N. Fullerton, Jr., "New Labor Force Projections, Spanning 1988–2000," *Monthly Labor Review* 112 (November 1989), p. 8.

Note: "Hispanic persons" is not a racial category. In the 1980 decennial census, however, persons of Hispanic origin identified themselves by race as follows: white, 93%; black, 5%; Asian and other, 2%. These proportions are applied to the data in Table 2.1 and the results are reflected in the above diagrams. See also Bureau of the Census, Current Population Reports, Series P-25, No. 1045 (Washington, DC: United States Government Printing Office, 1983).

---

minorities increased from 16% of the work force to 21%. They are expected to make up 25% of the work force in the year 2000. Stated another way, minorities represented 39% of the growth in the labor force between 1976 and 1982, but are expected to account for 52% of the growth between 1982 and 2000.

Table 2.2 (page 116) presents the changing composition of the U.S. population by age, racial background, and Hispanic origin in 1976 and 1988, with projections to 2000. As a consequence of the aging of the baby-boom cohort and the low fertility rates after 1965, the population between the ages of 25 and 54 grew relatively rapidly between 1976 and 1988. Although the rate of growth in the total population older than 16 years of age will slow between 1988 and 2000, the 35-to-54 age group is expected to grow faster than any other category. And, generally, older groups will grow faster than will those younger than 24. Note also, however, that minorities are expected to grow much faster than whites between 1988 and 2000.

The effect of these changes on the age, sexual, racial, and Hispanic-origin composition of the labor force is shown in Table 2.3 (page 117). Men's proportion of the work force will decline from 55% in 1988 to 52.7% in 2000; women's proportion will increase from 45% to 47.3%. The white proportion will decline from 86.1% to 84.3%, and the 25–54 age group will rise from 69.1% to 71.8%, after having been only 60.8% in 1976.

Blacks and Hispanics constituted 19% of the United States population in 1984 but are expected to increase to 34% in 2020. It is not clear, though, how quickly these population changes will be translated into labor-force percentages. The composition of the American population for the next 100 years will depend on immigration and the extent to which high minority-group fertility rates converge with those of whites. If immigration stabilizes at around one million a year and the fertility rates of minorities converge with the non-Hispanic white rate of 1.8 by 2030, the non-Hispanic white proportion of the United States population would drop to just under 50% by 2080. Asians would constitute 12%; Hispanics, 23% (they would surpass blacks in 2010); and blacks, approximately 15%.[9]

Other Demographic and Labor-Market Trends

1. *Many more old people and considerably fewer young ones will make up the work force.* Because of the baby bust that started in the late 1960s and lasted for 20 years, in 1995 the number of teenage workers will be 20% less than it was in 1975. In 1990, there were 4.3 million fewer people 18–21 years old than there were in 1980. The labor-market share of 16- to 24-year-olds declined from 30% of the work force in 1985 to 18.4% in 1990 and is projected to be 16% by 2000. The average age of the work force will increase from 35 in 1985 to 39 in 2000.

2. *The increased labor-market participation of women will continue to challenge prevailing employment practices.* Women will become much more important actors in political and economic affairs. They will, in addition, continue to expand their participation in nontraditional, male-dominated jobs. In large part, these changes will occur because well-educated workers will be in shorter supply and the increased educational levels of women relative to men probably will give women greater political power to challenge sex-based discrimination.

The increased labor-force participation of women will accompany continued changes in family structures. These will be summarized here and analyzed in greater detail in subsequent chapters. The main changes include the following: In 1950, 70% of American families were headed by men whose wages were the sole source of income. Today only about 10% fit that description and fewer than one in eight families consists of a married couple with children in which the mother does not work outside the home.

- Half of all marriages in the 1980s will end in divorce. Divorce rates in the United States are the highest in the industrialized world.
- Women will continue to marry at later ages and have fewer children.
- Sixty percent of the children born in the 1980s will spend at least part of their lives with only one parent. Ninety percent of single-parent families

Minorities increased from 16% of the work force to 21% between 1976 and 1988. They are expected to make up 25% of the work force in the year 2000.

In 1950, 70% of American families were headed by men whose wages were the sole source of income. Today only about 10% fit that description and fewer than one in eight families consists of a married couple with children in which the mother does not work outside the home.

Members of minority groups will constitute more than half of the work-force growth until 2000, and increasing proportions of it thereafter. This means that their poor levels of education and training will be a serious and growing national problem.

are headed by women, and these families are much more likely than are two-parent families to be poor.
- The upward trend in children born to unmarried mothers will continue. The rates are particularly high for blacks but are increasing for all segments of the population. The pregnancy rate of white teenagers in America is higher than the rate for all teenagers in any major industrialized country.
- In more than two-thirds of all two-parent families with children, both parents work, as do 70% of mothers raising children alone. Approximately 40% of all children will grow up in broken homes. Divorce is likely to be a particularly serious economic blow for mothers and children; living standards for divorced mothers fall dramatically, whereas the standards for divorced men rise. This creates special problems for children, who ordinarily remain with their mothers following divorce. About half of divorced fathers do not support their children and rarely see them. Children in poor families headed by women often are caught up in cycles of poverty that tend to be self-perpetuating. Approximately two-thirds of unwed teenage mothers drop out of school and have lifetime earnings that are less than two-thirds of those of women who wait until after they are 20 to have children. The children of teenage mothers achieve academically and economically at rates substantially below those of children born to adults. These family problems are serious for children of all races and income levels. In 1989, for example, about two-thirds of teenage births were to white teens. However, the incidence of teenage births, particularly to unwed mothers, was much higher for minority teens. Teenage births to unwed mothers were about 90% for blacks, 57% for Hispanics, and 49% for whites.

3. *The problems of minorities with limited education will cause youth unemployment to continue to be a serious problem, despite the declining numbers of young workers.* The fact that members of minority groups will constitute more than half of the work-force growth until 2000, and increasing proportions of it thereafter. This means that their poor levels of education and training will be a serious and growing national problem. In fact, the nation's future depends heavily on how we deal with issues of equity in education and training. Minorities have lower overall scores on standardized tests for educational achievement. In some urban areas, the dropout rate, which runs to 30% nationally, is 40% to 50% for minorities.[10]

4. *Family-structure developments have clear implications for education and the economy.* For children to learn most effectively, they require supportive family and home environments and parental involvement in their schools. Schools often have been called upon to compensate for inadequate and chaotic home environments in which, for example, only one parent is present, incomes and education levels of parents are low, parents abuse drugs or alcohol, or parents have to spend so much time making a living that they have little time for school activities or to help their children learn.

Teachers, school administrators, and political leaders must understand the background problems of students and their families if educators are to provide effective learning experiences. Educational difficulties will be particularly serious for the children of poor mothers with limited education, who are less likely than are affluent mothers to have healthy babies or to give their children adequate nurturing before they enter school. Many poor children start school behind other children in educational achievement. Thus it is not surprising that studies have consistently found that family income is a major predictor of educational achievement. These matters, explored at greater length below, likewise make it clear that educational improvements will require high-priority attention to preschool and early childhood development services to break the intergenerational nature of poverty and poor educational achievement.

5. *Some observers expect the lower proportion of young people to create labor shortages in coming decades.* Whether this happens depends on the flexibility of the work force, the rate of economic growth, and the rate of immigration. Immigration is expected to continue at high rates for the rest of this century—at least 500,000 immigrants a year and 25% to 40% of labor-force growth—because of the economic conditions in Mexico and other developing countries and because of the difficulty of developing effective immigration policies. In the labor markets where they are concentrated, some immigrants will compete with and depress the wages of undereducated U.S.-born Americans, especially young people and minorities. However, shortages of technically trained, educated workers are likely. Those who are well educated, trained, and highly motivated will have much better economic prospects.[11]

6. *The challenges for the United States created by these population changes are immense.* Demographic changes will present the nation's policymakers with some major concerns and challenges. Until 2010, the maturing of the baby boomers—the best educated, most privileged generation in United States history—will be a positive force. Because they will be fully absorbed into the work force during the 1990s, the baby boomers should greatly improve productivity and innovation. Immigration also presents the United States with some important demographic advantages. The immigration of younger, highly motivated, better educated people whose early development costs have been borne by other countries represents a net gain for the American economy.

Unfortunately, both demographic changes and immigration will create some serious problems for America during the 1990s and later, especially after 2010, when the baby boomers start retiring. Other difficulties will be created if immigration continues to add to the nation's growing underclass, which, without major policy shifts, is not likely to be prepared for jobs requiring higher-order thinking skills. As noted previously, minorities, many of whom have serious social and educational disadvantages, will constitute a growing proportion of the nation's work force during the next 50 years.

These demographic shifts will create a real challenge for the United States after 2010, when the economic burdens of the aging baby boomers and a dramatic shift in the number and proportion of people older than 85 could greatly burden American economic resources. At present, approximately 28% of federal resources are spent on the elderly; by 2015, the proportion is likely to be 40% or higher. The number of people older than 85 will increase from 2.7 million in 1985 to 4.9 million in 2000, 6.6 million in 2010, and 16 million in 2050. The proportion of the population older than 85 will increase from 1% in 1985 to 5% in 2050. This change will produce higher proportions of nonworkers to workers. In 1988, there were about five workers for each nonworker; in 50 years this ratio will be five to two. The aging of the population also means that families increasingly will have elder-care as well as child-care responsibilities.

The extent to which these changes result in marked declines in national power and personal welfare depends heavily on how we strengthen our international competitiveness during the 20-year period between 1990 and 2010, a period the demographic indicators suggest will be favorable for economic growth. The key to competitiveness is the quality of our work force, which will depend on the extent to which our policies improve the context within which families operate.

Demographic shifts will create a real challenge for the United States after 2010, when the economic burdens of the aging baby boomers and a dramatic shift in the number and proportion of people older than 85 could greatly burden American economic resources.

The extent to which these changes result in marked declines in national power and personal welfare depends heavily on how we strengthen our international competitiveness during the 20-year period between 1990 and 2010.

FIGURE 2.2

Percentage Distribution of Nonagricultural Employment by Major Industry in 1950 and 1989

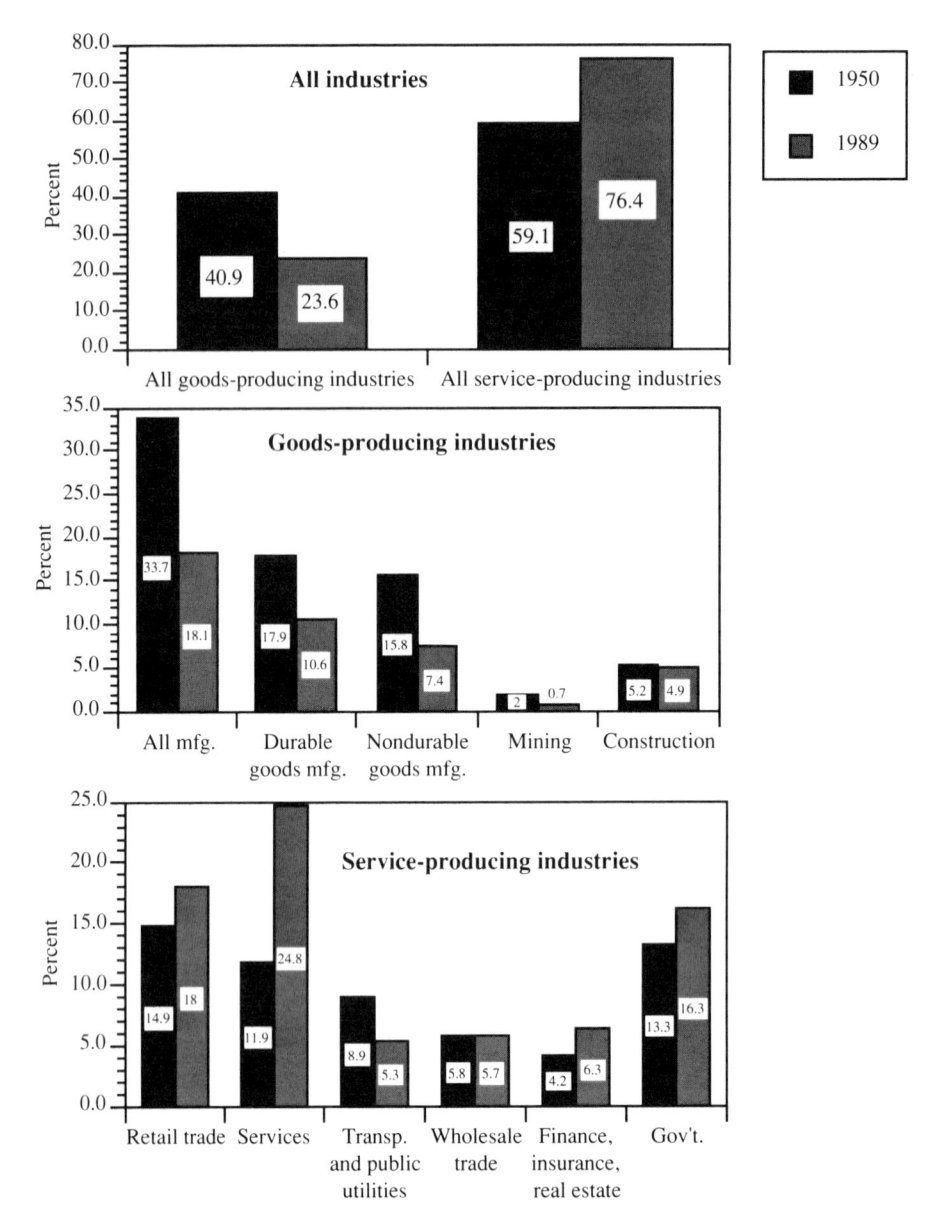

All industries

	1950	1989
All goods-producing industries	40.9	23.6
All service-producing industries	59.1	76.4

Goods-producing industries

	1950	1989
All mfg.	33.7	18.1
Durable goods mfg.	17.9	10.6
Nondurable goods mfg.	15.8	7.4
Mining	2	0.7
Construction	5.2	4.9

Service-producing industries

	1950	1989
Retail trade	14.9	18
Services	11.9	24.8
Transp. and public utilities	8.9	5.3
Wholesale trade	5.8	5.7
Finance, insurance, real estate	4.2	6.3
Gov't.	13.3	16.3

Source: Executive Office of the President, *1990 Economic Report of the President* (Washington, DC: United States Government Printing Office, 1990), pp. 342–43.

Employment and Wages

The job-growth trends in the United States for the rest of the century probably will continue to be what they have been—90% of all new jobs will be in services, and goods-producing jobs will decline. In 1989, more than 75% of America's workers were employed in service and service-related activities, and only

FIGURE 2.3

Average Weekly Earnings by Industry

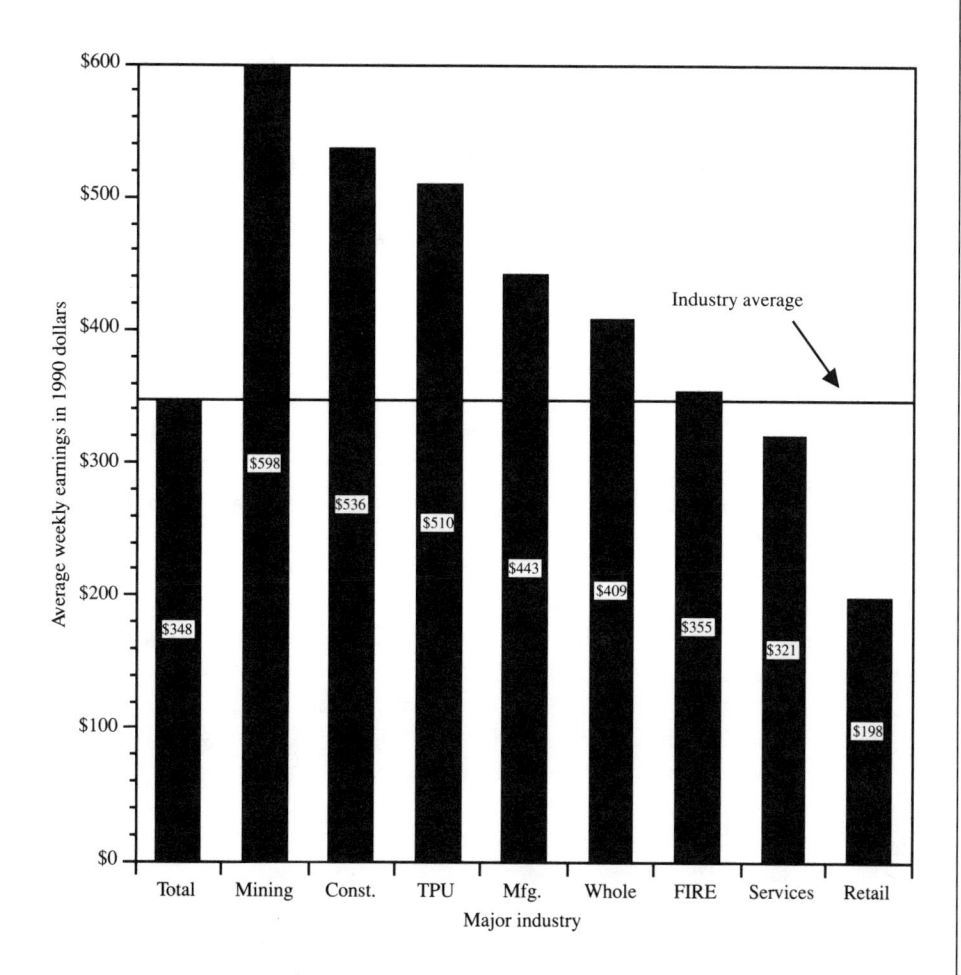

[Bar chart showing average weekly earnings in 1990 dollars by major industry:
- Total: $348
- Mining: $598
- Const.: $536
- TPU: $510
- Mfg.: $443
- Whole: $409
- FIRE: $355
- Services: $321
- Retail: $198

Industry average line indicated on chart.]

Source: Bureau of Labor Statistics, "Real Earnings in August 1990," USDL News Release 90–479 (Washington, DC: U.S. Department of Labor, 18 September 1990).

Notes: Graph is based upon average weekly earnings data for production or nonsupervisory workers on private nonagricultural payrolls only. TPU stands for transportation and public utilities; Whole stands for wholesale; FIRE stands for finance, insurance, and real estate.

---

approximately 25% were in manufacturing (see Figure 2.2, top panel). Manufacturing employment fell from 34% of all jobs in 1950 to 25.1% in 1959 and 18% in 1989. The total number of manufacturing jobs declined from a peak of 21.04 million in 1979 to 19.61 million in 1989. Indeed, this country has created no net additional manufacturing jobs since the late 1960s. In terms of output, manufacturing declined from 38.2% of gross output in 1969 to 35.2% in 1981 and 34.5% in 1984. Thus, manufacturing's share of total output has declined less than its share of total employment.[12]

Paralleling the decline of manufacturing work has been the rise of service employment. Although this development has been widely bemoaned, it is important to remember that service jobs vary greatly. Some, particularly those in producers' and business services, pay well and require high skills. Producers' services—legal, accounting, computing, business, and engineering—have experienced rapid growth, albeit from a relatively small base. Other sectors—retail services, consumer and personal services, and wholesaling—have generated mostly low-paying jobs, as Figure 2.3 suggests. These jobs have increased most in absolute number while the producer-services jobs have grown more rapidly in percentage terms.[13] In net terms, relatively more low-paying, low-skilled jobs have been created in services. The result of these changes has been a reduction in middle-level jobs. Services tend to have a more bipolar occupational distribution (i.e., some high-skill jobs, many low-skill jobs, and few in between) than manufacturing does. However, on the average, services have lower productivity[14] and pay lower wages.[15]

Productivity

The decline in productivity growth in the United States since the 1960s is a particularly important cause of our decreasing competitiveness. Productivity growth, which was approximately 3.2% per year between 1945 and 1965, declined to 2.2% between 1965 and 1973 and to approximately 1% since 1973. It now takes approximately three years to achieve the same productivity improvement we used to achieve in one year. With much lower productivity growth than other countries, American companies can achieve competitive unit labor costs only by reducing wages. The combination of low productivity growth and international competition is one of the reasons for declining real wages in the United States absolutely and relative to other countries. The United States once had the highest wages of any industrial country, but, in 1989, 12 other countries had higher wages.

However, the United States still has the highest average productivity in the world. The problem is that productivity in several other countries is higher in some strategic industries and the decline in productivity growth makes it more difficult for U.S. companies to improve their real wages and to compete in international markets.

Economists do not agree on all of the reasons for declining productivity growth, but several aspects of this problem are important for our purposes.

1. *The long-term productivity trend has been mainly responsible for higher economic growth, higher standards of living, and more leisure time.* Between 1950 and 1980, productivity approximately doubled in the United States, despite the slowdown in growth that began in the 1960s. This increase in productivity has made it possible to reduce the amount of time people spend working. Average working hours declined from 53 per week in 1900 to 35.5 in 1979. In the past 50 years, the number of hours of labor required to produce a product of a given value declined approximately 3% per year, while the number of hours worked declined at about 0.5% per year. This does not mean, however, that wages will increase as productivity increases. No necessary relationship exists between short-term changes in productivity and wages. However, productivity determines the room for wage increases, depending on the degree of competition in product and labor markets.

2. *Technology and the quality of labor (i.e., workers with greater education and better health) have been major factors in productivity improvements.* These factors have accounted for approximately three-fourths of productivity improvement since 1929, when we first began keeping such statistics. Enhancement of physical capital accounts for less than 20% of the productivity improvement.

3. *The productivity of management and white-collar workers in the United States has been declining, whereas that of blue-collar workers continues to increase at approximately 3% a year.*[16] Moreover, despite their rapid growth in

With much lower productivity growth than other countries, American companies can achieve competitive unit labor costs only by reducing wages. The United States once had the highest wages of any industrial country, but, in 1989, 12 other countries had higher wages.

number, white-collar workers have declining productivity growth, whereas that of goods-production workers is increasing. Relative to other countries, especially the Japanese, the work forces in U.S. companies have much larger proportions of managerial, supervisory, and white-collar workers. American companies and schools are top-heavy with managers and inspectors—an index of their failure to adapt from mass production to more modern management systems.

Unemployment

Despite the more rapid growth of jobs in the United States compared with other major industrial countries, unemployment has risen, even with a slower rate of increase in the work force. In addition, more and more workers are becoming marginal to the work force; they are unemployed, working part time although they want to work full time,[17] or have dropped out of the labor force because of the lack of employment opportunity. The real unemployment rate in the United States (unemployed, discouraged, involuntary part time) increased from 8.2% in 1973 to 9.7% in 1979 and 11.2% in 1987.

Income Distribution

Signs also indicate that the income distribution in America is becoming bipolar, to the detriment of the middle class. The share of income received by the middle quintile of families has declined to its lowest level since 1947. Lester Thurow calls the middle class "an endangered species."[18] To Thurow, the major reasons for this polarization are clear: the increasing growth of female-headed households, the diminishing skills of workers, the movement of jobs to nonunion areas, and our decreasing international competitiveness.

Frank Levy, one of the country's leading experts on income distribution, also has found growing inequality in income during the 1980s. He believes that the best way to understand income-distribution changes is to track the income of a typical 40-year-old man for a 10-year period as he ages to 50 years. A typical man's real wages increased 36% from 1953 to 1963 and 25% from 1963 to 1973. Between 1973 and 1983, however, a typical 40-year-old man's real income fell by 14% by the time he reached 50.[19] In addition, Levy has shown that average family-income distributions became more unequal between 1979 and 1986, despite the fact that average family incomes increased slightly in real terms during this period—by $1,000, to $34,924. For the wealthiest fifth of the population, however, real incomes increased from $70,260 to $76,300, a gain of $6,040. For the poorest fifth, by contrast, average family income fell from $8,761 to $8,031.

A 1989 study released by the House Ways and Means Committee confirmed this finding for the 1979–87 period. In real terms, average family income for the poorest fifth of the U.S. population declined by 6.1% from 1979 to 1987, while family incomes of the highest fifth rose by 11.1%. Because of the increased labor-force participation of women, personal incomes changed more than family income: they increased 15.6% for the richest fifth and declined by 9.8% for the poorest. Besides the growth of low-wage jobs, a major reason for these mounting income disparities is the rising proportion of children younger than 18 who live with never-married single parents: from 0.4% of the population in 1960 to 6.8% in 1987.[20]

Levy offers several reasons for these changes in average family-income distribution.

1. The income of men who did not graduate from college has shown a marked deterioration relative to the income of those who did. In 1979, an average male high-school graduate 25 to 34 years of age earned only 18% less than did a male college graduate of the same age. In 1986, this gap had grown to 43%

White-collar workers have declining productivity growth, whereas that of goods-production workers is increasing. Relative to other countries, U.S. companies have much larger proportions of managerial, supervisory, and white-collar workers.

Income distribution is becoming bipolar, to the detriment of the middle class. The major reasons for this polarization are the increasing growth of female-headed households, the diminishing skills of workers, the movement of jobs to nonunion areas, and our decreasing international competitiveness.

and it remained at about that level through 1988. The earnings gap has widened for women, but not as dramatically.

2. Female-headed households have grown from one-ninth of all families in the early 1970s to one-sixth in 1986; average income for female-headed households was $13,500 in 1986, compared with $39,240 for all families.

3. The tax structure has become more regressive. This means that high-income persons pay a lower percentage of their income in taxes and low-income persons pay a higher percentage of their income in taxes than they did in the 1960s and '70s.[21]

Poverty

Given the decline in real income and increasing inequality in income distribution, it should not be surprising to find that poverty has increased. Although the United States made great strides toward reducing poverty in the late 1960s and the 1970s, poverty rates have increased since 1979. Poverty, clearly, is a major obstacle to human-capital formation. Except for some inspiring exceptions, poor families are not very efficient learning and nurturing systems. The rising incidence of poverty in the United States during the 1980s ought to give us pause. In 1987, despite five years of economic recovery, the poverty rate was 13.6%, compared with 11.4% for 1978. The 1987 poverty rate for blacks was 33.1%, and the Hispanic rate was 28.2%; the white rate was 10.5%.

The high proportion of American children who are poor is especially alarming. According to census data, more than 20% of all American children under 18 years of age were poor in 1988, compared with 15% in 1978 and 18% in 1980. The problem is particularly serious for minorities: nearly half of all black children and 40% of all Hispanic children lived in poverty in 1988. Moreover, a large proportion of these children live in very poor families. In 1987, 51% of poor black children and 44% of all poor children lived in families with incomes below half of the poverty line. Not only are the poverty rates for children high and rising in the United States, but they are much higher than in other major industrial countries.[22]

Conclusion

This chapter has reviewed a complex constellation of interrelated economic and social factors that affect families in fundamental ways. Historically, as industrialization accelerated, economic activity became increasingly external to the family. At first, mainly men became involved in the market economy, because the economic advantages of the mass-production system allowed one earner to support a family, especially after governments developed social safety nets and means to prevent deep depressions. However, during the course of the 20th century, new technology, changing family structures, and rising aspirations drew more and more women into the work force, and their earnings became increasingly necessary to maintain family living standards. Simultaneously, beginning in the 1960s and '70s, a larger number of women began to consider paid employment not only a financial necessity but also a major means of self-fulfillment and identification.

These changes interacted with certain fundamental economic forces to change the nature of work and therefore family incomes. Technological innovations and internationalization changed the requirements for economic success. National leaders could no longer stimulate consumption through monetary-fiscal policies and keep the system running at nearly full employment.

Both the U.S. government and private companies must now be concerned with international competitiveness. This presents the country with a stark choice: we can either compete by reducing wages or by improving productivity and quali-

More than 20% of all American children under 18 years of age were poor in 1988, compared with 15% in 1978 and 18% in 1980. The problem is particularly serious for minorities: nearly half of all black children and 40% of all Hispanic children lived in poverty in 1988.

ty. Unlike most of our competitors, the United States is following a low-wage strategy. This is being done as much by default as by conscious choice—mainly because America, almost alone among industrialized nations, has been opposed to explicit national goals and objectives and conscious strategies to achieve them. This means we have followed passive policies and have let "nature take its course." When nature takes its course, most employers will follow low-wage strategies. This chapter outlines the necessary steps to develop high-performance systems to pursue a high-wage strategy. This requires a fairly complete restructuring of work, especially lean management processes, positive incentives, and much greater attention to the education and training of non–college-bound workers.

This chapter also documents in some detail the consequences of not pursuing a national strategy to encourage high performance and discourage low-wage strategies. Real wages in the United States are not only declining but are becoming more unequal. In fact, U.S. incomes are not only more unequal than at any time since World War II, they are more unequal than in any other major industrial, market-oriented economy—almost all of whom have adopted high-wage strategies. This inequality creates very serious economic, social, and political problems.

Family incomes have not declined as much as wages mainly because more women are working more time and in higher-paying jobs. However, this process is self-limiting—because of slower work-force growth, we will not be able to sustain national or family incomes by increasing the supply of labor. Instead, we must increase productivity growth if we want to improve incomes. But we also must give greater attention to equity in employment, education, and training opportunities. Members of ethnic and racial minority groups, who have not been well served by our economy or our education and training systems, are becoming a larger and much more important component of the work force and our population. Educated, trained, healthy, motivated people are an almost unlimited asset, but the opposite also is true: uneducated, untrained, unhealthy, or unmotivated people will be serious liabilities in a more competitive, knowledge-intensive world.

One other reality documented in this chapter, the aging of our population and work force, has very important implications for family and national welfare. The aging of the well-educated baby boomers between 1990 and 2010 should improve economic performance. But failure to strengthen the economy over the next 20 years will create serious problems as the baby boomers start retiring after 2010.

The trends documented in this chapter have other important implications for families that will be analyzed in chapter 3. More women are working, which has both positive and negative consequences for families. The family is our most basic learning system, so how well it functions will fundamentally affect the development of children, which, in turn, will determine our economic future. Similarly, economic factors influence both the formation and functioning of families: the number and spacing of children; the ability of families to educate and nurture children; the ability of our society to provide early childhood education and other supportive services; and the availability of resources for public family-support services. These matters will be explored at greater length in the following chapter.

Notes

1. Sidney Webb and Beatrice Webb, *Industrial Democracy* (London: Longman Green & Company, 1897).

2. Anthony Carnevale, *Human Capital: A High-Yield Corporate Investment* (Washington, DC: American Society for Training and Development, 1983); Theodore Schultz, *Investing in People: The Economics of Population Quality* (Berkeley, CA: University of California Press, 1981).

3. Bureau of Labor Statistics, Washington, DC, unpublished data, May 1990.

4. Shoshona Zuboff, *In the Age of the Smart Machines* (New York: Basic Books, 1988).

5. National Center on Education and the Economy, *America's Choice: High Skills or Low Wages,* Report of the Commission on Skills of the American Workforce (Rochester, NY: National Center on Education and the Economy, 1990).

6. Several different definitions of fertility exist, but for the purposes of this book, unless otherwise noted, total fertility rate is defined as the average number of children that would be born per woman if all women lived to the end of their childbearing years and at each year of age experienced the birth rates occurring in that specified year.

7. For a discussion of these matters, see Paul Demeny, "The World Demographic Situation," in Jane Mencken, ed., *World Population and U.S. Policy* (New York: W. W. Norton, 1986), pp. 27–67.

8. Ray Marshall, "Jobs: The Shifting Structure of Global Employment," in John Sewell and Stuart Tucker, eds., *Growth, Exports and Jobs in a Changing World Economy: Agenda 1988* (Washington, DC: Overseas Development Council, 1988), pp. 167–194.

9. Leon Bouvier and Robert Gardner, *Immigration to the U.S.: The Unfinished Story* (Washington, DC: Population Reference Bureau, 1986), p. 27.

10. Action Council on Minority Education, *Education That Works: An Action Plan for the Education of Minorities* (Cambridge, MA: Massachusetts Institute of Technology, 1990).

11. Of course, the concept of labor shortages is relevant only at specified salaries and qualifications. Some observers argue that there will be no teacher shortage because rising salaries and educational reforms are attracting more people into teaching. Those who contend that no shortage will occur also argue that the salaries of teachers are not out of line with those of comparable college graduates. However, these arguments assume that marginal changes in our present educational system are adequate. Those of us who believe that radical improvements are needed in the education system in order to make it world class believe it is not enough just to get warm bodies to stand before classes and "teach." Indeed, we do not believe baccalaureate degrees in education are adequate preparation for teaching. In this latter sense, a serious teacher shortage will occur in the absence of radical changes in teachers' compensation, status, working conditions, and power. For an elaboration of this point, see the Carnegie Forum on Education and the Economy, Task Force on Teaching, *A Nation Prepared* (Washington, DC: Carnegie Corporation, 1986).

12. Ronald E. Kutscher and Valerie A. Personick, "Deindustrialization and the Shift to Services," *Monthly Labor Review* 109 (June 1986), pp. 3–13.

13. For a discussion of the service sector, see Thomas M. Stanback, Jr., Peter J. Bearse, Thierry J. Noyelle, and Robert A. Karasek, *Services: The New Economy* (Totowa, NJ: Allenheld, Osmun, and Co., 1981); Thierry J. Noyelle, "Services, Urban Economic Development and Industrial Policy: Some Critical Linkages," presented at the conference "The Industrial Policy Questions: State and Local Issues," University of North Carolina at Chapel Hill, May 1984.

14. For instance, the American Productivity Center reports that manufacturing productivity grew five times faster than did services' productivity from 1979 to 1983.

15. Herbert Runyon, "The Service Industries: Employment, Productivity, and Inflation," *Business Economics* (January 1985), pp. 55–63; Bureau of Labor Statistics, "Real Earnings in August 1990," USDL News Release 90-479, September 18, 1990.

16. Lester Thurow, "Review of the *Positive Sum Strategy*," *Scientific American* 255 (September 1986), p. 26.

17. The Bureau of Labor Statistics calls these people employed part time for "economic reasons."

18. Thurow, "Review," p. 26.

19. Frank Levy, *Dollars and Dreams: The Changing American Income Distribution* (New York: Basic Books, 1987).

20. Martin Talchin, "Richest Get Richer and Poorest Poorer," *New York Times*, March 23, 1989, p. 1.

21. Frank Levy, "A Growing Gap between Rich and Poor," *New York Times*, May 1, 1988, p. F-3.

22. Timothy Smeeding, Barbara Torrey, and Martin Rein, "Patterns of Income and Poverty: The Economic Status of Children and the Elderly in Eight Countries," in John Palmer, Timothy Smeeding, and Barbara Torrey, eds., *The Vulnerable* (Washington, DC: Urban Institute, 1988), p. 95.

3

Changes in Family Structure

Dramatic changes have taken place in American families in this century, especially since the 1950s. The main trends include:
- decline in the proportion of people living in family households
- decline in fertility rates
- increased divorce rates
- increased proportion of households headed by single parents, especially single mothers
- much lower proportions of households with children younger than 18

It's important, however, to keep these developments in perspective. Despite dramatic relative changes, most households and a large proportion of family households continue to be maintained by married couples. This section explores some of the quantitative dimensions of these changes.

Trends in Family Composition

In order to examine the long-term trends in family composition for early years, data limitations force us to rely on decennial census statistics on households rather than families. A household is any separate living unit occupied by one or more persons. The number of households in the United States for various years were:

1910	20.3 million
1950	43.6 million
1989	92.8 million

The main long-term changes in households include the following:

1. *Fewer people in family households, particularly "traditional" nuclear families, than was the case early in this century.* The decline in the proportion of people living in families is due to three main factors: delayed marriages among young adults; higher divorce rates among all adults; and more older widows, because women live longer than men.

2. *Fertility rates have declined because women have fewer children during*

FIGURE 3.1

Composition of American Households, 1960–1988
(in percentages)

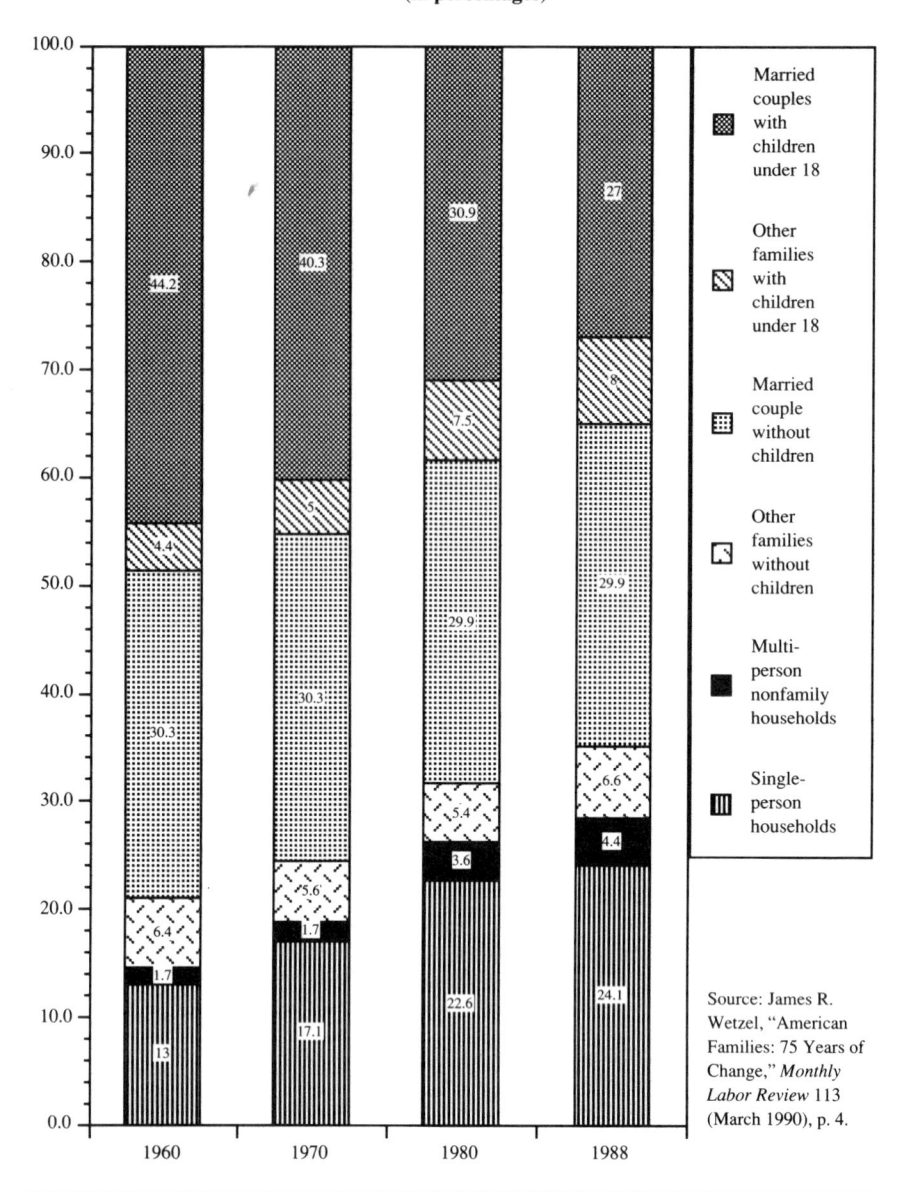

	1960	1970	1980	1988
Married couples with children under 18	44.2	40.3	30.9	27
Other families with children under 18	4.4	—	7.5	8
Married couple without children	30.3	30.3	29.9	29.9
Other families without children	6.4	5.6	5.4	6.6
Multi-person nonfamily households	1.7	1.7	3.6	4.4
Single-person households	13	17.1	22.6	24.1

Source: James R. Wetzel, "American Families: 75 Years of Change," *Monthly Labor Review* 113 (March 1990), p. 4.

their lives and have children at older ages. The total fertility rate (the number of children an average woman is likely to have in her lifetime) in the United States has been below the population replacement rate of 2.1 since 1972.

3. *Although a substantial majority of people still live in families, families are more dynamic and heterogenous than they were earlier in this century.* Because our life expectancies are longer now, more generations are likely to exist in kinship networks that include spouses and former spouses, in-laws, and former in-laws as well as children and stepchildren.

One of the more important long-term trends has been a decline in the proportion of adults who are married at any given time and in the proportion of households maintained by married couples (see Figure 3.1 above and Table 3.1 on page 118). As a result of these changes, 60% of today's children will live for some time with a single parent, although only about one-fourth of all children lived in single-parent households at any time during the late 1980s. Note also that many young people now live in "nonfamily" households as couples, with other adults, or alone. See Table 3.1 for specific figures on these increases.

One reason for the lower incidence of married couples at any time is the long-term rise in divorce rates. Since the mid-1970s, almost 50% of all marriages have ended in divorce, which is about triple the rates of the 1920s and '30s and more than double the 1950–65 rate. Low marriage rates also result from increases in the age at which people get married. During the 1940s, the age of first marriage of men and women dropped sharply. During the 1970s and 1980s, however, it increased considerably. By the end of the 1950s, the median age of first marriage had fallen to 20.1 years for women and 22.5 years for men; first-marriage median age rose to 23.6 years for women and almost 26 years for men during the 1980s. These delayed marriage rates have roughly matched women's rising education levels and labor-force participation rates, a pattern observable in most industrialized countries.[1]

The higher ages at first marriage have important implications for fertility, divorce rates, and out-of-wedlock births. Higher ages at first marriage are associated with lower fertility rates.[2] From 55 births per 1,000 women in 1780, when such statistics were first recorded, birth rates dropped to a low of 18.4 in 1934, rose to 25.3 at the peak of the postwar baby boom in 1957, reached a low of 14.6 in 1975–76 during the "baby bust" period, and increased to 15.9 in 1988, mainly because of the large increase in the number of baby-boom women who were reaching their prime childbearing years. The total fertility rate (i.e., the number of children each woman has in her lifetime at rates prevailing in the reference year) were as follows: 3.3 in 1920, 2.1 in 1934, 3.7 in 1957, and below 2.1 since the early 1970s. In 1989 the rate was 1.9.

Another important trend is the rising number of children born to unmarried mothers. In 1987, for example, 933,000 births, almost one-fourth of the total, were to unmarried mothers.[3] Nearly three million children younger than 18 were living in the 1.75 million households maintained by never-married women with children of their own in 1988. An additional 1.1 million children of unmarried mothers lived in households maintained by other people.[4] The annual out-of-wedlock birth rate was only 7.1 per 1,000 women 15 to 44 years old in 1940. It more than doubled to 19.3 in 1955, rose to 26.4 in 1970, and to 36.1 in 1987—a rate more than five times as high as it was in 1940. In 1960, slightly more than 5% of all births were to unmarried women, but this rate reached almost 25% by 1987.[5] To some degree, out-of-wedlock births are related to delayed marriages by women, which increases the time they are at risk of becoming pregnant out of wedlock. But these changes also reflect changing social attitudes about both the cohabitation of unmarried couples and out-of-wedlock births.

These and other developments have resulted in dramatic shifts in the composition of American households. As can be seen in Figure 3.1, the main changes between 1960 and 1988 were:

1. *The proportion of households maintained by married couples declined sharply*. The most dramatic drop, however, was in the proportion of households maintained by married couples with children—from 44.2% in 1960 to 27% in 1988 and 26% in 1990. The proportion of all families with children younger than 18 fell from 48.6% in 1960 to 35% in 1988. Although the number of married-couple families with children increased slightly during the 1980s, from 2.42 million in 1980 to 2.45 million in 1990, the declining percentage of such families was due to the increase in the number of households. Stated another way, almost all of the increase in households was in households other than traditional families.

Families today are more dynamic and heterogeneous than they were earlier in this century.

One of the more important trends in family composition has been a decline in the proportion of adults who are married at any given time and in the proportion of households maintained by married couples. As a result, 60% of today's children will live for some time with a single parent.

The proportion of single-parent households in America has doubled since 1970 and almost tripled since the 1940s. Families headed by single parents are much more likely to be poor than are those headed by married couples.

Married-couple and male-maintained families are more likely to become poor because of factors associated with business cycles, whereas the higher poverty among households maintained by females is less affected by economic conditions.

2. *Single-person households increased from 13% of total households in 1960 to 24.1% in 1988.* There were 9.7 million single-parent households in 1990, about one-fourth of all households. However, the increase in single-parent households slowed to 41% between 1980 and 1990, after having increased by 82% during the 1970s. Women constitute 8.4 million, or approximately 87%, of the heads of these single-parent households. The rate of increase in households headed by single mothers declined from 82% between 1970 and 1980 to 35% between 1980 and 1990. These changes reflect a combination of higher out-of-wedlock births, higher divorce rates, and more single people living alone because they have never married or because their mates have died. Overall, the proportion of single-parent households in America has doubled since 1970 and almost tripled since the 1940s.

Families headed by single parents are much more likely to be poor than are those headed by married couples. The poverty rate for families maintained by single women in 1988, for example, was 44.1%, more than six times as high as the poverty rate for married couple families (7.2%). In 1988, almost 20% of all children were poor, nearly double the 10.7 rate of people older than 18 (10.7%).

About one-fourth (24%) of all households were classified as "single person" in 1989, representing 21.9 million households—13.1 million women and 8.8 million men. The gender composition of single-person households reflects age-related factors: between the ages of 15 and 55, men are more likely to live alone than are women; persons older than 55 living alone are predominantly women. There were only 762,000 multiperson households in 1950 but 5.1 million in 1989. Slightly more than half of these 1989 households (2.6 million) were maintained by unmarried couples, four times the level of such arrangements in 1970. Approximately 800,000 (30%) of these unmarried-couple households had children younger than 15. More than 60% of the partners in unmarried-couple households were younger than age 35 and more than 50% had never been married.[6]

The changes in household composition by race and Hispanic origin from 1960 to 1989 are shown in Table 3.2 on pages 119–122. The number of black and Hispanic households as a proportion of all households has increased since 1970, reflecting their increasing proportion of the U.S. population; the white proportion of all households declined from 90.3% in 1960 to 86.2% in 1989. It should be noted, however, that whites account for slightly larger proportions of family and married-couple households. A significant difference can be seen in the proportion of black married-couple households in 1989 (36.1%) relative to whites (59.4%) and Hispanics (56.2%).

Family Structure and Economic Well-Being

Family structure is an important determinant of economic status and quality of life, although different factors influence the economic well-being of some families as opposed to others. Married-couple and male-maintained families, for instance, are more likely to become poor as a result of factors associated with business cycles, whereas the higher poverty among households maintained by females is less affected by economic conditions. In 1989, the incidence of poverty was 37.4% for female-maintained families, 20.6% for people not in families, and 7.2% for married-couple and male-maintained households.

The impact of these family-structure factors on the incidence of poverty has changed over time. Before 1973, other factors, such as changing incomes and smaller families, reduced the incidence of poverty. But between 1979 and

1988, the overall poverty rate increased by 1.4 percentage points, half of which was due to family-structure factors and half to other factors.[7]

Despite the high incidence of poverty among black and female-maintained households, most (59.6%) of the increase in poverty in female-headed households between 1979 and 1986 was among whites. This phenomenon reflected a reversal of the 1973–79 experience, when whites accounted for only 35.4% of the increase in poverty in female-maintained households.

Moreover, despite the higher incidence of poverty among households maintained by women, only 38.7% of all poor persons were in female-maintained households in 1988. Considerable variation by race, however, exists within this segment of the population: 61.5% of poor blacks but only 24.5% of poor whites and 39.0% of poor Hispanics lived in female-maintained households in 1988.

Although most women who maintain households with children do not work, a large proportion (44% in 1988) do. Of these, approximately one-fourth worked 50 weeks or more. Single mothers who work tend to have higher levels of education and fewer children than do those who do not work. Whether mothers of young children work also depends on the number of children they have. More than one-third (35%) of the nonworking single mothers had three or more children; only 22% of single mothers who worked part time and 13% of those who worked full time had three or more children.

Clearly, more children are living in single-parent families. Demographic analysts have found that the proportion of white children in single-parent families was about 20% in the late 1980s, more than double the 1970 rate. More than 60% of black children lived in single-parent families in the late 1980s, up from 41% in 1970. These changes are remarkable both for their size and the speed at which they have occurred. The main reason a larger percentage of children are in single-parent households is that the number of such households has increased, not that single-parent households are having more children.

Poverty among Children

American children are much more likely to be poor than are children in any other industrialized country. Regrettably, the well-being of children in America has generally deteriorated during the past 15 years, absolutely and relative to older people. The elderly lived and worked through America's golden era of rapid economic growth, which made it possible for them to accumulate more wealth. As will be demonstrated in chapter 4, higher real interest rates during the 1980s contributed significantly to increasing the wealth accumulated earlier. Older Americans also are the major beneficiaries of government Social Security and health programs that provide income support. As a consequence, the elderly face a smaller probability of being poor than at any time in the nation's history.[8]

Among children, by contrast, poverty increased from 14% of the child population in 1969 to 20% in 1987. The United States Bureau of the Census reported 32.5 million poor people in this country in 1987; of that number 13 million were children younger than 18 and 5 million were children younger than six. Thus, while a fifth of all children are poor, children are 40% of the poor. Nearly one-fourth (23%) of children younger than six are poor, and they represent more than 15% of the poor. A 1990 report from the National Center for Children in Poverty of the School of Public Health at Columbia University, *Five Million Children*,[9] summarized some of the major factors about poor children younger than six years old in the United States:

American children are much more likely to be poor than are children in any other industrialized country. The well-being of children in America has generally deteriorated during the past 15 years, absolutely and relative to older people.

While a fifth of all children are poor, children are 40% of the poor. Nearly one-fourth (23%) of children younger than six are poor, and they represent more than 15% of the poor.

Poor children are at greater risk for health problems, school failure, delinquency, early childbearing, and adult poverty.

Most poor households are not very good nurturing, protecting, and learning systems for children. Multiple physical and social risk factors for poor families are closely interrelated.

1. In 1987, nearly one-fourth of children younger than six (23%) were below the poverty line. The number of poor people in the United States declined between the 1960s and the early 1980s, but the number of poor children younger than six increased.

2. Children younger than six are more likely to be poor than any other age group; they are more than twice as likely to be poor than are adults aged 18 to 64.

3. Minority children younger than age six were much more likely to be poor than were white children. In 1987, 58% of poor children younger than six were from minority groups: 32% were non-Hispanic blacks, 21% were Hispanic, and approximately 5% were other races, predominantly Asian or American Indian. The poverty rates for different racial and ethnic groups were 48% for blacks, 42% for Hispanics, 29% for other minorities, and 13% for whites.

4. Child poverty varies substantially by geographic area. In central cities of U.S. metropolitan areas, it was 31%; in suburban areas, 13%; and in rural areas, 28%. Child poverty is higher in the South but is growing faster in other regions of the country.

5. Although 38% of poor young children lived in married-couple families, young children living with single mothers were more likely to be poor. The proportion of poor young children living with single mothers has gradually increased since 1979. Children born out of wedlock to teenage mothers are at the greatest risk. Although the teenage birth rate has decreased since the 1960s, the proportion of teenage births out of wedlock increased from about 15% in 1960 to 60% in 1986. It should be noted, however, that single teenage mothers account for less than 5% of all single mothers.

6. Children living in large families are more likely to be poor, but a smaller proportion of children currently live in large families than did in 1970. In 1986, slightly more than one-half of poor children younger than six lived in families with no more than one other child. And the average number of children per poor family declined dramatically between 1970 and 1986.

7. Poverty rates vary inversely with education. In 1987, 62% of the children of parent(s) who had not completed high school were poor, contrasted with 19% of children having at least one parent who had completed high school.

8. The great majority (72%) of poor children younger than six had at least one working parent. Only a little more than one-fourth (28%) of such children lived in families that rely exclusively on welfare. Approximately 16% lived in families whose income was supplemented by public assistance, 19% lived in families with a mix of earned and unearned income, and more than one-third (37%) were in families that relied exclusively on income from employment. In mother-headed families, 20% of mothers were employed full or part time. When mothers worked, children were much less likely to be poor.

9. Abundant evidence documents that poor children are at greater risk for health problems, school failure, delinquency, early childbearing, and adult poverty. As noted previously, most poor households are not very good nurturing, protecting, and learning systems. Multiple physical and social risk factors for poor families are closely interrelated. Poor medical care for pregnant women and young children causes health problems for infants, especially low birth weight, that tend to retard intellectual and physical growth. These problems, in turn, contribute to school failure and other social pathologies.

Evidence also suggests that teen parenting tends to become both expensive and self-perpetuating. Of all AFDC mothers younger than 30, 71% had children as teenagers. Annual welfare expenditures for these families (AFDC, food stamps, and Medicaid) are estimated to have been $16.65 billion in 1985.[10] The baby of a teenage mother also faces serious personal perils; it is more likely to be born prematurely, to have problems at birth, to be of low birth weight, and have fragile health generally—all of which often require expensive, intensive neonatal care. Although the exact causes are disputed, there is no disagreement that these children are more likely than those born to older women to be handicapped in their cognitive, social, and emotional development.

10. Failure for poor children is not inevitable. Indeed, even some of the most disadvantaged children survive and thrive socially and academically. As will be discussed later, educational achievement of poor children is determined by the nature of relationships within the family, not just the family's economic or social structure. Moreover, outside interventions, like the Women, Infants and Children (WIC) and Head Start programs, can make an important difference in the intellectual, emotional, social, and physical development of children.

Conclusion

As this chapter has documented, some dramatic structural changes have occurred in families over the past 30 years. Most notable is the decline in the number and proportion of traditional two-parent families with children, from 44.2% of all families in 1960 to only 26% in 1990. Simultaneously, the proportion of single-parent households has increased. The decline in the proportion of people living in families is due to three main factors: delayed marriages, higher divorce rates, and more older widows. The decline in the proportion of families with children reflects the fact that women are having fewer children. Although a majority of people still live in families, these families are much more dynamic and heterogeneous than they were earlier in this century.

Moreover, it is important to note that family structure is related to economic well-being. Poverty increased during the 1980s, especially among children, a factor with serious consequences for their future development. In addition, economic status of a family is directly related to whether two parents are present, whether the parent(s) work, the level of parental education, the race of the parents, and where they live.

The increase in poverty among children—from 14% in 1969 to approximately 20% in 1987—is a factor of considerable importance for America's future. Children account for more than 40% of the poor. The poverty rate for children under six is almost one-fourth (23%) and is twice the rate of adults aged 18 to 64.

Considerable variation exists in poverty among family structures. The rate for female-headed households is 44%, more than six times the rate for married-couple households (7.2%). In addition, considerable variation in poverty by race exists in female-headed households: 61.5% for blacks, 39.4% for Hispanics, and 24.5% for whites. However, most (59.6%) of the *increase* in poverty in female-headed households between 1979 and 1986 was in households maintained by white women; this reverses the trend between 1973 and 1979, when only 35.7% of the increase in poverty was in households maintained by white women.

The poverty rate among children under six varies inversely with the education of the parents: the rate is 62% for young children whose parents have not completed high school, whereas it is 19% for children with at least one parent who has completed high school. Poverty for children under six also varies substantially with geographic area—it is much higher in central cities (31%) and rural areas (28%) than it is in the suburbs (13%).

Although single teenagers account for only about 5% of the births to single mothers, the proportion of teenage births to unwed mothers increased from 15% to 60% between 1960 and 1986.

The economic status of a family is directly related to whether two parents are present, whether the parent(s) work, the level of parental education, the race of the parents, and where they live.

Finally, poor children are at greater risk of negative lifetime outcomes than are those in more affluent families—especially those born to unwed mothers, living in single-parent or minority households, or whose parents have little education. Obviously, however, failure for poor children is not inevitable. A variety of interventions can greatly improve their life chances. Toward that end, chapter 5 will examine family policies in other countries for the insights they might provide for dealing with the family issues in the United States. Priorities for assisting poor children and their families will be discussed in chapters 6 and 7.

Notes

1. Constance Sorrentino, "The Changing Family in International Perspective," *Monthly Labor Review* 113 (March 1990), pp. 41–58.

2. Arthur J. Norton and Jeanne E. Moorman, "Current Trends in Marriage and Divorce among American Women," *Journal of Marriage and the Family* 49 (February 1987), pp. 3–14.

3. National Center for Health Statistics, "Advanced Report of Final Natality Statistics, 1987," *Monthly Vital Statistics Report* 38 (3, suppl., 1989), pp. 32–34.

4. U.S. Bureau of the Census, *Household and Family Characteristics: March 1989*, Current Population Reports, Series P-20, No. 437 (1989), pp. 79, 83.

5. National Center for Health Statistics, "Advanced Report of Final Natality Statistics, 1987," pp. 32–34.

6. U.S. Bureau of the Census, *Households, Families, Marital Status and Living Arrangements: March 1988*, Current Population Reports, 1989, p. 63.

7. Lawrence Mishel and David Frankel, *The State of Working America* (Washington, DC: Economic Policy Institute, 1990), p. 185.

8. John Palmer, Timothy Smeeding, and Barbara Torrey, eds., *The Vulnerable* (Washington, DC: Urban Institute Press, 1988).

9. National Center for Children in Poverty, *Five Million Children* (New York: Columbia University, School of Public Health, 1990).

10. M. R. Burt and Frank Levy, "Measuring Program Costs," in National Research Council, Panel on Adolescent Pregnancy and Childbearing, *Risking the Future: Adolescent Sexuality, Pregnancy and Childbearing*, Vol. 2 (Washington, DC: National Academy Press, 1987).

4

Family Employment, Income, and Wealth: Growing Inequalities

The decline in real wages and the consequent growing inequality in wealth and income are major problems for American families. Family incomes have not fallen by as much as real wages, mainly because women are working more and in higher-paying occupations. This, however, cannot be a permanent solution for American families, because there is a limit to the amount of labor each family has to sell. The main reasons for the decline in real wages are related to the declining competitiveness of the American economy, detailed in chapter 2, though some income problems are due to changes in family structures. Unless economic performance improves, wages will continue to stagnate and polarize, with negative consequences for the nation's economic, political, and social health. This chapter analyzes some of the most important changes in family employment, income, and wealth. It begins with a discussion of the increased labor-force participation of women, a fundamental factor affecting family relations and income.

The Increased Labor-Force Participation of Women

The extent to which women have entered the paid labor force is clearly the most important labor-market development of this century. Women have always worked, of course, but in preindustrial times the family was the main producing unit and the work of women was an integral part of that unit. With industrialization, the labor market spread and production was increasingly external to the family. In this system, women were considered to be peripheral and temporary participants in the male-dominated market economy. Market values gave inadequate attention to work in the home, and the rules for the determination of wages and working conditions in the market economy were made on the assumption that men would be the main source of a family's money income.

At present, however, the conflict between this assumption and the reality that women have become permanent, integral, important participants in the labor market is the source of considerable tension in employment as well as in family relations and public policy. The way family members (especially men), govern-

FIGURE 4.1

Civilian Labor-Force Participation Rate of Women, Selected Years, 1900–1989

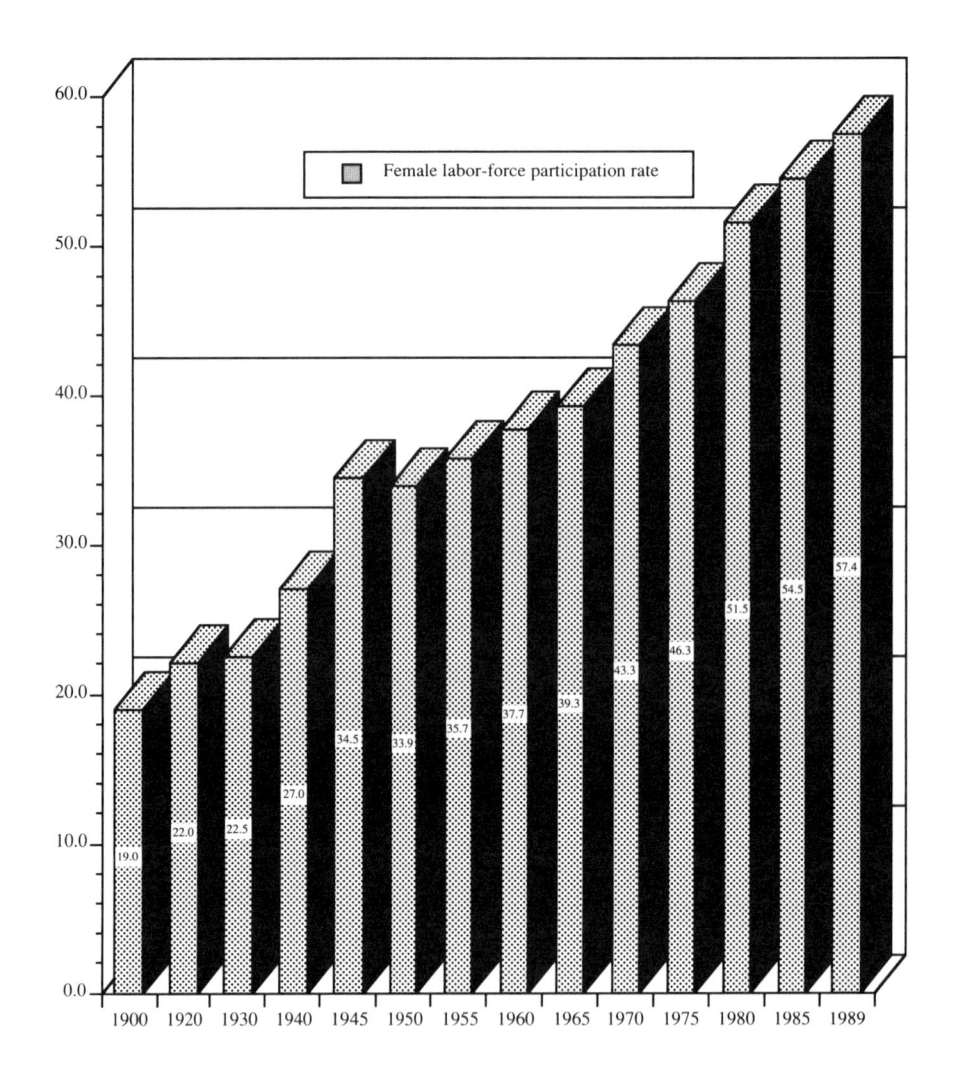

Year	Female labor-force participation rate
1900	19.0
1920	22.0
1930	22.5
1940	27.0
1945	34.5
1950	33.9
1955	35.7
1960	37.7
1965	39.3
1970	43.3
1975	46.3
1980	51.5
1985	54.5
1989	57.4

Sources: U.S. Bureau of the Census, Current Population Reports, Series P-20, No. 441 (Washington, DC: United States Government Printing Office, 1989), pp. 6–9; U.S. Bureau of the Census, *Statistical Abstract of the United States: 1990*, 110th ed. (Washington, DC: United States Government Printing Office, 1990), p. 46.

ments, and employers respond to the employment of women has important implications for families as well as for the nation's economic and social health.

The proportion of women in the paid work force increased gradually during the 1930s and 1940s until it peaked at 35% at the end of World War II. As Figure 4.1 shows, the rate declined to 34% in 1950, then increased sharply, reaching 57% in 1989. By the year 2000, 63% of working-age women probably will be in the work force. Women will constitute more than 60% of the work-force growth during the decade of the 1990s (see Figure 4.2, which displays these changes graphically). In contrast, Table 4.1 (page 123) indicates that the labor-force participation rates of men have declined steadily. Participation rates have increased steadily for every female age cohort, though they tend to decline for the 25-to-34 age cohorts and to rise for older age groups (see Table 4.2, page

FIGURE 4.2

Percentage Distribution of the Civilian Labor Force by Gender (top)
Percentage Distribution of the Growth in the Civilian Labor Force by Gender (bottom)

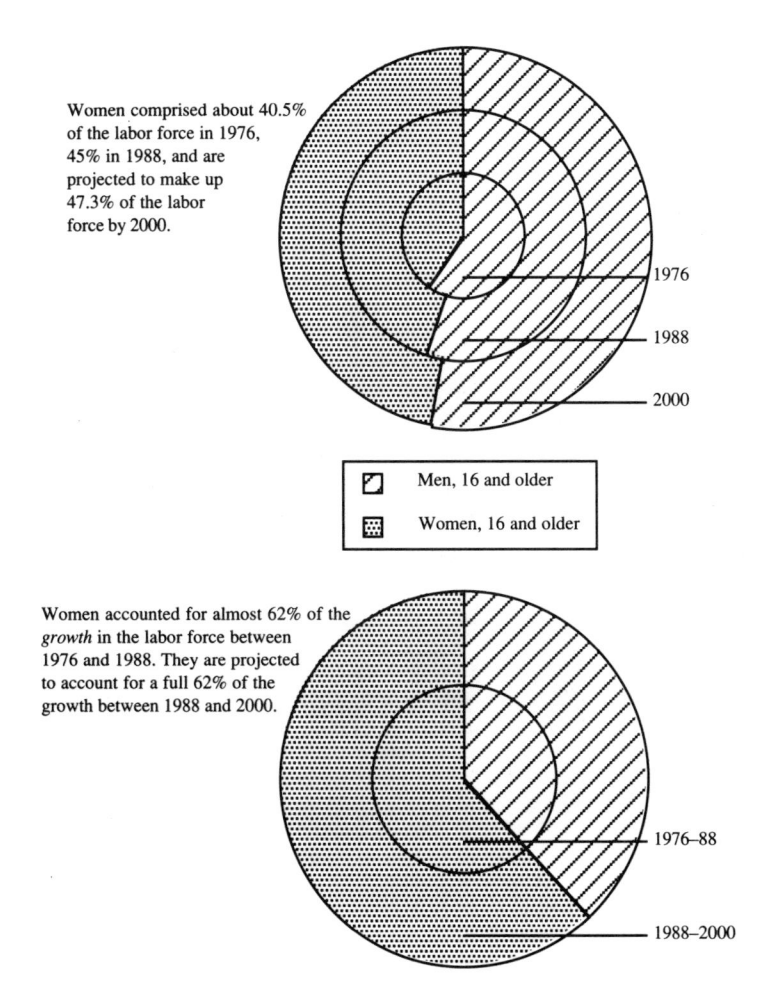

Women comprised about 40.5% of the labor force in 1976, 45% in 1988, and are projected to make up 47.3% of the labor force by 2000.

1976
1988
2000

☐ Men, 16 and older
☐ Women, 16 and older

Women accounted for almost 62% of the *growth* in the labor force between 1976 and 1988. They are projected to account for a full 62% of the growth between 1988 and 2000.

1976–88
1988–2000

Source: Howard N. Fullerton, Jr., "New Labor Force Projections, Spanning 1988–2000," *Monthly Labor Review* 112 (November 1989), p. 8.

124). Note, however, that delayed marriages and the rapid reentry of women into the work force following childbirth have caused this pattern to be much less pronounced in the 1970s and '80s than it was in the 1950s and '60s. Table 4.3 (page 125) shows the number of men and women in the labor force and the proportion of women as a percentage of all workers. Women have increased from 33.4% of the labor force in 1960 to more than 45% in 1989.

A number of forces are associated with the increased employment of women. One of these has been the growth of technology, which has increased service and light manufacturing jobs, both considered to be more appropriate for women. Also, technology and industrialization have interacted to increase life expectancies and make it possible for families to control more effectively the number and spacing of children. Technology also has reduced the amount of time required to do housework. These developments have greatly increased the amount of time women have available for paid work. In 1900, for example, the

FIGURE 4.3

**Mean Money Earnings of Year-round Full-time Workers
By Sex and Years of Schooling, 1987**

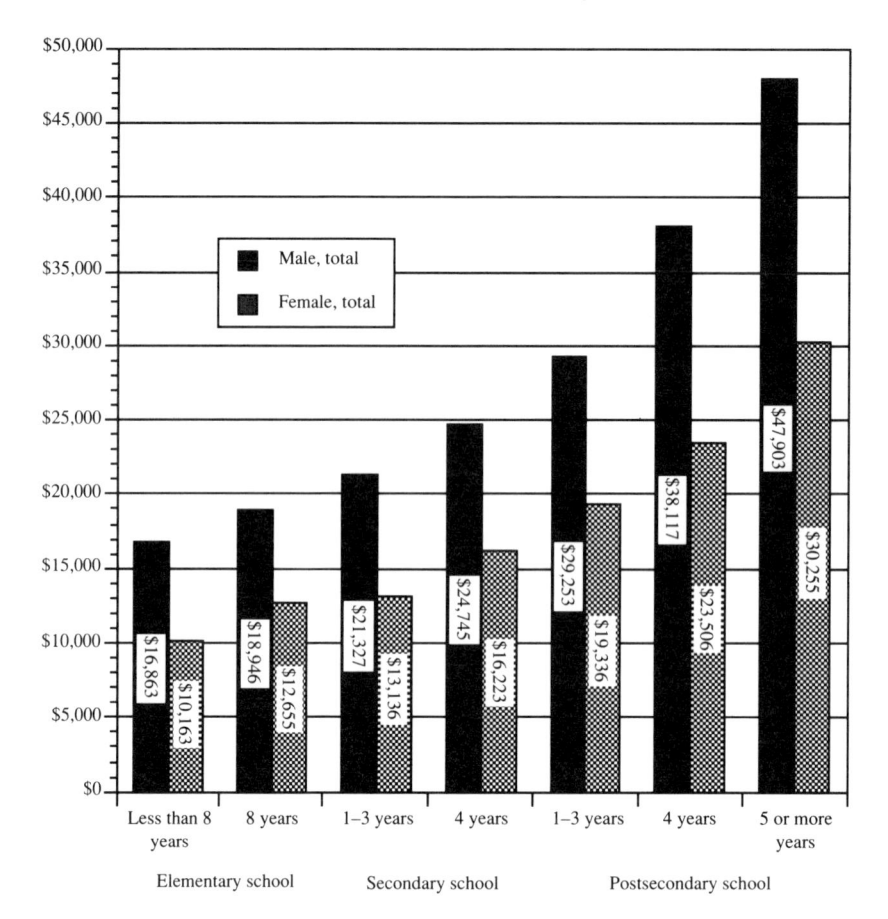

Education Level	Male	Female
Elementary school, Less than 8 years	$16,863	$10,163
Elementary school, 8 years	$18,946	$12,655
Secondary school, 1–3 years	$21,327	$13,136
Secondary school, 4 years	$24,745	$16,223
Postsecondary school, 1–3 years	$29,253	$19,336
Postsecondary school, 4 years	$38,117	$23,506
Postsecondary school, 5 or more years	$47,903	$30,255

Source: U.S. Bureau of the Census, Current Population Reports, Series P-60, No. 162 (Washington, DC: United States Government Printing Office, 1990).

---

life expectancy of a white woman in the United States at age 20 was about 64 years. She could expect, on the average, to be widowed at age 52 and to die before her last child left home. In 1980, a white woman who married at 22 could expect to live about 79 years and to stop having children at age 30. Her last child would leave home when she was 48. There was, however, a 47% chance that her first marriage would end in divorce. What this means, of course, is that social and demographic changes have reduced the importance of marriage in the life of most women. The chances are high that the average woman will spend two-thirds of her adult life without children at home and one-half to two-thirds without a husband.[1]

These demographic and economic forces have interacted with changing social attitudes to increase the power and independence of women. An important step in achieving this greater independence was for women to gain access to education and then to gain greater political and economic power. This process can be expected to accelerate because women have closed the general education gap and have narrowed the gaps in many more traditional fields. Between 1970 and 1986, for example, the proportion of women architects increased from 4% to 8%; of lawyers, from 5% to 20%; of doctors, from 10% to 18%; of computer scientists, from 14% to 28%; and of college teachers, from 29% to 37%.[2] As the economy has become more knowledge intensive, the importance of education for career success has increased. As can be seen from Tables 4.4 and 4.5 (pages 126 and 127), young women are less likely to be high school dropouts than are young men and also are more likely to have four or more years of college.

The occupational distribution of women from 1972 to 1989 is detailed in Table 4.6 (page 128). Some important shifts have occurred in women's employment patterns. In 1972, 17% of women were employed in managerial and professional specialties. But women are still heavily concentrated in sales and administrative support positions and services. In fact, in 1989, women held more than 80% of clerical and administrative support positions, about one-half of sales positions, and more than 60% of service occupations.

The earning patterns of men and women, in general and by level of education, are displayed in Table 4.7 and Figure 4.3. Table 4.7 (page 129) shows that women's median earnings relative to men increased gradually during the 1980s, partly because women's earnings were higher, but also because men's earnings fell. In 1989, the median full-time, year-round earnings for women were two-thirds those of men. Men earn more than women at every level of education. Indeed, despite the general correlation between more education and higher earnings for the population as a whole, male high school graduates earned more than female college graduates.

Not surprisingly, the experts do not agree on the reason for the earnings differential between men and women. Many believe, however, that even though part of the gender wage gap is due to factors other than discrimination against women, there is no doubt that part of the difference is due to discrimination. Almost all studies that attempt to account for the differential between men's and women's earnings by citing labor-market factors such as continuity of employment, education, experience, and so forth leave large unexplained residuals. These findings suggest that labor-market discrimination against women persists despite antidiscrimination legislation, improved attitudes about the employment of women, and some progress in closing the gender wage gap.

Family Employment Characteristics

In the first quarter of 1990, of the 65.3 million families in the United States, 53 million (81%) had employed members in the work force. Approximately 50 million of these families (76%) had members employed full time. Five million (7.8%) had a member unemployed, but 71% of these had other members employed. Approximately 10.9 million families had no one in the work force, but most of these families were composed of persons older than 60.[3]

In the 1940s and '50s, almost all American children lived in what has been called the "traditional" family, in which mothers worked in the home and fathers worked in the paid labor force. As the previous two chapters make abundantly clear, the traditional family is no longer the norm.

By 1990, only about one-fourth (26%) of all families with children were supported solely on the father's earnings, down from approximately 70% in 1940. Between 1975 and 1988, however, the percentage of working mothers in married-couple families with children went from 45% to 65%. In 1988, the mother and father worked in 63% of these families, up from 43% in 1975.[4]

Another significant change occurred in the labor-force participation of female-headed families with children younger than 18, which increased from

Social and demographic changes have reduced the importance of marriage in the life of women. The chances are high that the average woman will spend two-thirds of her adult life without children at home and one-half to two-thirds without a husband.

By 1990, only about one-fourth of all families with children were supported solely on the father's earnings, down from approximately 70% in 1940.

approximately 15% to 21% of all families between 1975 and 1988. Approximately 60% of these mothers were in the work force in 1975 and 67% in 1988.

Although they are relatively few, the single-parent families maintained by men more than doubled between 1975 and 1988, from 454,000 to 1,070,000, from 1.6% of all families with children younger than 18 to 3.3%. The proportion of such fathers in the work force increased from 87% to 90.2%.

By 1988, less than half of all families (48.6%) had children younger than 18 years of age. Of these 31.8 million families, 88.7% had employed parents and 61.6% had employed mothers. Only slightly more than one-fifth of all families (14.8 million or 22.7%) had children younger than six years old. Almost all of these families with young children (87%) had employed members and more than half of the mothers (53.7%) were employed.

Racial Composition and Family Employment Characteristics

Of the 65.3 million American families in 1990, 7.4 million were black and 4.8 million were of Hispanic origin (see Table 4.8, page 130). Hispanic families were most likely to have at least one member in the work force (85.4% of families, compared with 83.7% for whites and 79.6% for blacks). Hispanics and whites had about the same proportion of families with one member employed, but whites and Hispanics were substantially more likely than were blacks to have a member employed full time: 72.1% for whites, 69.7% for Hispanics, but only 59.8% for blacks.

Of the nation's families, more than three-fourths were married-couple families, whereas 11 million families were maintained by women and 2.9 million by men (see Table 4.9, page 131). In about half of husband–wife families, both husband and wife were employed; in approximately one-fifth, only the husband was employed; and in 5.2% only the wife was employed.

The employment patterns of whites, blacks, and Hispanics vary considerably (Table 4.10, page 132). Labor-force participation rates of whites (66.8%) were higher than were those of Hispanics (64.5%) or blacks (62.6%). Note, however, that black married-couple families have participation rates of 66.9%, about equal to that of white married-couple families (67%) and higher than for Hispanics (65.6%). The highest participation rate for husbands in these families is among Hispanics (83.2%), compared with 77.9% for whites and 75.9% for blacks. However, black wives have by far the highest participation rate: 65.6%, compared with 57.5% for whites and 52.8% for Hispanics. Blacks also have the highest unemployment rate. The unemployment rate for white family members in 1990 was 5%, compared with 11.7% for blacks and 8.2% for Hispanics.

Number of Earners

These data make it very clear that what we know anecdotally is true: the employment of two parents greatly improves family income. The median weekly wages of families with two or more earners are more than double those of families with only one earner ($841 versus $387) (see Table 4.11, page 133). Married-couple families had much higher weekly earnings if both husband and wife worked ($836) than if only the husband worked ($490) or only the wife worked ($267). In approximately 27% of married-couple families, only the husband worked; in 7%, only the wife worked; and in 46.4%, both the husband and wife worked. However, 64% of married-couple families had two or more work-

The employment of two parents greatly improves family income. The median weekly wages of families with two or more earners are more than double those of families with only one earner.

ers; in families in which husband, wife, and one other member worked (10.4%), weekly family wages were $1,131.

Of the families maintained by women, 67.9% had only one earner and wages averaged only $284 a week. Less than one-third of such families had two or more earners, and weekly wages averaged $614. The families maintained by men were somewhat more likely to have two or more earners (38.8%) and had higher weekly earnings ($769).

In the postwar period, the number of households maintained by persons not in the work force has increased significantly, from approximately 7 million in 1960 to 16 million in 1988. Married couples represented 51% of these households in 1950, but more than 69% in 1988. The great growth of such married-couple households undoubtedly reflects the tendency for husbands to retire early, especially after 1955.[5] However, married-couple families in which the wife but not the husband was in the work force increased considerably—4.5% of families were in this category in 1940 and 14.8% in 1988.[6]

Unemployment and Temporary Workers

Unemployment levels have increased for both men and women since the 1960s, though the situation improved somewhat between 1979 and 1989. Unemployment rates for various groups were as follows:

	Total	Male	Female	White	Black	Hispanic
1967	3.8%	3.1%	5.2%	3.4%	NA	NA
1979	5.8	5.1	6.8	5.1	12.3	8.3
1989	5.3	5.2	5.4	4.5	11.4	8.0

Lower unemployment rates in 1989 were due mainly to slower growth in the work force, not to a faster growth in jobs. Full-time-equivalent employment grew by 2.28% a year between 1973 and 1979, but slowed to 1.64% between 1979 and 1988.

The proportion of persons holding "involuntary" part-time jobs—that is, people who would rather be working full time—also rose from 3.8% of nonagricultural employment in 1979 to 4.7% in 1988. At the same time, the proportion of part-time workers increased from 17.6% in 1979 to 18.4% in 1988. The proportion of part-time workers who would prefer full-time jobs rose from 33.7% of part-time jobs in 1973–79 to 43.1% in 1979–88. Involuntary unemployment rates were significantly higher for women in 1988 (5.6%) than for men (3.9%), especially for married women (4.8%) relative to married men (2.6%). These rates also were much higher for blacks than they were for whites (7.2% vs. 4.4%).

Lower wages have, in addition, increased the small but growing proportion of workers who hold more than one job for hardship reasons, especially among women. The percentage of men and women combined who do this increased from 3.6% to 5.5% between 1979 and 1989. In 1989, 48.2% of the workers who held multiple jobs for hardship reasons were women, up from 33.7% in 1979. Only about 41% of female multiple job holders for hardship reasons were in the "married with spouses present" category—the rest were single, widowed, divorced, or separated.

A growing proportion of the work force is classified as "contingent" workers hired on a temporary basis. Temporary and personnel-service workers increased from 0.3% of total U.S. employment in 1973 to 0.6% in 1979 and 1.2% in 1989. In 1989, women constituted more than one-half (58%) of the per-

The proportion of persons holding "involuntary" part-time jobs rose between 1979 and 1988.

Lower wages increased the small but growing proportion of workers who hold more than one job for hardship reasons, especially among women.

sonnel services component of the temporary employment industry. Tem-porary women employees increased their share of total employment from 0.3% in 1982 to 0.7% in 1989.

Changes in Family Income Distribution

Income inequality was more prevalent during the 1980s and in 1987 it was greater than at any time since 1947.[7] The income of the richest 20% of families increased by 28.9% in the 1980s, and the income share of the wealthiest 1% was greater in 1987 than that of the poorest 40%. Capital gains accounted for 40% of the income growth by the upper 1% of families. The bottom 90% of families realized an average of $9 from capital gains between 1980 and 1990; the average family in the upper 1% of income recipients gained $91,842 and the next 4% gained $5,421. Thus, only the very rich benefited much from capital gains.

These income inequalities were caused by a number of factors. The rapid growth in nonlabor income was due mainly to higher interest income, which rose from 9.2% of market-based income in 1973 to 12.0% in 1979 and 16.2% in 1989. Rent income actually declined from 1.8% in 1973 to 0.2% in 1989. These changes were due to the growth of capital income by a whopping 68.5% between 1979 and 1989, compared with an increase of 24.9% for all labor income and a growth of 9.4% in the income of business and farm owners.

Labor's share of national income, which is the aggregate of labor and property earnings that arise in the current production of goods and services, also fell during the 1980s. It was 71.1% in 1989, down from 74.6% in 1979 and 74.7% in 1973. Other functional shares in 1989 were capital, 19.3% (up from 13.6% in 1973 and 14.9% in 1979), and income from business and farm ownership, 9.6% (down from 11.7% in 1973 and 10.4% in 1979).

Although the United States consumed approximately 4% more of the gross national product than it produced during the 1980s, this was due mainly to a slowdown in real disposable-income growth per capita, not because of an increase in average family personal consumption. The growth of personal-consumption expenditures per capita actually fell from 3.14% between 1967 and 1973 to 1.74% between 1979 and 1989, the lowest of any postwar decade. However, the growth in consumption by the highest fifth of income recipients between 1972–73 and 1988, the only dates for which data are available, was 2.18%, compared with 1.35% for the households with the lowest fifth of income and 1.61% for all households.

A major determinant of the economic well-being of American families has been the decline in real wages since the early 1970s. Wages are important, of course, because they account for more than 70% of American family income and for much larger percentages among low-income families. Declining real wages have been a particularly serious problem for young men, minorities, those without college educations, and households maintained by single women.

Real wages declined by 9% between 1980 and 1989. Fringe benefits (pensions, insurance, health benefits) fell even more (13.8%). Wages and income have declined since the early 1970s, but by how much depends on the measures used. Total hourly compensation, excluding taxes, fell from $14.42 in 1980 to $13.01 in 1989, a drop of $1.41 or 9.8%. The average weekly earnings of front-line nonsupervisory and production workers were $40.53 less in 1989 than they were in 1973. Family incomes have been sustained mainly because the average family with children worked more than 20% more average weeks in 1989 than in 1979.

The wage changes, moreover, were different for men and women. The median weekly wage for men fell from $486.10 in 1973 to $451.50 in 1988. Wages were diminished for the entire lower three-fourths of male workers. For the top 10% of wage earners, real weekly wages rose from $921.00 in 1973 to $929.60 in 1979 and $964.20 in 1988. But between 1979 and 1989, hourly wages for this group increased only from $21.17 to $21.97.

For women, wages increased more than they did for men, thus narrowing the differential between median hourly real wages of men and women. Women's wages rose from 62.3% of men's in 1979 to 66.0% in 1988. Overall, the proportion of workers earning a poverty wage has significantly increased—from 26% in 1979 to 32% in 1987. Still, a much higher proportion of women than men earn the poverty wage (35.2% in 1979 and 39.5% in 1989 for women versus 17.8% in 1979 and 24.4% in 1989 for men).

Another cause of growing wage inequality is the widening wage gap between workers by level of education. The economic return for increasing years of schooling remains high, but the average wage of all high school graduates fell by 4% between 1979 and 1987, while the average for college graduates increased by 8%. The wage gap between college and high school graduates therefore rose by 18.7% between 1979 and 1987, after having narrowed between 1971 and 1979. This widening educational wage gap between 1979 and 1987 was not due to rapid growth in the wages of college graduates. Between 1979 and 1987, college-educated workers' wages grew by 8%, but this was only about one-fourth as much as the increase in the 1960s. In fact, the average college graduate earned less in 1987 than in 1971. The main reason for the growing gap between high school and college graduates was the large decline in the wages of lower-paid workers: wages for those with 8 to 11 years of schooling declined 6.3% and for high school graduates, 4%. The decline has been more dramatic for young male high school graduates with one to five years of experience, whose weekly wages were 18% lower in 1987 than they were in 1979. The weekly wages of young female high school graduates were 3.5% lower in 1989 than in 1979. Male high school graduates with 26 to 30 years of experience had weekly wages only slightly lower in 1987 than in 1979 (a decline of 2.0%), whereas wages for women in this category were 11.3% higher in 1987. Between 1963 and 1971 the wages of experienced (26 to 30 years) men and women rose 18.1% and 21.5%, respectively.[8]

Wage changes have, in addition, been influenced by the fact that 1.7 million jobs were lost in higher-paying manufacturing and mining industries between 1979 and 1989, while the lower-paying retail trade service sectors gained 14.4 million jobs. The high-wage manufacturing, mining, government, transportation, and communications share of the work force dropped 7.7% between 1979 and 1989. In the 1981–87 period, industries with expanding employment had average annual per-worker compensation of $21,983, compared with $32,387 for declining industries, a difference of $10,404 a year, or 47%.

Thus, the main picture that emerges is that (1) the real wages of men are declining, (2) family incomes are being held up mainly because more women work longer hours, and (3) U.S. income distribution, already the most unequal of any major industrial economy, has become markedly more unequal since the 1970s. There are, however, variations on these patterns according to race, age, family structure, and education.

Table 4.12 (pages 134–136) and Figures 4.4 and 4.5 confirm the concentration of blacks and Hispanics in the lowest income categories. In 1988, blacks constituted 11.4% of all households in America but accounted for 22.6% of

The average wage of all high school graduates fell by 4% between 1979 and 1987, while the average for college graduates increased by 8%.

Wage changes have been influenced by the fact that 1.7 million jobs were lost in higher-paying manufacturing and mining industries between 1979 and 1989, while the lower-paying retail trade service sectors gained 14.4 million jobs.

FIGURE 4.4

1988 Income Distribution of Black and Hispanic-origin Married-couple Households

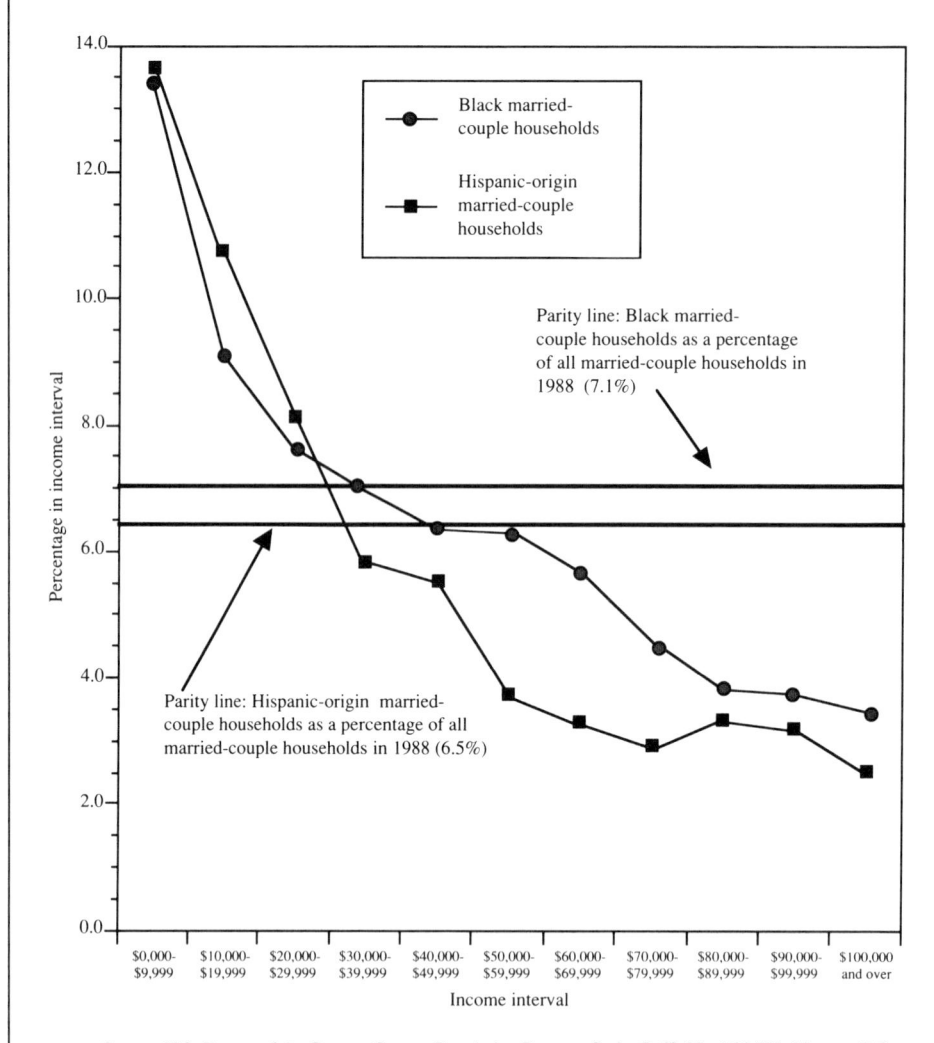

Source: U.S. Bureau of the Census, Current Population Reports, Series P-60, No. 166 (Washington, DC: United States Government Printing Office, 1989), pp. 25–26.

households with income below $10,000 a year. They were, moreover, underrepresented in all higher-income categories. Also, blacks accounted for only about 7% of all married-couple households but approximately 30% of all female-headed households. Both black married-couple and female-headed households were overrepresented in low-income categories. Although blacks made up 7% of married couples, they represented 13.4% of married couples with incomes less than $10,000. Black families maintained by females were 30% of such households but accounted for 42% of those with incomes less than $10,000.

Hispanics were not as overrepresented in the low-income categories as were blacks but their incomes also were heavily skewed toward the lower end of the scale. Hispanics accounted for 6.4% of households and a slightly higher proportion of all married-couple families (6.5%). They represented 10.2% of fami-

FIGURE 4.5

1988 Income Distribution of Black and Hispanic-origin Family Households

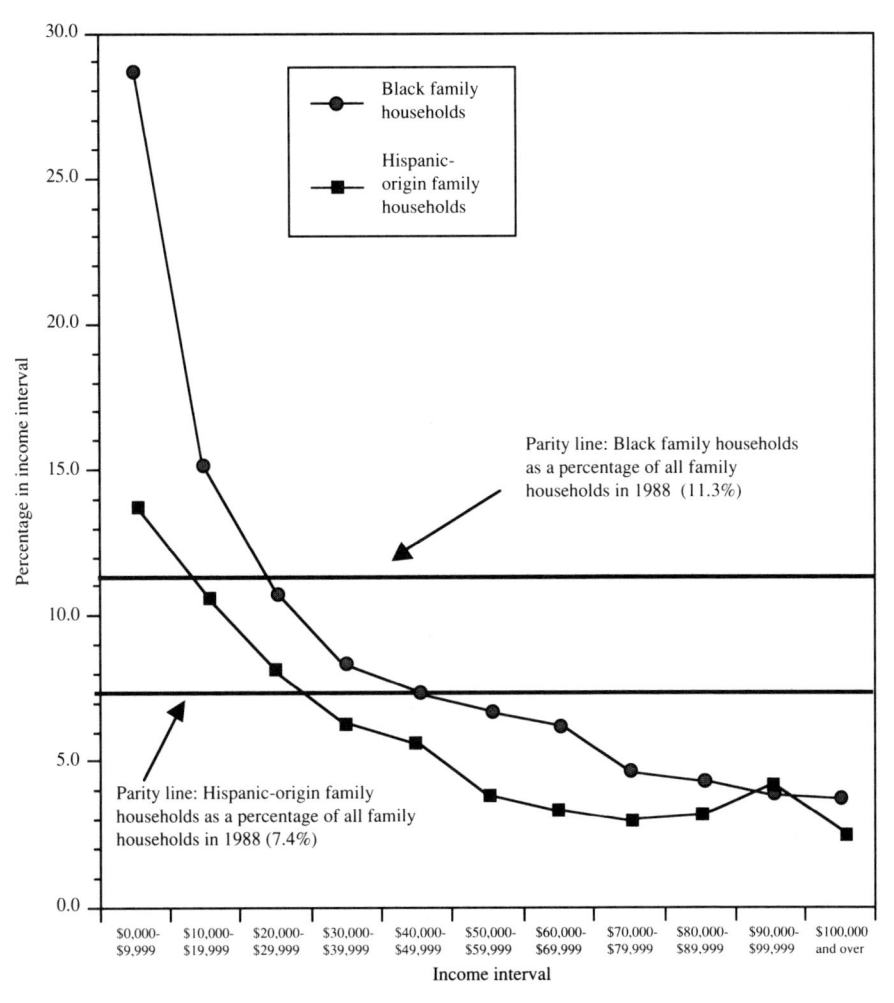

[Figure: Line chart showing percentage in income interval (y-axis, 0.0 to 30.0) by income interval (x-axis, $0,000-$9,999 through $100,000 and over) for Black family households and Hispanic-origin family households. Two horizontal parity lines are shown: Black family households as a percentage of all family households in 1988 (11.3%), and Hispanic-origin family households as a percentage of all family households in 1988 (7.4%).]

Source: U.S. Bureau of the Census, Current Population Reports, Series P-60, No. 166 (Washington, DC: United States Government Printing Office, 1989), pp. 25–26.

---

lies headed by females. However, Hispanics accounted for 8.8% of all households with incomes less than $10,000, and Hispanic married-couple families accounted for 13.6% of all such households. Only 2.4% of Hispanic married-couple families had incomes of $100,000 and more in 1988.

Table 4.12 also shows the distribution of household incomes by race. Approximately 27% of blacks and 20% of Hispanics, but only 8.2% of whites, had incomes less than $10,000. Note, however, that although lower percentages of black and Hispanic married-couple families were in this low-income category—10.6% and 11.8%, respectively—only 5.2% of white married-couple families had incomes less than $10,000. In general, the racial proportions in the $20,000–$40,000 income brackets were more equal for married-couple families, as can be seen from a comparison of Figures 4.3 and 4.4. As noted earlier, however, married couples accounted for a much smaller percentage of all black households in 1989 (36.1%) than of white or Hispanic households (59.4% and 56.2%, respectively). In 1988, black median family income was $18,098, compared with $32,274 for whites. Approximately 30% of blacks and only 8% of whites had incomes below the poverty line.

Young Families

Because they depend almost entirely on income from work, young families (headed by persons aged 25 to 34) were particularly hard hit by falling real wages during the 1980s. Income deterioration was especially serious for young families headed by workers without college degrees (55% of all young workers) as well as for those headed by blacks. After having grown by 0.5% a year between 1973 and 1979, median incomes of young families fell by 0.5% a year between 1979 and 1988. The typical (median) young family consequently had $629 less income in 1988 than did its counterpart in 1973. The decline in median income was at least twice as fast for young black families, who had $3,300 (16%) less income in 1988 than did their 1973 counterparts.

The deterioration of median incomes of young families varied by levels of education. Families maintained by high school graduates had a median income $2,300 less than they did in 1973. The median income for families maintained by college graduates, by contrast, was 10.8% higher in 1987 than it was in 1973. Among blacks, young families headed by college graduates were better off relative to black families maintained by persons with less education, but they were not any better off in 1987 than their demographic counterparts were in 1979. For the typical black family head with less than a high school education, income was 33% lower in 1987 than it was in 1979; for black families headed by college graduates, income was down by only 0.6%. Among whites, the typical family headed by a college graduate had 13.6% more income than its 1979 counterpart.[9]

Young families have maintained their per-capita incomes by having fewer children and working more hours. In 1973, 66% of young families had children; in 1987 only 50.3% of them did. Between 1973 and 1987, the proportion of married couples with children dropped from 56.5% to 37.5%, while the proportion of single mothers with children increased from 9.1% to 11.3%.[10]

As noted earlier, the main reason for the slowdown in the earnings of young families was their heavy reliance on wages, which have declined relative to nonlabor income. In 1987 the average young family got nearly all (94.3%) of its income from earnings; the average family of all ages received 72.3% of its income from this source. The average young family got only 2.8% of its income from capital investments and 2.1% from government transfers.[11] Young families with children headed by single parents received disproportionately more income from government transfers. The average family headed by a single woman got 16.5% of its income from government transfers; those headed by single men got 6.3% from that source. For all young families, average government transfers declined 2.3% between 1979 and 1987, after having risen 0.4% between 1973 and 1979. In 1988, all families received 16.6% of their income from capital, 72.3% from labor, and 6.8% from government transfers.

As Table 4.13 (page 137) shows, the average young married couple with children had a slightly higher income in 1987 than in 1979, despite their lower weekly wages, mainly because they worked more weeks. Note, however, that the average adult woman worked 5.3 more weeks at higher wages, whereas men had lower wages and were employed almost one week less.

Young families were particularly hard hit by falling real wages during the 1980s, especially young families headed by workers without college degrees as well as those headed by blacks.

The average young married couple with children had a slightly higher income in 1987 than in 1979, despite their lower weekly wages, mainly because they worked more weeks.

FIGURE 4.6

Full-time Equivalent Wage Growth of Young Workers, Aged 25–34, 1979–1987

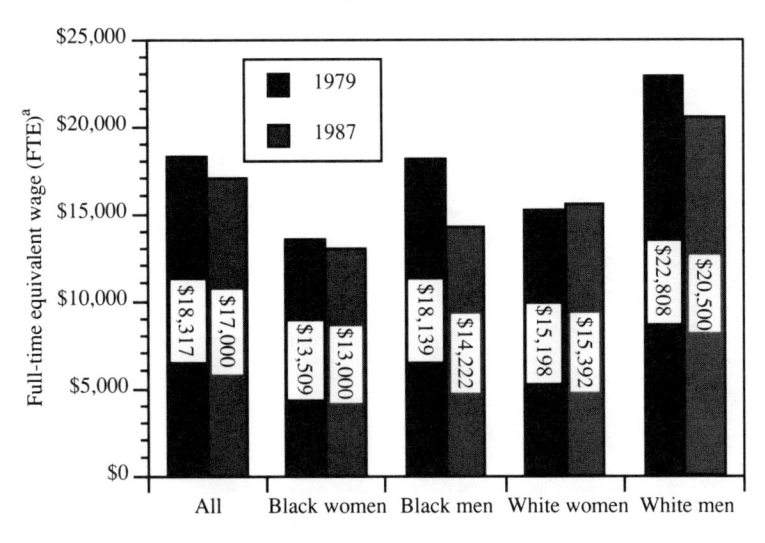

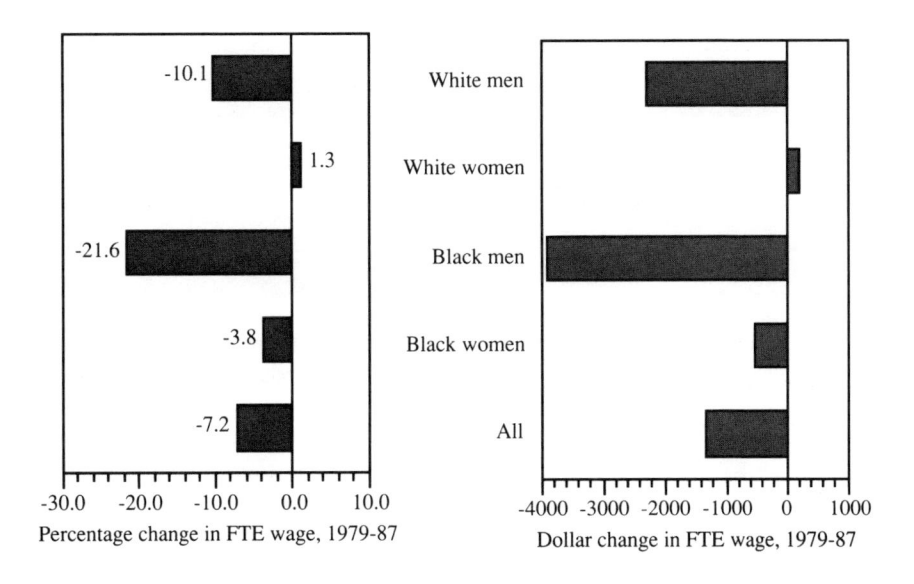

[Bar chart: Full-time equivalent wage (FTE)[a], comparing 1979 and 1987]

Group	1979	1987
All	$18,317	$17,000
Black women	$13,509	$13,000
Black men	$18,139	$14,222
White women	$15,198	$15,392
White men	$22,808	$20,500

Percentage change in FTE wage, 1979-87:
- White men: -10.1
- White women: 1.3
- Black men: -21.6
- Black women: -3.8
- All: -7.2

Dollar change in FTE wage, 1979-87 (approximate, from chart):
- White men: ~ -2300
- White women: ~ +200
- Black men: ~ -3900
- Black women: ~ -500
- All: ~ -1300

Adapted with permission from Lawrence Mishel and David Frankel, *The State of Working America* (Washington, DC: Economic Policy Institute, 1990), p. 212.

[a]Annual wage working full-time, full-year, at the average hourly wage.

Young married-couple families without children had higher overall earnings in 1987 than in 1979, despite a small decline in weekly wages for men. Table 4.14 (page 138) details these changes. Adult women in these families had 10.3% higher earnings but worked about half a week less, on average, than they did in the 1970s. Single women had the fastest wage growth between 1977–87 (5.2%) of any group and worked slightly more than half a week longer.

Thus, among young married couples with children, the wives' higher earnings prevented incomes from being lower than they would have been in 1979.

FIGURE 4.7

Full-time Equivalent Wage Growth of Young Workers, Aged 16–24, 1979–1987

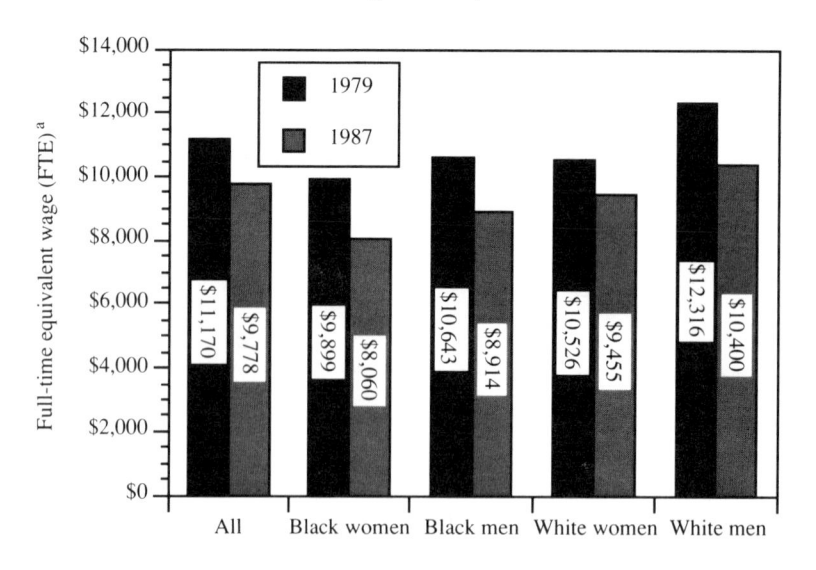

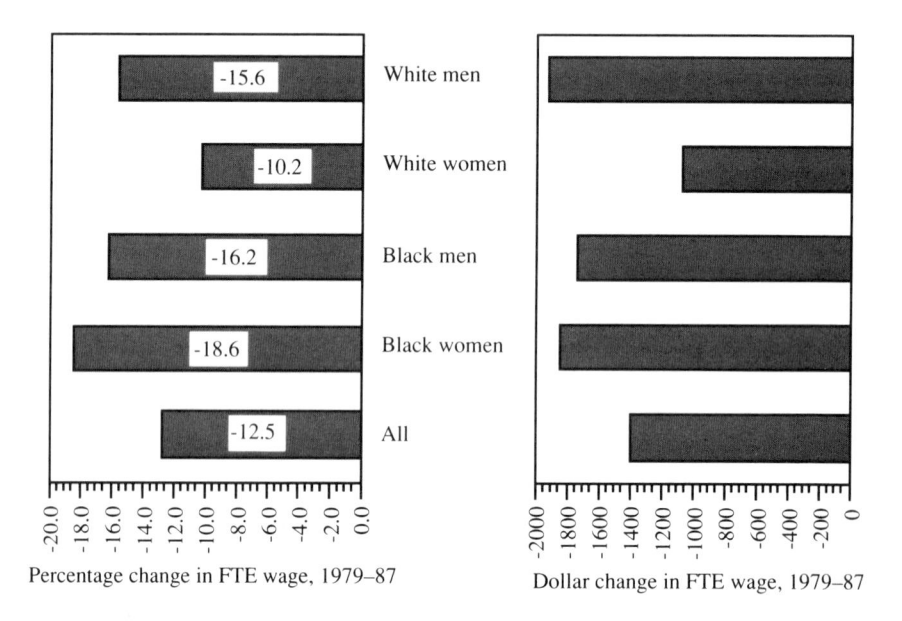

[Bar chart showing Full-time equivalent wage (FTE) for 1979 and 1987:
- All: $11,170 / $9,778
- Black women: $9,899 / $8,060
- Black men: $10,643 / $8,914
- White women: $10,526 / $9,455
- White men: $12,316 / $10,400]

[Percentage change in FTE wage, 1979–87:
- White men: -15.6
- White women: -10.2
- Black men: -16.2
- Black women: -18.6
- All: -12.5]

[Dollar change in FTE wage, 1979–87]

Adapted with permission from Lawrence Mishel and David Frankel, *The State of Working America* (Washington, DC: Economic Policy Institute, 1990), p. 212.

[a] Annual wage working full-time, full-year, at the average hourly wage.

Several points are worth emphasizing about these developments. Obviously, it will be harder in the future to sustain family incomes by having more wives work, because few families have additional wives who can enter the work force. Second, approximately three-fourths of the higher earnings of wives in these families were the result of working more hours; only about one-fourth were due to higher wages, though not necessarily higher wage rates for the same jobs. In other words, women have entered new jobs with higher wage rates; the wage rates have not increased as much for the jobs women traditionally have held.

It also is instructive to look at changes in full-time equivalent wages of young workers by race and gender.[12] For all young workers aged 25–34, earnings were 7.2% less in 1987 than they were in 1979; they declined 21.6% for all blacks and 10.1% for white men, as shown in Figure 4.6. Wages increased slightly only for white women (1.3%) but fell 3% to 8% for black women. Earnings declined substantially for the youngest age groups (16–24) of black and white males and females. The sharp decline in wages for young workers reflects the rapid shift to low-wage work by these workers during the 1980s. Figure 4.7 shows this decline in graphic terms.

Clearly, the downward shift in wages was particularly dramatic for non–college-educated young workers. The full-time earnings gap between college and high school graduates increased from 16% in 1979 to 33% in 1987. The annual wages of a college graduate rose by 9.2%, whereas a high school graduate earned 8.6% less. Lawrence Mishel and David Frankel offer two explanations for these changes: (1) young workers who have completed only high school worked in lower-wage industries in 1987 than in 1973 and (2) their numbers increased relative to college graduates.[13] They conclude that deunionization and the shift to lower-wage industries largely account for the growth in the college–high school graduate wage gap.[14]

Impact of Women's Earnings on Family Income

As the foregoing suggests, one of the main ways the average family has sustained its income is by selling more labor. This is especially true for low-income families. Between 1979 and 1987, for example, the average number of income earners per family rose by 22%, from 1.34 in 1979 to 1.64 in 1989. For the bottom two-fifths of families (i.e., the two lowest quintiles) in terms of income, the number of earners per family grew by 26% and 32%, contrasted with only 15% and 16% for the top two quintiles.

In every income class, higher incomes have been due mainly to the increased earnings of women. The earnings changes in married-couple families between 1979–87 by member and quintile (size adjusted for married couples with children) were:[15]

| | Highest-paid adult | | |
Quintile	Male	Female	Total family earnings
Top	12.0%	51.9%	16.9%
Fourth	0.8	44.1	7.3
Middle	-2.5	39.5	3.5
Second	-7.6	37.9	-1.4
Lowest	-15.4	18.4	-10.8
Total	1.9	44.4	07.8

Overall, the earnings of highest-paid females grew by 44.4%, males by 1.9%, and total family incomes by 7.8%. If we deduct the earnings of the highest-paid female in married-couple families, the increase in family income would have been only 0.2%. Thus virtually all of the increase in family incomes for this period was due to this factor. Indeed, for all except the top 20% of married-couple families (in which the highest-paid woman contributed 7.6% of the

Earnings declined substantially for the youngest age groups of black and white males and females. The sharp decline in wages for young workers reflects the rapid shift to low-wage work by these workers during the 1980s.

One of the ways the average family has sustained its income is by selling more labor. In every income class, higher incomes have been due mainly to the increased earnings of women.

9.1% increase in family incomes), family incomes would have declined as follows without the earnings of the highest-paid woman:[16]

Quintile	Earnings without top female
Top	-7.6%
Fourth	-1.0
Middle	-3.0
Second	-6.7
Lowest	-11.6

However, the increased earnings of wives do not represent a net gain in the standard of living for these families in that the increased work of women requires additional expenditures (child care, transportation, clothing, food, and so forth) as well as reduces leisure time for working mothers. This can be illustrated by examining the work-related expenditures of one- and two-earner families. In 1990 dollars, one-earner low-income families had incomes of $12,952, whereas two-earner families had $21,990. Work-related expenditures were $4,802 for one-earner families and $7,128 (48% higher) for two-earner families; in both cases, the bulk of work-related expenses were for transportation ($3,795 and $5,225, respectively). The comparable figures for middle-income families were:

	One-earner	Two-earner	Difference
Income	$27,876	$38,475	38%
Work-related expenses	5,933	9,139	54
Transportation	4,503	6,435	43

Thus, the real incomes of families are higher if there are two earners (by 70% and 38% for low- and middle-income families, respectively), but work-related expenditures reduce the advantage for two-earner families (to 18% and 27%, respectively).

The inability to find adequate child care is a major constraint on the employment of mothers. Approximately two-thirds of women do not pay for child care because they can leave their children in school or with friends, neighbors, and relatives. For those who do pay (32% of working women), average monthly family incomes are $3,586 and average weekly child-care expenses are $53.18, or 6.4% of income. The costs are higher for children younger than one year old ($62), but average family monthly incomes are also higher ($4,218). Average costs for one child younger than five ($54 or 6.6% of income) are, as should be expected, lower than they are for two or more children younger than five ($74.12 or 8% of income). Of course, a much larger percentage of families with young children (younger than five) must pay for child care (from 54.7% to 61.3% of families), compared with only 32% of all families with children; child care absorbs from 6.4% to 8.0% of the income of families with young children.[17]

Taxes and Family Income

Taxes as a percent of gross domestic product in the United States are low relative to other countries. Also, changes in taxes have contributed to the growing inequality of family incomes in America. On the first point, U.S. tax revenues as a percent of GDP were the lowest of any major country in 1987 (30%), compared with 30.2% for Japan, 37.5% for the United Kingdom, and 44.8% in

The inability to find adequate child care is a major constraint on the employment of mothers.

France. United States taxes also increased less between 1967–87 (2.7%) compared with 5.4% for West Germany, 11.9% for Japan, 4.6% for the United Kingdom, and 10.1% for France.

Second, federal tax changes in the 1980s made American family incomes more unequal. The top fifth of all families got 49.9% of income after federal taxes in 1990, up from 44.8% in 1980. The share of the middle fifth of families fell from 16.2% in 1980 to 14.9% in 1990. The effect of federal tax changes between 1977 and 1990 was to increase the after-tax incomes of the top fifth by 0.8%, and the top 1% by 1.3%, and to reduce the after-tax incomes of the bottom four-fifths of families from 0.4 percentage points for the fourth quintile and by 0.3 points, 0.2 points, and 0.1 points for the lowest three quintiles, respectively.

Federal taxes have therefore become more regressive since the 1970s. The 1986 tax reform made the system somewhat more progressive, but not enough to alter the basic character of the other changes in the 1980s.

Wealth

The economic welfare of families is determined by wealth as well as by income. In America, wealth is even more unequally distributed than is income, because more than half of all families (54%) in 1983, the most recent year for which data are available, had negative or zero financial assets. The top 0.5% of wealth holders owned 46.5% of all corporate stocks, whereas the bottom 90% owned only 10.7%. The top 10% owned 90% of all stocks and bonds. The average net worth of the top 0.5% of families rose 6.7% between 1979 and 1989, while the average net worth of the bottom 90% of families fell by 8.8%.

Wealth is also very unequally distributed between black and white households, regardless of type. The median net worth of various types of households in 1984 were:

	Black	White	Black/white ratio
All	$ 3,397	$39,135	.09
Married couples	13,061	54,184	.24
Female head	671	22,500	.03
Male head	3,022	11,826	.26

Poverty

After declining from 22.4% of the population in 1959 to 11.1% of it in 1973, poverty rates increased slightly to 11.7% in 1979 and then to 13.1% in 1988. These rates have increased regardless of whether the value of noncash benefits is included. For example, including food and housing benefits provided by governments at market value changes the poverty rates to 9.7% in 1979 and 12.0% in 1987. Not only are there more poor family members, but the mean income deficits (i.e., the gap between actual incomes and the poverty line) also have increased from 8.9% per family member in 1973–79 to 15.5% in 1979–88.

Although females have a higher incidence of poverty (14.6% in 1989 versus 11.5% for males), the poverty rates for both sexes have increased since 1973. The only group to experience reductions in poverty rates have been people older than 65. The main reason for the reduction in poverty among the elderly has been expanded transfer payments, particularly those adopted between 1967 and

Federal tax changes in the 1980s made American family incomes more unequal. Tax changes between 1977 and 1990 increased the after-tax incomes of the top fifth, and reduced the after-tax incomes of the bottom four-fifths of families.

Wealth is even more unequally distributed than is income. More than half of all families in 1983, the most recent year for which data are available, had negative or zero financial assets.

1973, which generally were indexed for inflation. Poverty rates before and after transfers for various groups and years were:[18]

	All persons		Persons aged 65 and older	
Year	Before transfer	After transfer	Before transfer	After transfer
1967	19.4%	14.3%	58.3%	28.7%
1973	19.0	11.1	58.0	16.1
1979	20.4	11.6	58.9	15.1
1988	21.2	13.0	52.0	12.0

Thus, without transfer payments, poverty among the elderly in 1988 would have been 52.0% instead of 12.0%.

The increase in poverty during the 1980s has occurred largely because of more regressive taxes and declining government assistance to the poor, especially the working poor, due to cuts in federal programs. The percentage of persons removed from poverty by government assistance declined from 48.2% in 1979 to 40.5% in 1988. For single-parent families with related children younger than 18, 39.7% were removed from poverty by such payments in 1979, but only 22.8% were in 1987. Among persons in married-couple families with children younger than 18, 33% were removed from poverty by these programs in 1979 and 24.4% in 1988.[19] Indeed, for single-parent families with related children younger than 18, 8.6 percentage points were added to their income by changes in government programs; market forces and demographics actually would have reduced poverty by 0.5 percentage points. For married couples with children younger than 18, market and demographic forces increased poverty by 1.1 percentage points and government program changes by 0.5 percentage points.

Contrary to popular assumptions, many poor people who can work do so. However, only about one-third (34.4%) of the poor were employable in 1988. Of these, 40.3% worked—33.7% of poor workers worked year round and 22.9% worked full time year round.

Housing, Health, and Education

Housing—one of the basic needs of individuals and families—significantly affects family well-being. Adequate housing is particularly important for providing an environment for the education and development of children. During the 1980s, home ownership fell, mainly because of high costs of housing and interest rates. Housing-cost increases have been especially detrimental to young families with children. The cost of housing as a percentage of income rose from 7% in 1970 to 22% in 1988 for home owners and from 23% to 30% for renters.[20] Home ownership declined for families maintained by persons in all age groups, as indicated by the following statistics:

	Percent of home ownership	
Age	1980	1988
Under 25	21%	15%
25–29	43	36
30–34	61	53
35–39	71	63

The increase in housing costs has created a particularly nasty hardship for low-income renters. A census survey reported that in 1985, 45% of all poverty-level renters, more than three million households, paid more than 70% of their income for housing and utilities; 55% of such households paid 60% or more of

The increase in poverty during the 1980s has occurred largely because of more regressive taxes and declining government assistance to the poor, especially the working poor, due to cuts in federal programs.

their income for housing in 1985, up from 44% in 1978.[21] The typical (median) poor renter household had an income of less than $5,000 in 1985 (about $5,500 in real terms in 1988) and spent 65% of its income on housing.

Poor home owners were not much better off. The typical poor home owner's household had an income of less than $5,000 in 1985 and paid 47% of its income for housing. Nearly half of poor home owners paid 50% of their income for housing and almost three-fourths paid at least 30%. Approximately 60% of all poor households were renters and 40% were owners.[22]

Conclusion

During the past 20 years, American families have experienced some very important changes in employment and income. Probably the most important of these changes has been the increased labor-force participation of women. The increased employment of the mothers of small children became especially significant during the 1970s and 1980s. Indeed, most mothers of preschool children are now in the work force. This trend is expected to continue so that by the year 2000, 80% of children under one year of age will have working mothers. Other implications of this development will be discussed in chapter 6. This chapter emphasizes that women work mainly for economic reasons and that the increased employment of women has prevented family incomes from falling as much as real wages for all except the wealthiest families. This is so because the real wages of men have declined since the early 1970s, mainly due to the changing composition of jobs and the fact that most American companies are competing with low-wage strategies rather than reorganizing to become high-performance companies.

The decline in real wages has been particularly sharp for young families, minorities, and workers without college educations. The main increases have been experienced by college-educated white workers, especially women. On the whole, however, women's incomes have risen mainly because they are working more and in higher-paying occupations, not because of an increase in the wages of the occupations where they are concentrated. The gender wage gap has narrowed mainly because men's wages have fallen, not because women's wages have increased.

Black and Hispanic families are worse off than whites on every major economic indicator. However, black college graduates are relatively better off than are those with lower levels of education. Between 1979 and 1987, the incomes of young black college graduates declined by 0.6%, while the incomes of their white counterparts increased by 13.6%. College graduates in all race and sex categories gained relative to high school graduates and dropouts, but the greatest gains were made by white women. Similarly, black married-couple families are better off relative to whites than are those headed by single parents. As noted, however, most white and Hispanic households (54.4% and 56.2%, respectively) were maintained by married couples, but only a little more than one-third of black households (36.1%) were maintained by married couples.

In addition to deleterious economic forces, the economic welfare of families deteriorated during the 1980s because of changes in family structures. Divorce, separation, and out-of-wedlock births to single women, especially single teenagers, create particularly serious problems for families with children.

Growing inequalities in wealth and income have resulted from policy changes during the 1980s that shifted the tax burden from high- to middle- and lower-income groups and reduced real expenditures for programs to help the poor, particularly the working poor. Policy changes also increased real interest rates and, together with international competition and structural changes, shifted

Probably the most important change American families have experienced in employment and income has been the increased labor-force participation of women.

Growing inequalities in wealth and income have resulted from policy changes during the 1980s that shifted the tax burden from high- to middle- and lower-income groups and reduced real expenditures for programs to help the poor, particularly the working poor.

the composition of income from labor to capital. These changes were particularly devastating for young families, who got almost all of their income from wages. Moreover, the rising cost of housing has been particularly devastating for poor families. Housing costs increased from 7% of average family income in 1970 to 22% in 1988. The median poor renter family spent 65% of its income on housing and utilities in 1988 and the median poor home owner family spent 47% of its income for these purposes.

The policy issues raised by these changes in the economy and in families will be discussed in chapter 6. Before turning to that subject, however, it is useful to compare changes in family structures among the United States and some other industrialized democratic countries as well as to examine some of the policies developed by other countries to support families. Such comparisons deepen our understanding of both the causes of the changes in family structure and the effectiveness of various family-support policies.

Notes

1. See Ray Marshall, *Work and Women in the 1980s* (Washington, DC: Women's Research and Education Institute of the Congressional Caucus for Women's Issues, 1983).

2. *Washington Times*, May 7, 1987, p. 8C.

3. Bureau of Labor Statistics, "Employment and Earnings Characteristics of Families: First Quarter 1990," USDL News Release 90-202, April 1990, Table A.

4. Howard V. Hayghe, "Family Members in the Work Force," *Monthly Labor Review* 113 (March 1990), Table 3, p. 17.

5. Howard V. Hayghe and Steven Haugen, "Profile of Husbands in Today's Labor Market," *Monthly Labor Review* 110 (October 1987), pp. 3–11.

6. Hayghe, "Family Members in the Work Force," Table 2, p. 17.

7. Lawrence Mishel and David Frankel, *The State of Working America* (Washington, DC: Economic Policy Institute, 1990).

8. Ibid., p. 98.

9. Ibid., Table 7.2, p. 198.

10. Ibid., Table 7.4, p. 202.

11. Ibid., Table 7.7, p. 204.

12. Ibid., Table 7.12, p. 213.

13. Ibid., p. 218.

14. Ibid., p. 223.

15. Ibid., p. 39.

16. Ibid., p. 40.

17. Ibid., p. 45.

18. Ibid., Table 6.9, p. 172.

19. Ibid., Table 6.14, p. 176.

20. Joint Center for Housing Studies, *The State of the Nation's Housing, 1989* (Boston: Joint Center for Housing Studies of Massachusetts Institute of Technology and Harvard University), Appendix Table 1, p. 22.

21. Paul A. Leonard, Cushing N. Delbeare, and Edward Lazere, *A Place to Call Home: The Crisis in Housing for the Poor* (Washington, DC: Center on Budget and Policy Priorities, 1989), Table 1, p. 51.

22. Ibid., pp. xi–xii.

5

International Perspectives

Comparisons of family developments in several countries make it possible to distinguish between trends that are fairly widespread and those that are confined to particular countries or regions. Such comparisons thus help avoid the common fallacy of attributing all changes to developments within a particular country. The experiences of other countries also provide insights into policies that might be effective in dealing with family issues in the United States.

Among the industrialized countries of the world, several common demographic patterns may be seen.

- Fertility rates have declined in all major industrial countries. As Table 5.1 (page 139) shows, all 10 of the countries represented have had total fertility rates below the replacement rate since the early 1970s. Declining fertility rates imply smaller rates of population growth and smaller families.
- All industrialized countries likewise have aging populations, because mortality rates as well as fertility rates have fallen.

The age distributions of the population of 10 countries between 1950 and 1990 are detailed in Table 5.2 (page 140). All the countries have experienced dramatic declines in the proportions of their population younger than 14 years of age. Because the U.S. population is somewhat younger than those of Western Europe and Japan, mainly because of immigration and the high proportion of minorities in our population, a larger proportion of our population is younger than 14. Germany has by far the lowest proportion of young people, followed by Denmark. A relatively high proportion of Germany's population also is aged 65 and older. Japan has the highest proportion of people 15 to 64 (70.3%), followed by Germany, the Netherlands, and Italy. Sweden, Germany, and Denmark all have about the same proportion of elderly as they do children younger than 15. In the United States, Canada, and Japan, by contrast, the proportion of people aged 15 and younger is substantially larger than that 65 and older. For all other countries listed, the proportion of the population younger than 15 is larger than the proportion of people 65 and older.

The aging of populations has important implications for the economy. For one thing, large percentages of young and old people increase the proportion of the population that must be supported by persons in the work force. Second, older populations increase the number of single-person households, because in all industrialized countries pension systems and the growth of incomes since the 1930s have made it possible for more elderly people to live alone.

Declining fertility rates, the aging of populations, increased divorce rates, and delayed marriages have all contributed to fewer people per household in Europe as well as in the United States. Table 5.3 (page 141) displays the decrease in household size among 10 industrialized countries over the past three decades. Japan has the highest number of persons per household (3.1) and Sweden the least (2.2), followed closely by Germany (2.3) and Denmark (2.3).

Marriage and Divorce

The United States has much higher marriage and divorce rates than do the other industrialized countries (Table 5.4, page 142). However, marriage rates have declined for all countries since 1970. Extreme declines in marriage rates have occurred in the United States and Sweden.[1] European countries have all experienced delayed and less frequent marriages since the 1970s, a pattern that one can see beginning in the United States in the 1950s.

European countries also have much higher proportions of cohabitation by unmarried persons than does the United States, a factor reflected in the higher American marriage and divorce rates. This cohabitation pattern is particularly common in Scandinavia, but also in France, the United Kingdom, and the Netherlands.

Although divorce rates have increased in all industrialized countries, they are much lower in Europe than in the United States. Japan and Italy have very low divorce rates. In the United States, as noted earlier, a marriage during the 1970s had about a 50% chance of ending in divorce. European marriages had a 25% to 33% chance of ending in divorce.

The United States also has a relatively high rate of births to unmarried women (Table 5.5, page 143). However, the rate here is much lower than in Denmark and Sweden, where rates are about double that of the United States. Although almost half of Swedish and Danish children are born to unmarried mothers, it is important to note that almost all are born to parents who live together.[2] In Sweden, for example, in the early 1980s only 0.5% of all live births were children whose fathers were not identified and not required to pay child support.

One of the most striking differences between the United States and Europe is our country's large proportion of out-of-wedlock births to teenagers (33%, compared with 6% in Sweden and 10% in France and Germany). The United Kingdom also has a relatively high proportion of out-of-wedlock births to teenagers. Stated another way, the number of teenage pregnancies in America has been approximately one million per year in recent years. The rate of teen pregnancies in the United States has been 96 per 1,000 women aged 15 to 19, compared with 14 per 1,000 in France and the Netherlands, 44 per 1,000 in Canada, 45 per 1,000 in England and Wales, and 35 per 1,000 in Sweden. As Margaret S. Gordon has pointed out,

> According to a study by the Guttmacher Institute, the countries with the lowest teenage pregnancy rates were those that had the most open attitudes about sex, the most extensive sex education programs, and the readiest access to contraception for young people.[3]

As can be seen in Table 5.6 (page 144), the United States has a larger percentage of single-parent households than does any of the European countries listed. As might be expected from their low marriage rates, Denmark and Sweden have somewhat smaller proportions of married-couple families compared with most other countries, which have proportions ranging from 67.4% in Japan to 41.0% in Denmark.

The United States also has a higher proportion of single-parent households with children (22.9% in 1988) than do most other countries. Japan has the lowest, 5.9%. Table 5.6 presents the changing proportions of such households in nine countries over three decades. Note that the proportion of single-family households with children has increased in every country listed.

The labor-force participation rates of women have increased in all industrialized countries but are relatively high in Scandinavia (80% in Sweden and 79.2% in Denmark, for example) and in North America, where the rate in the United States is 68.5% and in Canada, 66.8%. Italy, in contrast, has a very low rate of women in the work force (43.3%). Germany's rate is somewhat higher (55.8%), but still much lower than that in the United States, Canada, and Scandinavia.

Family Policies

In addition to highlighting demographic trends, international comparisons provide some insight into questions of family policy. Why do some countries give family and women's issues high priority? In a study of family policy in 18 countries, Harold Wilensky constructed an index of innovative and comprehensive or "expansive" family policies in these countries for the years 1976–82. Wilensky considered three policy "clusters":

- existence and length of paid and unpaid family leave
- availability and accessibility of day care and government efforts to expand day care
- the flexibility of retirement systems

He found that Sweden, France, Belgium, Norway, and Finland had the most expansive and innovative family policies. Denmark, Germany, Austria, Italy, and, marginally, the United Kingdom and the Netherlands had moderately helpful family policies. The countries that scored the lowest in terms of supportive family policies were the United States, Japan, Switzerland, Canada, New Zealand, Australia, and Ireland.[4]

The priority afforded to family and women's issues in a country depends heavily on the extent to which these matters relate to the political parties' priorities and the degree of industrialization. Industrialization is important because, in general, the labor-force participation rates of women rise with economic development; concomitantly, the need for supportive policies to aid their families rises as well.

Wilensky's findings confirm these observations for most countries. Although national differences exist, high labor-force participation rates for women are associated with stronger pressures for governments to help parents balance the demands of family and work. A somewhat surprising finding, however, is Wilensky's discovery that "the more aged [in a country], the higher the score on family policy."[5] This finding is contrary to the assumption that parents with young children are a potent political force behind family policy, whereas older persons in retirement might tend to oppose government expenditures on the young. Obviously, this is not true. As Wilensky points out, "An aging population is a powerful source of family policy, including the support of child care."[6]

How do we explain this almost counterintuitive outcome? Wilensky provides three observations:

The priority afforded to family and women's issues in a country depends heavily on the extent to which these matters relate to political priorities and the degree of industrialization.

High labor-force participation rates for women are associated with stronger pressures for governments to help parents balance the demands of family and work.

(1) Grandparents want to relieve pressures on both their working adult children and themselves. (2) Wisdom about childbearing pressures, we hope, comes with experience; the aged, having been through it themselves, may simply be more sensitive to the troubles of harried parents and more open to government help. (3) The numerous nonaffluent young parents with schoolchildren (especially children in preschool) are at a stage in the family life cycle in which they experience least job satisfaction, lower participation in community life, greatest financial and family burdens, and the greatest psychological tension—a condition of life-cycle squeeze hardly conducive to intense political action, even on behalf of their own interests.[7]

Thus, industrialization and the increased labor-force participation of women are almost universal forces driving the development of family policies in many countries. In several industrialized countries, however, certain factors—especially fragmented, decentralized, political decision-making processes—militate against the development of strong family policies. We can see this in the United States, Switzerland, Canada, and New Zealand, for example. The term fragmented, in this context, means that policy decisions are divided among different branches and levels of government. As it is in the United States, fragmentation is often associated with a bias against government intervention in the society or economy. Fragmented countries also oppose public–private consensus processes to get agreement on the facts, develop common goals, and agree on strategies to achieve those goals. Consensus processes focus attention on common interests; adversarial political processes focus attention on differences, however trivial. The United Kingdom—a fragmented country—scored somewhat higher than expected on Wilensky's index, probably because of both high female labor-force participation rates and a high proportion of older people in its population. The United Kingdom also had a strong Labour Party in the immediate postwar period, a political factor associated with expansive family policies. However, the British Labour Party was relatively weak during the 1980s, which may account for some slippage in family-policy development.

As with most international comparisons, Japan is an exception. It has strong national consensus-building processes, but weak family policy. This contradiction might be explained by the fact that Japan's families are still strong and have not yet experienced the same kinds of tensions between work and family and the need for family support systems evident in all other industrialized countries. Eventually, however, industrialization and the increased labor-force participation of married women probably will produce the same kinds of pressures in Japan as are evident in all other industrialized, market-oriented economies. Nonetheless, Japan's unique culture and institutions will undoubtedly shape that country's family policies, as they emerge, in ways that will support the competitiveness of the Japanese economy.

Sheila Kamerman and Alfred Kahn, noted social policy analysts, have studied the conditions of families and children in considerable depth and in an international context.[8] Their work provides insight into various kinds of policies developed to handle common problems, such as helping families deal with the tensions created by conflicting employment and family responsibilities or providing adequate support for single-parent families.

With respect to support of single-parent families, Kamerman and Kahn found considerable diversity in countries' treatment of single-parent families, especially mother-only families, which are increasing in number in all Western industrialized countries. They note that in all countries, single-parent families are no longer created mainly by the death of a parent, as was the case earlier in this century, but occur as a result of divorce, separation, or the birth of children to unwed mothers. The economic conditions of families headed by widows—once a critical problem—have been improved by advances in health care that have reduced death rates of men and by transfer payments that sustain widows.

Although divorced mothers head as large a proportion of families in Europe as they do in the United States, more European couples opt to live together without marrying. Similarly, unwed mothers are as prevalent in Europe as in the United States, but births to unwed teenagers are much more common in the United States. This difference is due more to the higher use of contraceptives by European teenagers than to degrees of sexual activity. Finally, in Europe single mothers receive social benefits but are not perceived to be as much of a "welfare problem" as they are in the United States. This is undoubtedly due to the developmental attitude taken by most European countries. They do not regard welfare as a "necessary evil" or a drag on the economy, as is often the case in the United States. Instead they consider it to be an investment in human resources that will pay rich dividends in the future. Most European countries also have more homogeneous populations than does the United States and thus are less likely to oppose welfare on racial or ethnic grounds. As Kamerman and Kahn point out, in Europe single mothers are aided rather than stigmatized.

> Some countries' poverty is a real or potential issue, but social policy often provides them with a protected status and subsidized income. While single mothers in Europe are likely to have relatively low incomes, they are not truly poor. Earnings and/or income supports protect them and their children.[9]

Kamerman and Kahn note, however, that there is no uniform European policy strategy for single mothers. They identify four major policy models:

1. *An anti-poverty strategy to meet the general needs of the poor, exemplified by Britain, which makes it possible for most single mothers to stay home with their children.* Working mothers are given wage supplements and mother-only families are helped through child allowances, the national health service, and priority access to public housing. However, the plight of mother-only British families became worse after 1979, absolutely and relative to two-parent families. This is probably due to the same kinds of developments that made single-parent families worse off in the United States. Economic conditions in the 1980s and the policies of the Thatcher administration put great pressure on wages, especially for young and less educated workers, and weakened income-support systems.

2. *A categorical strategy for single mothers, which provides financial aid to enable single mothers to remain at home with their children*, was the original purpose of Aid to Families with Dependent Children (AFDC) in the United States. This policy is illustrated by Norway, which provides the most generous benefits to mother-only families of any country. Norway expects most mothers to stay at home until their children are 10 years old. Income support for mother-only households is sufficient to eliminate poverty, but not enough to permit the same standard of living as for husband–wife families. As a consequence, single mothers have far lower labor-force participation rates than do married mothers. A negative side effect of this policy, however, is that single mothers have difficulties entering or reentering the work force when their children reach age 10 and the benefits taper off.

3. *Strategies to provide universal cash benefits to all children, especially those younger than three.* This model is exemplified by French policy, which makes it possible for parents to choose to stay home when their children are young. The French use universal income-tested, but nonstigmatizing, family support, including housing assistance, maternity and paternity leaves, and special allowances for mothers of very young children. French policy is specifically designed to facilitate child

---

Unwed mothers are as prevalent in Europe as in the United States, but births to unwed teenagers are much more common in the United States.

In Europe single mothers receive social benefits but are not perceived to be as much of a "welfare problem" as they are in the United States. They are aided rather than stigmatized.

Sweden's objective is not just to reduce poverty, but to provide more equitable incomes for all families. A major instrument of that policy has been well-organized education, training, and labor-market systems and incentives for people to support themselves through work.

Europeans recognize the benefits of investment in people rather than viewing social expenditures as necessary evils.

rearing and employment, to promote child development, and to encourage parents to have a third child. French policy is especially concerned with the development of children three years old and younger, during the period when it is particularly hard for mothers to work. Governmental support makes it possible for parents to either stay home or to pay for child care. However, mothers, including single mothers, in poorer families are expected to work once their children reach age three.

4. *The fourth model combines labor-market and family policies*, illustrated by the Swedish experience. Sweden has the most developed labor-market policy of any industrialized, market-oriented country. The Swedes, as a consequence, have been more successful than most in maintaining relatively high wages in a full-employment economy. Unlike the United States and Britain, Sweden's social policy objective is not just to reduce the incidence of poverty, but to provide high and more equitable or "solidaristic" incomes for all families. A major instrument of that policy has been well-organized education, training, and labor-market systems and strong incentives for people to support themselves through work rather than to rely on "doles" of any kind. The Swedish family-support system is formed on the basis of that philosophy. Cash and other benefits are provided to families, but young mothers are encouraged to enter and to remain in the work force in order to improve their family incomes. Sweden's benefits to families with young children are designed to maintain the children, not to support the parents; adults are expected either to support themselves or to engage in education and training that will make it possible for them to be self-supporting.

As a consequence of this philosophy, the Swedes expect earned income, not transfer payments, to be the main source of family support. Transfer payments, even unemployment compensation, are considered to be "last resorts" to be used only when jobs or training cannot be found. Sweden nevertheless provides a generous array of social supports to supplement earned income. These supports include health care, education and training, labor-market information, relocation assistance, counseling, and a variety of services designed to facilitate work and parenting. Single parents have basic family supports, including child and housing allowances, one year of guaranteed parental leave following childbirth, special leaves to care for sick children or for school visits, and reduced working hours when children are young. Swedish single parents also collect child support from the noncustodial parent or receive a generous child-support benefit from the government.

Comparisons with the United States

Clearly, some major differences exist between American and European social policies. For one thing, the Europeans, especially the Scandinavians and Western European countries, have integrated their social and economic policies much better than we have in the United States. Moreover, they take a more developmental approach to family-support policies. They recognize the benefits and high returns to investment in people rather than viewing social expenditures as necessary evils or public charity, as we have in the United States. Europeans, therefore, tend to give greater attention to education, training, and support for children and parents, and these services are more likely to be universal. Even when they are income tested, European social programs are less likely to be stigmatizing.

Europeans have, in addition, been much quicker to deal with the negative impact of divorce on women and children. In the United States, very few families receive child support from noncustodial parents. All of the Nordic countries, by contrast, guarantee child support to custodial parents, either by governments or from the absent parents, regardless of income. Divorce is thus regarded as a social as well as an individual risk.

In the United States, according to the Bureau of the Census, only 39% of custodial mothers were awarded child support in 1985. Of these, payments were not made in 26% of the cases, and only partial payments were made in another 26% of cases.[10] Even when child-support payments are made, they are relatively small—averaging only $2,215 a year in 1985. Child-support awards in the United States are not only inadequate, but inequitable as well, depending largely on the vagaries of a grossly inadequate court system. The only alternative is an equally inadequate and inequitable AFDC system, wherein benefits are set by the individual states at much less than the official poverty level. Unlike the European system, AFDC is not developmental in that it encourages dependency by reducing the earnings of recipients who work. Of course, every European country provides national health care to all citizens regardless of income.

Family Policy in America

International comparisons also provide some perspective on the important policy question of how to make family policies in the United States more acceptable politically and more effective in achieving their objectives. Traditionally, social policy debate has been over whether benefits should be universal or selective. Universal programs, such as the Social Security system, or those that have wide coverage, such as student loans, have broader political support but are resisted out of fear of raising budgetary costs.

Budgetary constraints usually have caused American programs to be allocated on the basis of "means" tests—that is, restricting benefits to people with income and assets below a certain level. Means testing has the presumed advantage of allocating scarce resources to those most in need. However, this procedure has the very serious disadvantage of being stigmatizing, causing many needy families or individuals not to participate. In addition, means testing often requires cumbersome, degrading, inequitable, and costly investigation and surveillance procedures. Careful research by Irwin Garfinkel and his associates casts considerable doubt on the assumption that income testing leads to greater program efficiency and does the most for those in greatest need of the program. Garfinkel notes that "empirical evidence does not support the intuitive view that income testing is likely to be more efficient."[11]

On the basis of their extensive studies of family policies in a number of countries, Kamerman and Kahn conclude that universalism versus selectivism in social programs is an erroneous dichotomy. They note that "policy strategies reflect a far more complex, subtle, and sophisticated elaboration of the options. In effect, the state of the art has gone well beyond a simplistic choice between two extremes."[12] With respect to child-support programs, for example, countries that provide generous benefits to vulnerable families (e.g., Sweden, France, the Federal Republic of Germany) do so by adopting a universal, nonstigmatizing approach that provides benefits to all children. These countries generally consider child development to be in the national interest and necessary to the development of valuable human resources. Other countries (the United States, Australia, Canada, and Israel) are more likely to use means-tested programs and to treat their vulnerable families less generously. These latter countries are, in addition, more likely to take a nondevelopmental, "charity" approach to family-support programs, stigmatizing recipients and maintaining large investigatory and administrative systems to check eligibility and to prevent cheating.

Child-support awards in the United States are not only inadequate, but inequitable as well, depending largely on the vagaries of a grossly inadequate court system. The only alternative is an equally inadequate and inequitable AFDC system.

Means testing has the presumed advantage of allocating scarce resources to those most in need. However, this procedure has the very serious disadvantage of being stigmatizing.

59

> *While the question of child care is still hotly debated in the United States, Europeans have recognized the importance of high-quality preschool programs for the social and cognitive development of their children.*

A more effective policy would be to provide income supplements to low-wage earners coupled with a system of universal benefits. The government's costs for such a universal system could be limited by taxing these benefits on a progressive basis or by providing refundable tax credits instead of tax allowances. Sweden, for example, has eliminated personal income-tax deductions for children because these deductions gave much larger benefits to families with high marginal tax rates. The United States provides refundable earned-income-tax credits (EITC) of up to $920, which will be discussed in the next section. This small amount can be very significant to low-income families. Kamerman and Kahn point out that income testing is simpler than means testing (i.e., checking on assets as well as income in determining support eligibility levels).

Nowhere is the contrast between the European developmental and the American *laissez-faire*, welfare approach to services more evident than in the provision of preschool programs for children. While the question of child care is still hotly debated in the United States, Europeans have recognized the importance of high-quality preschool programs for the social and cognitive development of their children. Although preschool programs in Europe vary somewhat from country to country, they generally are universally available and are not limited to children with special needs or to those with working mothers. Europeans recognize the mounting importance of preschool programs as socializing agencies at a time when families are having fewer children. The general pattern in Europe is to provide free, full-coverage preschools for four- to five-year-olds and nearly full coverage for children aged two and a half to three.

Finland and Sweden are unique in providing preschool for the full workday and not just the school day, as is the case in most other countries. The Swedish and Finnish programs are administered as freestanding, autonomous institutions by the departments of social welfare, whereas most others are administered by the education system.[13] The Swedish program provides "the highest quality available anywhere," with standards "based on extensive research" that are "rigorously set and enforced."[14] The Swedish programs are heavily subsidized, though parents pay small, income-related fees (generally less than 10% of mothers' average incomes). All children are eligible, though in keeping with Sweden's work-oriented philosophy, preference is given to children of working parents, especially single mothers and immigrants (who form a larger proportion of the Swedish than of the U.S. population). Approximately 70% of three- to seven-year-olds are enrolled in these preschool programs, though this proportion is expected to rise during the 1990s. Beginning in 1991, all children aged 18 months or older will be guaranteed places in preschool or child-care centers. Sweden guarantees parental leave for up to 18 months and will guarantee care to all children up to 18 months old of working parents.

Conclusion

Like the United States, other industrialized countries have experienced changes in family structure related to declining fertility rates, aging populations, delayed and less frequent marriages, and an increase in single-parent households and out-of-wedlock births. Cohabitation without marriage is increasing in all major industrialized countries, but is more common in Europe, especially in Scandinavia, than it is in the United States.

Relative to the other industrialized countries studied, the United States has a younger population, higher marriage and divorce rates, and a larger proportion of births to unmarried women, except for Denmark and Sweden, than does

> *Like the United States, other industrialized countries have experienced declining fertility rates, aging populations, delayed and less frequent marriages, and an increase in single-parent households and out-of-wedlock births.*

Japan or any major Western European country. Similarly, the United States has a much higher rate of births to teenagers, a larger proportion of single-parent households, and a higher labor-force participation rate for women, except compared with Sweden and Denmark, and twice the proportion of children in poverty than does Japan or any major Western European country. The United States has higher poverty rates and a more unequal distribution of income than almost any other industrialized country, with the possible exception of France.

However, the greatest difference between the United States and other developed democratic countries is in the nature of the policies devised to support families. Economic and social policies in the United States are less explicit and coherent than those of any other major democratic industrial country. The United States is almost alone among major industrialized countries, for example, in not having strategies to achieve wage, income, and employment goals. This is one of the reasons, as noted in chapter 2, that most American companies have been free to compete by low-wage strategies instead of reorganizing production and improving work-force skills in order to improve productivity and income.

The United States has equally incoherent, and often perverse, family-support systems. The policies of all major countries studied are more comprehensive and more developmental than those of the United States. Other countries have responded much more quickly to changing family structures and the needs of high-performance companies by accommodating the employment and income needs of working parents, single-parent families, and especially families with children. These countries not only have universal health-care systems but also provide income-support and preschool programs for children, usually at little or no cost to parents. All of these countries recognize the importance of high-quality preschool programs for the cognitive and social development of children. The general pattern in these countries is to make preschool programs universal and nonstigmatizing. Programs are paid for mainly by progressive income taxes.

All of the reasons for these policy differences cannot be explored in this book. Nonetheless, it is important to note that the increased labor-force participation of women has been a major factor responsible for expansive family policies in all the countries studied, though, as the U.S. experience testifies, this alone is not sufficient. We have one of the industrialized world's highest female labor-force participation rates but probably the weakest family-support system. A second relevant factor, underlined in Wilensky's work, is the presence of centralized, consensus-based, policy-making mechanisms, which usually are the consequence of strong and politically active labor movements. The American labor movement is the weakest of any among the major industrialized countries. Open, consensus-based systems focus on high-priority national interests and make it difficult for policies to be dominated by narrow special interests, as they are in the United States. Consensus-based systems also generate much better factual analyses, making it very difficult for policies to be dominated by ideology, misconceptions, and trivia, as is true of much of American policy, especially at the federal level. Some of the dominant myths include:

- "There is no need for policy interventions to help low-income people because we have a level playing field and anybody in America can make it on his or her own."
- "It doesn't help to intervene with quality preschool, elementary, and secondary schools because learning is mainly due to innate ability."
- "It costs too much to have human resource development programs."
- "The country's family problems are caused by such deeply entrenched economic and technological forces that we can do nothing about them."

The greatest difference between the United States and other developed democratic countries is in the nature of the policies devised to support families.

Other countries have responded much more quickly to changing family structures by accommodating the employment and income needs of working parents, single-parent families, and especially families with children.

> - "Policy interventions aren't needed because (a) we don't know what to do, (b) whatever we do will have unintended perverse effects, or (c) it is best to let market forces develop our people."
> - "Money won't help a problem because we already spend more on elementary and secondary education than any other country."

My argument is not that these misconceptions don't exist in other countries; it is, rather, that a consensus-based system that requires factual analyses of social problems makes it harder for such myths to dominate policy. Consensual processes also make it possible to focus more clearly on long-term national interests such as making high-yield investments in children and developing human resources.[15]

A somewhat surprising factor correlated with expansive family policies was the high proportion of elderly in a population, as discovered by Wilensky. Perhaps the fact that the U.S. population is relatively young accounts for some of our reluctance to develop comprehensive family policies. However, I suspect that our history of *laissez-faire* ideology, business dominance, racial and ethnic diversity, and a more unequal distribution of income than in other democratic industrialized countries are more important reasons for our difficulty in developing world-class human resource development programs for any but our college-educated elites.

These international comparisons therefore raise the question of what family policy should be in the United States. Although the United States has no comprehensive policies, we do have some of the elements of such policies and are debating others. The specific issues raised by these debates are explored in chapter 6.

> *Our history of laissez-faire ideology, business dominance, racial and ethnic diversity, and unequal distribution of income are reasons for our difficulty in developing world-class human resource development programs for any but our college-educated elites.*

Notes

1. David Popenoe, *Disturbing the Nest: Family Change and Decline in Modern Societies* (New York: Aldine de Gruyter, 1989), p. 283.

2. Constance Sorrentino, "The Changing Family," *Monthly Labor Review* 113 (March 1990), p. 44.

3. Margaret S. Gordon, *Social Security Policies in Industrial Countries* (Cambridge, England. Cambridge University Press, 1989), p. 288.

4. Harold L. Wilensky, "Common Problems, Divergent Policies: An 18-Nation Study of Family Policy," *Public Affairs Report* 31, No. 3 (May 1990), pp. 1–3.

5. Ibid., p. 1.

6. Ibid., p. 2.

7. Ibid., pp. 2–3.

8. Sheila Kamerman and Alfred Kahn, "What Europe Does for Single-Parent Families," *Public Interest* 93 (Fall 1988), pp. 70–86.

9. Ibid., p. 80.

10. U.S. Bureau of the Census, *Child Support and Alimony 1985*, Current Population Reports, Series P-23, No. 152, 1987.

11. Irwin Garfinkel, ed., *Income-Tested Transfer Payments: The Case for and Against* (New York: Academies Press, 1982), p. 520.

12. Sheila Kamerman and Alfred Kahn, "Universalism and Income Testing in Family Policy: New Perspectives on an Old Debate," *Social Work* 32 (July–August 1987), p. 277.

13. Sheila Kamerman, "An International Overview of Pre-School Programs," *Phi Delta Kappan* 71 (October 1989), pp. 135–138.

14. Ibid., p. 137.

15. For an elaboration of this theme, see Ray Marshall, *Unheard Voices: Labor and Economic Policy in a Competitive World* (New York: Basic Books, 1987).

6

Family Policy Issues

The changes in family structure detailed in this book have generated a number of controversial issues concerning what governmental family-support policies ought to do and be. This is understandable, of course, because many family policy issues are based on deeply held religious and moral beliefs and because many public policies were molded by the needs of "traditional" families, in which relatively few women worked outside the home, families were larger and more likely to have children of diverse ages, divorce rates were lower, and fewer single-parent and unmarried multiperson households existed to complicate the picture of American family life. Families were much more stable and homogeneous, making it almost unnecessary to have "family policies." The similarity of experiences and the stability of families and neighborhoods caused attitudes to be more homogeneous and made public opinion and "expected behavior" the main regulators of family matters. However, since the 1960s, the dramatic changes in family structure and the growing diversity of family types and experiences have greatly reduced the regulatory significance of public opinion. Diversity of living arrangements has reduced the commonality of family experiences, and with that, public consensus about acceptable family relationships has diminished. At the same time, the increased importance of human resource development, the weakening of traditional family-support systems, and the increased interdependence of people in society combine to give the American public a big stake in what happens to families. It is unfortunate that the ferment in family affairs has not produced a consensus about what family policy should be, because such a consensus is almost a precondition to coherent, stable, and acceptable policies. This chapter seeks to clarify some of these emerging policy issues.

Divorce, Birth Control, Abortion

Some of the most heated family-policy controversies center on abortion. Although abortion has become common in the past 30 years, it is opposed by many for moral and religious reasons. Needless to say, the bitterest controversies involve clashes of moral principles. Such controversies, furthermore, raise the important question of whether laws can change behavior. Some analysts doubt that public policy can do much to influence family structures or the choices of particular families, arguing that these matters are determined by fundamental economic, social, or attitudinal forces beyond the reach of public policies. Indeed, some analysts even argue that attempts to support families often have perverse or unintended effects.

Since the 1960s, state laws regulating divorce, birth control, and abortion have become less restrictive, often because of U.S. Supreme Court decisions outlawing those restrictions. Particularly important was the 1973 Supreme Court decision of *Roe v. Wade*, which overturned state laws prohibiting abortion during the first trimester of pregnancy. And in *Griswold v. Connecticut* in 1965, the Supreme Court overturned state laws prohibiting the sale of contraceptives. In the meantime, states, on their own, made it much easier for married couples to get divorced.

In all of these cases, however, liberalization of laws affecting family life and family planning coincided with changing attitudes and behavior, making it difficult to discern cause and effect. The widespread practice of birth control, made possible by innovations in contraceptive technology, virtually nullified the impact of restrictive laws governing the sale of contraceptives. Moreover, less restrictive abortion laws undoubtedly have increased abortions, especially among young unmarried women, since the procedure was legalized. This has been borne out by experiences in other countries and by the fact that teenage births have declined while teen pregnancies continue to increase. The availability of cheaper, more accessible, less risky abortion technologies, like RU-486, the French abortion pill, which is currently banned in this country, undoubtedly would nullify restrictive abortion laws and regulations.

We must also question whether government programs have negative effects on the behavior of individuals and families. In some circles, social observers believe that child and family support systems increase out-of-wedlock births and the breakup of families. Charles Murray, for example, argued that welfare payments encourage fathers not to support their children and make it possible for mothers to support their children without getting married.[1] Murray supports his case by arguing that out-of-wedlock births, divorce rates, and welfare expenditures increased together during the 1970s.

Murray's conclusions have been challenged by a number of empirical studies. For instance, the real value of the maximum welfare payment in the median state dropped 33% between 1975 and 1985. In addition, program administration was tightened to make it more difficult for people to obtain benefits.[2] As a result, welfare case loads have remained constant, and the number of poor female-headed households has continued to increase, casting doubt on the existence of a causal relationship. Murray's reasoning should have resulted in a decline in case loads and female-headed households, because the real value of benefits declined. Second, interstate comparisons reveal no relationship between welfare-benefit levels in the various states and the number or proportion of female-headed households, divorce rates, and out-of-wedlock births. Indeed, the fact that some of the highest proportions of children in female-headed households are in states with the lowest welfare benefits suggests that other factors affect family structures. Similarly, more sophisticated analyses of state differences have found only small relationships between divorce levels, separation rates, and welfare-benefit levels. In one of the most influential studies on the subject, David Ellwood and Mary Jo Bane found no discernible relationship between births to unwed mothers and welfare-benefit levels, but they did find a small relationship between benefits and the number of households maintained by

In some circles, social observers believe that child and family support systems increase out-of-wedlock births and the breakup of families. However, analyses of state differences have found only small relationships between divorce levels, separation rates, and welfare-benefit levels.

single women with children. Ellwood and Bane concluded that the number of single mothers would increase by perhaps 5% in response to a large benefit increase of $100.[3] These findings imply that welfare benefits make it possible for single mothers to maintain independent households, which could be a very positive condition for the development of mothers and their children.

Although the jury is still out on this question, the evidence suggests that welfare is, at most, only a marginal factor contributing to the increased proportion of children in single-parent families. Moreover, the main effect of welfare appears to be that it increases the number of single mothers who can maintain households, not the number of births to single women. Thus other societal and economic forces, not just government support levels, affect public opinion, the options available to teenagers, and adult choices about living arrangements and whether to have children.

Increased Employment of Mothers and Changing Family Structures

The changes in family relationships that we have seen in the past three decades have had different effects on various family members. For one thing, it is fairly certain that the main negative effects of changes in family structure have fallen on children. Some analysts have concluded that children in the 1980s were worse off than they were two decades earlier. However, it is unclear how much of this decline is attributable to changes in family structure and/or the increased employment of mothers and how much to social and economic conditions. From an economic perspective, real family incomes have increased significantly since 1960, but, as noted in chapter 4, most of this increase came before 1973 and incomes have been stagnant since then. In fact, for almost all families, per-capita incomes have risen only slightly since 1973, due mainly to more women working longer and in better-paying jobs as well as having fewer children. Increased poverty for children has been associated with the growth of single-parent families, whose incomes are substantially lower than those of two-parent families. On the other hand, the increased employment of mothers outside the home has improved the economic welfare of children in two-parent families.

Impact of Divorce

Most observers agree that children are the main victims of divorce. Divorce reduces the family income of mothers, who obtain custody of the children in about 90% of all divorces. According to one study, in the year after divorce, women's living standards drop by an average of 30% while the father's living standards increase by 10% to 15%.[4] The drop is even greater for women in high-income families, who often have had little work experience and have relied on their husbands' incomes. However, few upper-income families drop below the poverty line as a result of divorce. Children in families just above the poverty line are not so lucky, and those families are much more likely to fall below the poverty line in the year following divorce.[5]

Unfortunately, very few families receive much support from the noncustodial parent following divorce. According to a 1985 survey by the United States Census Bureau, only 48% of mothers awarded child support were paid the full amount awarded. Twenty-six percent received nothing.[6] Even those who were paid something by the noncustodial parent got only $2,200 a year on average.

The longer-term effects of divorce depend on the mother's age and employability, whether she remarries, and whether she receives child support. Women

Very likely, welfare is, at most, only a marginal factor contributing to the increased proportion of children in single-parent families.

The main negative effects of changes in family structure have fallen on children. Some analysts have concluded that children in the 1980s were worse off than they were two decades earlier.

who remarry are more likely to regain economic parity with divorced men and married-couple families.

Divorce and separation clearly have emotional as well as economic effects on children. However, most experts agree that children generally recover and eventually resume their normal intellectual and emotional development. The long-term negative effects seem to be greatest for younger children.[7]

Family Instability and the Well-being of Children

The impact of divorce and separation on various social pathologies is difficult to discern because family instability has increased at a time when families have been increasingly plagued by many other problems—including drug abuse, increased teenage pregnancy, out-of-wedlock births, rising juvenile arrests, and higher suicide rates. The association of these problems with increased family instability and rising labor-force participation of women suggests a positive causal relationship to some analysts. In an influential article, for example, two demographers, Peter Uhlenberg and David Eggebeen, hypothesized that the deterioration in well-being for white adolescents during the 1970s was due to increased maternal employment and marital instability.[8] They based their conclusions on several indicators of problematic youth behavior at a time when material welfare improved because of smaller family size, higher family incomes, and increased public expenditures on education, welfare, and other programs designed to help youth. Despite this improvement in the material world for adolescents, these analysts assert there was "a uniform and serious decline in the well-being of adolescents between 1960 and 1980."[9] Uhlenberg and Eggebeen attribute these negative outcomes to a declining parental commitment to child rearing, evidenced by maternal employment and marital instability, which reflect "an erosion of the bond between parent and child—one characterized by parental commitment and willingness to sacrifice self-interest."[10]

As one might expect, the Uhlenberg-Eggebeen thesis has been challenged by a number of family experts. Frank Furstenberg and Gretchen Contran, for example, criticize Uhlenberg and Eggebeen's use of decennial data (i.e., 1960, 1970, and 1980), which obscured the year-to-year relationships among some of the variables.[11] Furstenberg and Contran disaggregated the data and examined longer periods of time. They pointed out that all of the negative developments, like declining Scholastic Aptitude Test (SAT) scores, have multiple causes, not all of which are necessarily related to maternal employment or family instability. For example, SAT scores are a function of the number of people taking the tests. Evaluations by the Educational Testing Service (ETS), which administers the tests, demonstrate that the decline in SAT scores between 1963 and 1970 was largely due to the increased number of students taking the tests. After 1970, only about one-fourth of the decline is attributable to this factor. The rest, according to ETS, is due to changes in school requirements and pedagogy, not family structure. Moreover, SAT scores began to rise after 1980 for minorities, who experienced no less family instability than whites did and who had higher maternal employment rates. Also, some biases exist in the SAT scores that are not evident in the National Assessment of Education Progress, a data-collection program administered by ETS, which shows a generally upward trend in achievement scores beginning in the mid-1970s. Similarly, data on drug and alcohol abuse show increases during the 1970s, but declines after 1979, despite rising maternal employment and family instability. Delinquency rates show similar trends, as do other indicators, except for births to unmarried whites ages 15 to 19, which rose in the 1950s and continued to rise more steeply in the 1980s.

> *Divorce and separation clearly have emotional as well as economic effects on children. However, most experts agree that children generally recover and resume their normal development.*

> *Family instability has increased at a time when families have been increasingly plagued by many other problems—including drug abuse, teenage pregnancy, rising juvenile arrests, and higher suicide rates.*

Furstenberg and Contran reach three conclusions:
- Annual data show less uniform patterns over time than do the decennial data used by Uhlenberg and Eggebeen.
- For all of the indicators, except out-of-wedlock births to teenagers and possibly suicide rates, declines during the 1970s were reversed in the late '70s or early '80s, despite rising maternal employment and family instability.
- Although the data have limitations, some indicators of adolescent well-being started declining long before the 1960s, before maternal employment and family instability accelerated.

Furstenberg and Contran conclude that their analysis casts serious doubt on Uhlenberg and Eggebeen's findings. Similarly, they believe Uhlenberg and Eggebeen misinterpreted opinion polls showing declining parental commitment to children. It is true, Furstenberg and Contran state, that

> Americans expressed more reservations and ambivalence about parenthood in 1976 than in 1957.... Yet these responses do not necessarily indicate that parents have devalued their role. Parents assigned a much higher importance to their family roles—marriage and parenthood—as sources of value fulfillment and social validity than to work or leisure activities in 1976.... Today's parents are probably more likely to view parenthood as voluntary and therefore may be more cognizant of the trade-offs or personal costs of having a family. But there is no evidence from the survey data that parents today are less committed to rearing children once they have decided to have them than were parents in the past.[12]

Finally, Furstenberg and Contran criticize Uhlenberg and Eggebeen for failing to note the large body of research on the linkages between marital stability, maternal employment, and the well-being of children. Despite Uhlenberg and Eggebeen's assertion that the research is "unclear," substantial and fairly consistent findings demonstrate that children of employed mothers generally experience no more developmental difficulties or behavioral disorders than do children whose mothers are not employed.[13]

The results of maternal employment on marital disruption are more ambiguous. According to Furstenberg and Contran, this is partly because it is hard to separate the effects of family instability from the general conditions surrounding the dissolution of a marriage, especially conflict between spouses preceding separation and economic deprivation of the divided family after divorce. In general, Furstenberg and Contran state,

> empirical research rising out of large, nationally representative samples of children has failed to document persistent and pervasive differences [between children of divorced or separated parents and other children]. Separation and divorce have moderate negative effects on a number of aspects of children's behavior, such as performance in school or reports of problem behavior at home or at school, but the expected powerful relationship between marital disruption and problem behavior has not been found as yet. In addition, a number of studies suggest that high conflict but intact marriages produce the same negative effects on children as disruption.[14]

In short, no evidence exists that maternal employment alone has a negative impact on children. Family breakup surely has negative effects, particularly when the divorce is acrimonious and results in lower living standards for mothers and children.

Furstenberg and Contran believe that a satisfactory explanation for the changes in the well-being of children during the 1970s is yet to be found. They agree with Uhlenberg and Eggebeen that "the situation of youth today is far

"Americans expressed more reservations and ambivalence about parenthood in 1976 than in 1957. Yet these responses do not necessarily indicate that parents have devalued their role. There is no evidence that parents today are less committed to rearing children once they have decided to have them than were parents in the past."

> *The depth of American social problems probably is more attributable to the heterogeneity of our population, the absence of coherent national policies, the decline in real wages, growing inequalities in wealth and income, and social disunity—especially racism—than to happenings in the family.*

> *Family relationships constitute the most basic, early, and essential learning experience in one's life. Within the family, most of us learn how to deal with other people and with the hazards and opportunities of the outside world.*

from ideal."[15] However, they reject maternal employment and marital instability as major causes. They also agree that the association between improved economic welfare and various youth-behavior problems is not well understood. They note, however, that the United States spends relatively smaller amounts on youth services than do most industrialized democracies and has relatively more problems. Moreover, social expenditures are an imperfect measure of well-being, as it is well known that American schools and other institutions lag behind those of other industrialized countries in terms of their efficiency in the delivery of services to their presumed beneficiaries.

Furstenberg and Contran suggest some possible explanations, especially having to do with the historical and cultural climate of the 1960s and early 1970s. Some events, such as the Vietnam war, "precipitated a cultural crisis that sent shock waves through a number of institutions."[16] Furstenberg and Contran also cite a growing skepticism toward authority during these years as well as the proliferation of counterculture life-styles. In addition, prohibitions against drug use, certain sexual behaviors, and divorce were also eroded.[17]

We must, however, be skeptical of explanations that focus only on the United States, because most of these trends were evident in Europe as well. Still, as we have noted, America has especially high rates of marriage, divorce, and poverty as well as greater economic instability, higher incidences of out-of-wedlock births to teenagers, and relatively high birth rates in comparison with Europe.

Nevertheless, the depth of American social problems probably is more attributable to the heterogeneity of our population, the absence of coherent national policies, the decline in real wages, growing inequalities in wealth and income, and social disunity—especially racism—than to happenings in the family. These factors are more likely to have been the causes of family instability than the consequences.

Some scholars attribute young people's problems to "the sharp imbalance in the size of cohorts [that] can create radical shifts in the availability of actual and perceived opportunities."[18] The problem with this explanation, of course, is its failure to explain why resources were limited and how these resource limitations affected different groups. In other words, economic conditions require explanations for the changes in the demand for labor as well as the supply. Explanations for resource limitations must be found in the broad economic changes discussed earlier. Moreover, the causes of social pathologies are likely to elude traditional techniques used by highly specialized academic disciplines. Reality is far more complicated than what a simple, unidimensional explanation can account for. Particular problems require comprehensive explanations and solutions.

Family Relationships and Academic Achievement

The evidence makes it very clear, however, that the nature of family relationships is a very important determinant of personal development, influenced by, but to some degree independent from, external environments. This is so because family relationships constitute the most basic, early, and essential learning experience in one's life. Within the family, most of us learn how to deal with other people and with the hazards and opportunities of the outside world. Here, too, is where many people learn negative lessons that cause them to abuse their own children or engage in destructive practices.

Mounting evidence suggests, for example, that educational achievement, a major determinant of success in life, can be predicted rather reliably by a combination of socioeconomic factors related to family background, such as parental occupation, education, income, marital status, number of children, whether mother works outside the home, and number of adults in the household. Although these characteristics predict *average* relations among variables, they do not explain the differences among individual families in very similar circumstances. They do not explain, for example, why some young people succeed against great odds. The explanation cannot be found in parents' aspirations, because many poor people, for example, have high aspirations for their children.

Studies that attempt to explain why some disadvantaged students succeed focus on family relationships or the "hidden curriculum" in the home. One study of successful achievers in poor black families concluded that such families had a number of common characteristics: they stressed explicit educational activities that included "reading, writing, topical dialogues, and the explicit practice of social etiquette as well as indirect literacy-enhancing activities such as word games and hobbies."[19] Other aspects of family relationships in supportive families include:

> interactive communication styles that provide opportunities for direct instruction and feedback opportunities. Affect, or emotional climate, is also important. It is crucial that the child can be afforded opportunities to develop academic and social skills through personally satisfying activities.[20]

In addition, the parents of high achievers were assertive in following their children's progress at school. In contrast, the parents of low achievers tended to avoid contact with school personnel unless they were summoned to the school.

Similarly, James Comer's highly successful model for restructuring predominantly minority schools to achieve high behavioral and intellectual performance stresses aggressive parental involvement.[21] Moreover,

> parents of high achievers appear to be more optimistic than the parents of low achievers and . . . seem to perceive themselves as persons who can cope with the current exigencies of life. The parents of low achievers do not perceive themselves as copers, and they tend to see the world around them as unmanageable and devoid of opportunities for self-improvement.[22]

Finally, Reginald Clark's research makes it very clear that it is not class that determines a family's educational competence; rather, "it is the quality of life within the home that makes the difference."[23]

The Welfare of Women and Men

The trends described in this and previous chapters have had important consequences for men and women as well as for children. Increased employment outside the home, divorce, fertility, and marriage have all had positive and negative effects on adult women and men. As noted in chapters 3 and 4, the average American woman in 1950 worked mainly in the home. Her husband's income was the sole source of family support. In 1990, most married women work outside the home. In the late 1980s, approximately 14 million women were married and working, compared with 10 million who were married with children younger than 18 and not working outside the home. An additional 6 million women with children younger than 18 maintained their own households; approximately 70% of them were separated or divorced, 10% widowed, and 20% had never married.

Studies that attempt to explain why some disadvantaged students succeed focus on family relationships or the "hidden curriculum" in the home.

It is not class that determines a family's educational competence; rather, it is the quality of life within the home that makes the difference.

> *Employed women generally enjoy greater independence and a higher standard of living than women who are not employed. However, for most women, employment has become an economic necessity.*

Employed women generally enjoy greater independence and a higher standard of living than women who are not employed. The women's movement and accompanying social changes have made it possible for educated women to enter professional fields other than teaching and nursing, where most professional women traditionally had been employed. Ironically, employers' ability to discriminate against women in pay probably has accelerated their employment relative to men in some growth occupations. Many women derive personal satisfaction and identification from paid employment. However, for most women, employment has become an economic necessity to maintain acceptable levels of living. A growing body of evidence shows that the degree of personal satisfaction a woman derives from work depends heavily on whether she wants to work outside the home and whether she receives adequate support from employers, family members, and other institutions for her dual role as worker and homemaker.

Considerable research has investigated the family stresses of dual-income families, especially for wives, who experience most of the stress. As Mavis Hetherington has pointed out, "A mother employed full time devotes over 50 percent more hours to her combined duties in the home and in the work place than do fathers or single men and women without children. Recent comparative studies show this is true across a broad range of industrialized countries."[24] Indeed, as Hetherington adds, "although mothers in all types of families devote more time to child care and household tasks than do fathers, the same time is spent in child care in single earner families and in dual earner families."[25]

A number of factors affect mothers' ability to cope with the multiple stresses of family and work, especially a cooperative spouse and a woman's own job satisfaction. Hetherington concludes, on the basis of extensive research on this subject, that

> [t]here are few differences between the parenting of satisfied full time homemakers and women who are satisfied in their dual roles as parents and workers with one exception. Employed mothers are more likely to emphasize early assumption of responsibility and independence in their children.[26]

This behavior, however, can place adolescents at greater risk of negative outcomes, as discussed later in this chapter.

> *Obviously, a major problem for many working women is inadequate support from husbands and employers. Personnel policies are often based on the outdated idea that most permanent workers are male heads of household.*

Obviously, a major problem for many working women is inadequate support from husbands and employers. Personnel policies are often based on the outdated idea that most permanent workers are male heads of household. Studies have demonstrated, for example, that working wives have better mental health when husbands share child-care tasks. In fact, one study found that under these conditions, working women had even better mental health than those who did not work; those who did not receive help with child care, by contrast, showed higher levels of emotional stress.[27]

Unfortunately, most studies show that husbands of employed women devote only slightly more time to family matters than do those whose wives do not work. This creates a double burden for employed mothers, resulting in a reduction of leisure time for working women, or what Sylvia Hewlett has called "a lesser life."[28] Clearly, however, these tensions are not inevitable—other family members, particularly husbands, as well as employers and supportive public policies and institutions, can facilitate maternal employment.

Men's behavior patterns resulting from their changed role as principal or sole providers of outside income for their families is what Frank Furstenberg has called the "good dad–bad dad complex." Fathers feel freer to get more heavily involved in the development of their children, and some do that. At the same time, other men perceive greater freedom to abandon their children, and many have.[29] Some men also suffer shocks to their egos when they are no longer the sole breadwinner, especially when their mates have higher earnings and occupational status. However, this seems to be more of a problem for people committed to the "traditional" family patterns than for younger men accustomed to more diverse living arrangements, and perhaps it is a problem that will lessen as families work out acceptable roles in more diverse family structures. Of course, women also have greater freedom to abandon marriages, but they have higher risks because they are usually left with the children and men generally have higher earnings. Some authorities have noted, however, that men's freedom to abandon their children has not necessarily caused them to be better off. Several studies have suggested that marriage is good for men's health and well-being. In general, married men live longer, have fewer illnesses, and report a greater sense of personal well-being than do unmarried men.

Family-Support Policies in the Workplace

Women have become permanent, important fixtures in the work force, and American companies increasingly realize that they should modernize personnel policies rooted in the assumptions of an earlier era.[30] Companies that want to attract and retain the best possible workers are therefore experimenting with a variety of policies to ease the tensions on families created by the employment of women. Most labor-market experts expect these corporate efforts to accelerate during the 1990s, when the rate of growth in the work force will be substantially lower than it was during the 1970s.

The policies of leading companies are driven by the realization that women employees have valuable skills, knowledge, and abilities at a time when skill requirements for high-performance companies are rising. Indeed, as noted earlier, during the 1990s, when shortages of highly educated workers are expected, young women entering the work force will be better educated than young men, and women are expected to fill more than 60% of new jobs created during this period.

Of course, working women will continue to be motivated by economic necessity as well as by desires for personal fulfillment. The extent to which family well-being depends upon working women is suggested by the fact that two-thirds of working women are either the sole supporters of their families or are married to men who earn less than $15,000 a year.

Companies are finding that their ability to attract and retain male workers also depends increasingly on the extent to which the jobs they offer allow men to meet their family responsibilities. Many signs indicate that some "traditional" family values are likely to become more important in the 1990s than they were in the 1960s and '70s. If this is so, companies will have added inducements to accommodate family concerns. For example, more than half of the men surveyed by Robert Half International, a personnel recruitment firm, said they would sacrifice as much as a quarter of their salaries to have more family or personal time. Forty-five percent said they would likely refuse a promotion that involved taking away more time from their families.[31]

In anticipation of a changing work force, several leading-edge companies have pioneered family-support policies. Aetna Life and Casualty introduced more flexible work arrangements after a 1987 survey revealed that "21 percent of the women who left technical positions did so because of family obliga-

Companies that want to attract and retain the best possible workers are experimenting with a variety of policies to ease the tensions on families created by the employment of women. Most labor-market experts expect these efforts to accelerate during the 1990s.

Companies are finding that their ability to attract and retain male workers depends increasingly on the extent to which the jobs they offer allow men to meet their family responsibilities.

tions—and these women were rated as better than average performers by their supervisors."[32] Similarly, DuPont discovered that a fourth of its male and half of its female employees had considered seeking other jobs with more flexibility in dealing with family responsibilities. DuPont responded by lengthening maternity leaves, creating more flexible work schedules, and raising its funding for community child-care centers.

A number of high-performance companies have discovered that family-oriented policies are good investments. The American Bankers Insurance Group found that its Miami facility, with an on-site day-care center, had an absentee rate of 7% compared with 17% for the whole company. Sunbeam's company-based prenatal health program reduced the average cost per pregnancy from $25,000 to $3,500. Sunbeam learned that high health care costs were due to the fact that many employees who gave birth prematurely were not seeing doctors until the third to fifth month of their pregnancies, for reasons ranging from the cost of care to the lack of personal leave time.

Corporate family-support policies take four basic forms:

1. *Flexible working time.* This makes standard working time less rigid. Such arrangements can reduce costs, improve attendance, and attract good workers who want to work part time. The disadvantages for companies include making supervisory and pay practices more complicated. Despite these disadvantages, a 1988 Conference Board survey found that 93% of large American companies had adopted some kind of flexible work practice.

2. *Family leave.* Large and medium-sized American companies have traditionally given leave to full-time employees (FTEs) for such matters as vacation (97% of FTEs, according to a 1989 Bureau of Labor Statistics survey), funerals (84% of FTEs), and sick leave (68% of FTEs). Paid maternity leave, by contrast, was available for only 3% of FTEs and paid paternity leave was available for only 1%; unpaid maternity and paternity leave covered 37% and 18% of female and male employees, respectively. A number of major companies are beginning to grant parental leave, however. Merck, for example, provides maternity leave of six weeks with pay and another six months unpaid leave for both parents. IBM provides three years of unpaid child- or elder-care leave, with flexible options for returning to work. American Telephone and Telegraph's collective bargaining agreement provides one year of leave for child or elder care and one-day leaves in two-hour increments to handle family matters. The director of labor relations at AT&T believes that "every dollar spent [on family leave], we get back in productivity."[33]

3. *Dependent care.* Although dependent care is provided by a relatively small number of American companies, this is a growing employee benefit. Only an estimated 4,000 employers now offer dependent care, but this represents a 400% increase during the decade of the '80s, according to the Child Care Action Campaign.[34] Child care takes a number of forms—direct payments, on-site day care, referral services, and other options. Some companies also provide prenatal as well as child-care resource and referral services. One increasingly popular benefit is financial assistance for dependent care. A simple and low-cost option is the Dependent Care Assistance Plan (DCAP), which permits pre-tax deductions of up to $5,000 a year from employees' salaries to cover predictable care for children or other dependents. Companies' only expense for a DCAP is the administrative cost of organizing and managing these benefits. In addition, some employers reimburse employees for child-care costs or make payments to child-care centers. In its collective bargaining agreement, AT&T has allocated $10 million to support dependent-care programs in communities where AT&T

employees live. International Business Machines reported that it would spend $25 million between 1990 and 1995 on dependent-care activities in communities where IBM employees live. These funds will help develop and expand child-care centers as well as finance programs for school-age and mildly ill children and other relatives.

4. *Sick-child care.* Another high-yield employee benefit is to provide for the care of sick children or other relatives. According to a report in *Pediatrician Magazine*, businesses lose 6 to 29 days a year per parent with children younger than six because of sick children; the estimated costs to all businesses is $2 billion to $6 billion a year.[35] Honeywell estimated that it saved $45,000 in nine months by underwriting 80% of the cost of emergency care for its employees. Apple Computer provides an "isolation room" in its day-care center for noninfectious sick children. In New York, Colgate-Palmolive, Time, Ernst & Young, and four other companies have developed a joint program to place emergency child-care workers in the homes of employees whose usual child-care arrangements have been disrupted.

Teenage Pregnancy

Unwanted teenage pregnancies can cause great difficulties for teenage mothers, their children, and society. What, if anything, can be done about the problem is a controversial policy issue. It is important, however, to keep the teenage-pregnancy problem in perspective. While it has received a lot of media attention, teenagers actually account for less than 5% of all single parents. Moreover, the incidence of births to teenagers is down 25% for blacks and 35% for whites for women born between 1940 and 1960.[36]

Nevertheless, the problem is serious for the families involved and for society. Many question, however, how effective preventive interventions are likely to be. Mary Jo Bane and Paul Jargowsky find that prevention programs "are not . . . likely to have important effects on the number of single mothers even if they are successful, and examples of successful programs are not easy to come by."[37] Other analysts, by contrast, are more optimistic about interventions. The National Academy of Sciences, for example, reports that contraception and abortion services can clearly reduce teen pregnancy and parenthood. Moreover, two school-based projects, one in Baltimore and the other in St. Paul, reported positive results in reducing teen pregnancy.[38]

Examples of other kinds of successful interventions include programs like the Job Corps, which has been effective in preventing teen pregnancies. Probably the Job Corps and residential education and training programs succeed because they involve comprehensive support services in a setting where young people are removed from traditional, negative peer pressures. Similarly, attaching basic and behavioral education to federal summer youth employment and training programs can reduce the large loss in learning most disadvantaged children experience in the summer as well as reduce dropout rates and teen pregnancies, drug abuse, and involvement with the criminal-justice system. The Philadelphia-based organization Public/Private Ventures (P/PV) has had some success in this regard. This intervention, the Summer Training and Education Project (STEP), was carefully tested by P/PV in five sites initially and by 1990 was in 50 locations. Such programs are predicated on the finding that a strong correlation exists between educational achievement and positive social outcomes, including the reduction of teen pregnancy.[39] Improved education and training of parents, especially mothers, is one of the most effective ways of making it possible for poor teenage mothers to escape poverty.[40]

It is important to keep the teenage-pregnancy problem in perspective. While it has received a lot of media attention, teenagers actually account for less than 5% of all single parents.

A strong correlation exists between educational achievement and positive social outcomes, including the reduction of teen pregnancy. Improved education and training of parents, especially mothers, is one of the most effective ways of making it possible for poor teenage mothers to escape poverty.

Fertility, Family Structure, and Public Policy

Can comprehensive family-support systems affect family structure and behavior? European countries have sometimes sought to use family-support programs to reverse declining fertility rates. One review of these efforts concluded, however, that the effects of these programs had been "nil or negligible."[41] Similarly, analyses of fertility rates across various countries show little relationship of those rates to policy differences.[42]

Some analysts believe family structure to be based mainly on economic factors and therefore not likely to be influenced very much by policies that ignore fundamental economic principles. Gary Becker, for example, argues that marriage and childbirth can be viewed as economic decisions.[43] According to this theory, marriage is a good deal for men and women, on the basis of comparative advantages. Women get access to men's higher earnings, and men get access to services from women they do not want to perform themselves or get those services on better terms than they could find in competitive markets. As career opportunities for women improved, however, marriage made less economic sense, so women either delayed marriage, divorced more often, or cohabitated without marrying. Similarly, according to this theory, having children is a cost–benefit decision. The benefits include ego enhancement, old-age security, and future income from children's earnings. The costs include the forgone wages for the caretaking parent and the costs of having and raising children. As women's earning capacities increase, the opportunity costs of children rise relative to the benefits, resulting in lower fertility rates.

The problem with this theory is that relying on presumed subjective cost–benefit calculations and adding catch-all variables such as "ego enhancement" make it difficult to prove or disprove the theory with empirical evidence. To some extent, of course, all decisions are cost–benefit calculations, though it strains credulity to argue that decisions about family matters are restricted to purely economic calculations. Unfortunately, a theory that explains everything explains nothing.

Other economists advance more general hypotheses to explain fertility rates. One of the most influential of these was developed by Richard Easterlin, who argues that an age cohort's fertility rates are directly related to their perceived lifetime earnings potential and their aspirations concerning living standards. If expected earnings and aspirations are low, a cohort will have low fertility rates. If earnings expectations turn out to be higher than aspirations, cohorts will have more children, as happened with the parents of the baby-boom generation in the 1945–65 period, when earnings rose at an unprecedented rate for a relatively small cohort whose size and low aspirations were shaped by the Depression of the 1930s. The large baby-boom cohort, by contrast, entered the labor market at a time of slow growth in productivity and total output. The large increase in the supply of labor at a time of slow growth in demand depressed earnings below the requirements of the aspirations shaped by the living conditions of the baby boomers' more affluent parents. In order to sustain the living standards to which they aspired, the baby boomers therefore either delayed or avoided marriage, and wives in this cohort worked more and had fewer children.[44]

A more restricted economic analysis is the "marriageable pool" hypothesis, popularized by William Julius Wilson's influential book, *The Truly Disadvantaged*.[45] Wilson and his colleagues attempted to explain the low marriage rates of poor, black inner-city people in terms of a scarcity of marriageable males—

that is, males with adequate earnings to support families. The number of eligible males was reduced in these areas by high mortality rates, low wages, inadequate education and training, and high unemployment rates. In this analysis, most of the available males offer females few economic advantages, especially when women are able to support themselves and their children by a combination of welfare and low-wage service jobs.

What about these arguments? Unquestionably, economic conditions have affected birth and marriage rates in the past. Fertility rates fell during the depressed 1930s, rose during the prosperous 1940s and '50s, and declined during the economically stagnant 1970s and '80s. However, the correlation is not strong for the prosperous 1960s and early '70s, when marriage rates were declining despite good economic conditions. Similarly, the year-to-year changes in income and marriage rates are not highly correlated with the economy on a short-term basis. As predicted by orthodox economic theory, fertility rates for blacks and whites fell during the 1970s when male median incomes also fell. However, the decline in birth rates started while incomes were still rising.

Finally, just because broad economic changes and fertility have been highly correlated in the past does not mean these relationships will hold in the future. In other words, economic conditions are important determinants of fertility, but other factors—especially attitudes and behavioral patterns—also are at work and apparently have modified the formerly very strong relationships between economic conditions and marriage and fertility rates.[46]

As noted earlier, women's employment and income patterns differed markedly from men's during the 1970s and '80s. Women's labor-force participation rates continued to increase, while those of men continued downward. Presently, men's rates are higher than those of women, but the rates are converging. Men also were more concentrated in industries that faced downward wage pressures as a result of more intensive international competition and technological change. Women's income also increased because they worked more hours and in different occupations.

Improved economic opportunities for women have caused them to be less dependent on marriage and have increased the opportunity costs of both childbearing and homemaking. Some analysts suggest that this factor may have broken the long-standing relationship between business cycles and fertility.[47]

U.S. Policies

The United States, unlike most democratic industrial countries, does not have comprehensive or coherent family policies. However, most government policies affect families, albeit often unintentionally, and we do have a number of categorical programs that affect families. This section outlines some of the proposals that have been made to improve those programs.

Child allowances. Child allowances are the centerpiece of most European family-support programs. Child allowances have been proposed in the United States, with a variety of means suggested to pay for them. One option would be to raise the personal income-tax exemption for dependent children. This exemption, of about $2,000 to $4,000, has declined over the years because its nominal value has not kept up with inflation. A higher exemption clearly would help families with children, especially if the tax were made refundable—that is, if those who owed no tax got a payment from the government. This option has the added advantage of administrative simplicity—it would require no additional governmental administrative agency, and would not be as stigmatizing as some categorical programs, such as food stamps or AFDC.

Economic conditions are important determinants of fertility, but other factors—especially attitudes and behavioral patterns—also are at work and apparently have modified the formerly very strong relationships between economic conditions and marriage and fertility rates.

Improved economic opportunities for women have caused them to be less dependent on marriage and have increased the opportunity costs of both childbearing and homemaking.

However, a number of objections can be made to child allowances. One is that because such programs have broad eligibility conditions, they are fairly expensive; according to one estimate, doubling the $2,000–$4,000 exemption would cost about $19 billion a year.[48] A second objection is that child allowances are regressive, though the strength of this objection, ironically, has been diminished by the fact that the U.S. federal income tax has become less progressive. Nevertheless, this benefit would do little for poor families unless it were made refundable. Finally, there is no guarantee that children would be the beneficiaries of child allowances.

Child-support enforcement. A major policy problem is getting fathers to take greater responsibility for their children. Counseling and educational campaigns focusing on paternal responsibility might help, although the peer groups of many young males seem to encourage irresponsibility. However, efforts are beginning to try to make fathers more responsible for their children.

The Family Support Act of 1988 sought, among other things, to strengthen child support by requiring automatic and universal income withholding upon the award of child support, except where both parties agree to a waiver in court. As Pat Wong has noted, "Income withholding is a proven, efficient means of collecting payment, as evidenced by the success of the income tax system."[49] As will be noted below, the Family Support Act also attempted to emulate the Swedish system of providing work, job-search assistance, and education and training for welfare recipients. The difference, of course, is that Sweden and other European countries have incorporated human-resource-development policies as integral components of overall economic policy, whereas the United States still relies primarily on inadequate income-support programs that are justified by an amalgam of public charity donations and Keynesian economics.

The inadequacies of federal family policies have caused some states to initiate reforms on their own. One notable experiment is Wisconsin's Child Support Assurance System (CSAS). This experiment establishes a presumptive "percentage of income" standard for setting child-support amounts and a universal, immediate, income-withholding collection system. These provisions were introduced in 1983 and 1987, respectively. The CSAS also guarantees a minimum level of assured child support for all families with child-support awards. The state makes up any difference between the assured level and the amount paid by the noncustodial parent. In order to provide greater incentives for parents to work, the CSAS provides an hourly work-expense offset for all low-income child-support families not receiving AFDC. This offset is phased out for higher-income groups in a manner similar to the federal earned income tax credit. Wisconsin taxes the noncustodial parent to provide funds for the assured child-support amount.

However, the Family Support Act collection mechanism has several problems. The most obvious one is that noncustodial parents without income still will not support their children. Second, the act provides an exception by private consent for automatic withholding. This could cause the system to continue to be bogged down in litigation. Third, it is difficult to monitor this system because it is mainly private. Fourth, under present arrangements, the custodial mother has discretion in establishing paternity. One option would be to require that paternity be established at birth. At present, mothers who depend on public assistance are required to cooperate in establishing paternity, but others are not. Some experts therefore suggest that this requirement might be extended to all births. This practice would do much to extend the rights of out-of-wedlock children "beyond the need for current support to the areas of social insurance entitlement, health care coverage, inheritance, and family identity."[50]

No results are available from the Wisconsin experiment, but a mathematical simulation of that program suggests that it will decrease dependence on government support and decrease poverty, without a significant increase in public spending.[51]

Family Leave

The effort to establish a family leave policy for the United States was stalled in 1990 when President George Bush vetoed the Parental and Medical Leave Act, which would have required firms with more than 50 employees to provide up to 12 weeks of unpaid leave when a child was born or adopted or when a spouse, child, or parent had a medical emergency that required at-home care. The bill had widespread support but was vetoed because President Bush opposed "federally imposed conditions," which he thought would be too rigid and would hurt the competitive position of American business.[52] Without any valid statistical evidence—because we have no comprehensive information on how many employers already provide parental leave for comparison—President Bush said the bill's mandated benefits would "stifle the creation of new jobs and perhaps eliminate existing ones." The President argued, in addition, that such benefits should be negotiated by workers and companies and that competition for workers would force employers to provide the kind of benefits that workers want.

This argument has some merit, but the problem is that less than 20% of American workers actually have collective-bargaining rights. Moreover, relying on employer action and collective bargaining will do the most for workers who already have substantial economic power and least for workers who need help. As discussed in chapter 2, one of the reasons most industrialized democracies enacted laws to put floors under competitive labor markets was to moderate the market's natural tendency to produce inequality. Moreover, competitive markets can depress conditions as well as improve them. Employers in the most competitive and lowest-wage markets, for example, will be more reluctant to voluntarily grant parental leave or other benefits and they are less likely to face labor shortages than are employers in higher-wage industries. Labor standards, therefore, take these matters out of competition and force employers to compete by improving productivity, not by maintaining poor working conditions. One of the reasons the Commission on Skills of the American Workforce found that American companies were lagging behind their major competitors in productivity improvements is that those companies are much freer of governmental or collective-bargaining constraints than their competitors in most other countries are.[53] American companies are therefore freer to pursue low-wage strategies that might be in their short-term interest but are not viable strategies in the long run for countries that want to compete by maintaining and improving incomes. A more effective way to promote competitiveness would be to grant parental leave in order to help parents raise their children, our next generation of workers.

The opponents of parental leave also ignore the costs to the country in not having a medical- or family-leave policy. A congressional study estimated that the annual costs to employers of the Parental and Medical Leave Act of 1990 would have been approximately $200 million. On the other hand, the Institute for Women's Policy Research (IWPR) in Washington, D.C., estimated that the cost to American workers and taxpayers of not having family and medical leave is staggering. In a 1990 report, the IWPR concluded: "the costs borne by workers because of childbirth, illness and dependent care [come] to over $100 billion" and added that "the total earnings loss to all women who have babies

An effective way to promote competitiveness in productivity would be to grant parental leave in order to help parents raise their children, our next generation of workers.

The cost to American workers and taxpayers of not having family and medical leave is staggering—over $100 billion.

is estimated at $1 billion annually."[54] It is therefore hard to avoid the conclusion that the parental leave bill's economic benefits alone would far outweigh its costs.

After all, laws in 26 states already guarantee leave to employees for family and medical reasons. A survey of the first four states to pass parental-leave legislation (Oregon, Minnesota, Wisconsin, and Rhode Island) by the New York-based Families and Work Institute found that these states were experiencing "neither serious increases in costs . . . nor difficulties administering and implementing the laws."[55] The overwhelming majority (56% to 84%) of employers surveyed in these states said the laws had caused no change in training, unemployment insurance, or administrative costs.

Welfare Reform

The increased labor-force participation of women—especially the mothers of young children—has changed public attitudes about the desirability of providing incentives for low-income people to support themselves through work. Because most mothers work, it is hard to argue that welfare recipients should not also work. Support for employment-oriented programs likewise has been strengthened by federal budget constraints and the realization that low-income families could have higher incomes if public assistance were used to help people become self-sufficient rather than remain dependent. Finally, support for work programs has been strengthened by experience with a variety of such programs in the United States and other countries during the 1960s, '70s, and '80s.

These programs have taught us a number of important lessons. Low-income people respond to the same incentives as anybody else—a lesson that dispelled the idea in some circles that the poor had to be forced to work. The problem was not that the poor did not want to work, but that welfare recipients had few opportunities to improve their conditions through the kinds of jobs available to them. Mothers of young children were justifiably concerned about jobs that not only paid no more than public assistance but also could cause them to lose health care and other benefits for their children. Housing and health care are particularly important to low-income people, who, as noted in chapter 3, pay much higher proportions of their income for housing than do more affluent people. Also, the cost of health care accelerated rapidly during the 1980s, at the very time that federal income-support expenditures were being cut or allowed to lag behind the rate of inflation.

The welfare system in the United States has provided very little incentive for AFDC recipients to work. Because many low-income jobs provide no health insurance, the loss of Medicaid can be a particularly serious problem for low-income single mothers. For example, in 1990 a single mother with two children who took a job earning 90% of the poverty rate would experience a reduction in AFDC and food stamps to $2,566 (from $6,611, both in 1988 dollars) and would lose Medicaid after 12 months. When child-care expenses are added to this, the mother's incentive to work is clearly reduced.

The 1988 Family Support Act represents the first step in what could be a major reform of the nation's welfare system. The act stresses child-support enforcement, job training, and supportive services for families making the transition from welfare to work. The Family Support Act encourages parental support for children whenever possible. It strengthens child-support enforcement, as noted earlier, and requires all states to make AFDC benefits available to two-parent families facing economic difficulties because of unemployment.

One of the Family Support Act's basic provisions is the Job Opportunities and Basic Skills (JOBS) program, which creates education, training, and employment opportunities for AFDC recipients. The JOBS program will make some fundamental changes in the operation of state and local welfare employment programs. States are required to assess the employability of each participant and to provide a menu of training, job-search, and support services tailored to individual needs. The Family Support Act is based on the assumption that basic education has been a major barrier to the attainment of good jobs for many low-income people. It thus generally requires that education services be provided to teen parents and to adult participants who have not completed high school.

Chief among the supportive services the states are required to provide to families is child care, discussed in the next section. The Family Support Act permits unlimited federal matching funds to the states for child care at the Medicaid matching rate of 50% to 80%, depending on the state. The act also sets the rates per child that states must pay for these services. The rate cannot be below $200 a month for a child younger than two or $175 for a child older than two. Federal matching funds are available up to the "local market rate," defined as the 75th percentile of the rates for the providers of particular kinds of care.

Child Care

A number of developments have made child care an important national economic and social priority. The most obvious of these is the increased employment of mothers of young children, a trend that is expected to continue. By 2000, 80% of children under one year old will have mothers in the work force.

A second set of developments increasing the need for child care relates to changes in family structure. The dispersal of the extended family and the trend toward smaller family sizes, for example, have reduced the number of family members who can care for infants and toddlers. The increased number of children in single-parent households is another important factor. In 1990 approximately nine million children younger than 10 were in single-parent families. The limited financial resources available to these households, partly due to lack of support by noncustodial parents, has forced adult family members into the work force, as have state and federal welfare policies. Furthermore, the absence of day care is a major impediment to employment for many of these single parents. According to a recent survey in Washington state, two-thirds of single mothers receiving AFDC cited child-care problems as a primary obstacle to seeking employment.

Of course, child-care problems are not restricted to low-income mothers. The cost, quality, and availability of child care are serious problems for all working mothers. According to a recent report, 25% of nonworking mothers of infants and toddlers say they would seek paid employment if affordable day care were available.[56]

The growth of scientific knowledge about the impact of experiences in the first years of life on a person's lifelong physical, social, and cognitive development highlights the importance of high-quality early childhood care. Much of this research has centered on the relationship of parents to their children's development. The quality of mothers' prenatal care, diet, and habits all affect the growth of their children. Indeed, because most organs form during the first eight weeks after conception, drugs, alcohol, or other toxic substances can cause irreversible damage to these organs in a developing fetus, including the central ner-

According to a recent survey in Washington state, two-thirds of single mothers receiving AFDC cited child-care problems as a primary obstacle to seeking employment. The cost, quality, and availability of child care are serious problems for all working mothers.

vous system. Similarly, inadequate nutrition for pregnant and nursing mothers can cause problems for their children.

The attachment formed between infants and another human being, ordinarily the mother, is crucial. Longitudinal studies have shown that infants who are securely attached at one year or 18 months are more sociable and skillful with peers, do better in preschool programs, and are better learners as they grow older. According to Dr. David Hamburg, president of the Carnegie Corporation of New York, and one of the world's leading experts on early childhood behavior,

> Several years after the initial establishment of secure or insecure attachments, independent observations show the children who have had the benefit of more secure attachment in the first year of life are more curious, more exploratory, and effective both in relation to the social and physical aspects of their later environments. A kind of friendly and trusting curiosity seems to guide their behavior. This in turn gives them the basis for developing cognitive and social skills in later years.[57]

What parents need to do to develop secure attachment in the first five years of life is "simple in concept, though more complicated in day-to-day application." Hamburg outlines four basic orientations:

> 1) a loving parent, cherishing the life of the child and making a patient investment in the child's future; 2) an enjoying parent, finding focal points for interactions with the child that provide mutual satisfaction; 3) a teaching parent who understands enough about child development to interact constructively with the child, to become skillful as a mentor, and to sharpen the child's skills gradually as the child's capacity evolves; 4) a coping parent who knows how to seek help to develop skills for getting through the inevitable vicissitudes of life.[58]

The second year of life, when language develops rapidly, is another crucial stage in the child's learning cycle. At this stage, lively interactions with parents and other caregivers greatly improve a child's subsequent cognitive and social development. Children in poor families are particularly likely to miss out on these vital interactions. Ordinarily, the behavioral norms learned early in life, in the context of interpersonal warmth and trust, include (1) taking turns; (2) sharing with others; (3) cooperating, especially in learning and problem solving; and (4) helping others, especially in times of stress. Although, as Hamburg notes, these norms are established on a simple level in the first few years of life, they provide the basis for much more complex and beneficial relationships later in life.

Research has demonstrated the importance and usefulness of interventions to help poor children and their parents cope with developmental problems. Most of the negative factors can be overcome. Preventive programs that help poor parents improve their understanding of child development can pay exceptional dividends in breaking the cycle of poverty. These interventions can help overcome a cluster of factors associated with severely disadvantaged parents, including "an extreme sense that the locus of control in life is outside ourself, that one has little capacity to shape the events of greatest personal significance; low self-esteem; little perception of opportunity."[59] Children whose parents or caretakers have these characteristics, Hamburg points out, are most at risk for slower intellectual growth and behavior problems as well as for educational handicaps during their school years.

Clearly, however, even in the most disadvantaged environments, research has shown that stimulation to encourage learning that is responsive to children's expressions tends to enhance later learning capabilities when these infants are compared to controls. Similarly, studies have focused on social responsiveness to some of the main behaviors that infants produce, especially smiling and vocalizing. When caretakers are highly responsive to these infant generated behavior patterns, the infants tend to respond positively.[60]

Studies show, in addition, what most of us know intuitively to be true: "the same developmental influences predict child intellectual outcome in families of different social classes."[61]

One of the most important findings of child-development research seems to resolve the question of whether child care is less desirable than full-time care by at-home mothers, which formerly was assumed to be ideal for promoting child development. However, according to studies reviewed by the Ford Foundation,

> children placed in quality care outside the home develop as well as children in the full-time care of their mothers. Partly as a result of this new understanding . . . discussion now focuses on what constitutes quality child care rather than on whether mothers of young children should be employed.[62]

Greater understanding of the beneficial effects of preschool programs has also been fostered by child-development studies.

The availability of quality early-childhood care is a key issue in child care. To be most effective, child-care services must be accessible and affordable as well as high quality. No "best" model of services or facilities exists; instead parents' comfort with the facilities available seems to be an important factor in children's adjustment to them.

Federal and state agencies have attempted to ensure the quality of child-care programs mainly through regulation of such matters as the credentials of caregivers, staff–child ratios, and the nature of the physical facilities. Staff qualifications and training, however, clearly are the most critical factors in determining the quality of child-care programs. One of the most complete studies of such matters is the Abt Associates National Day Care Study, which found that

> the key variables affecting the quality of day-care center programs are the training of teachers or other care givers, specifically in early childhood education and child development, and class size. In classes supervised by staff with education or training in child development, teachers spent more time interacting with the children, and the children showed more cooperative behavior, greater persistence in completing tasks and more frequent involvement in class activities. In centers where teachers or caregivers had received training, the children also made greater gains on tests of intellectual functioning.[63]

Studies of family day-care centers have reached similar conclusions, though the findings have not been as strong or as consistent. In these centers, in addition to staff training, affiliation with a larger child-care network or provider association appears to be an important factor in quality of care. Homes that were part of such networks were 50% more likely to provide positive cognitive stimulation for children than were homes without such affiliations.[64]

School-age child care and preschool or "nursery school" services were formerly discussed as separate issues. Increasingly, however, parents and policymakers are becoming aware of the mounting evidence that quality learning environments help foster the growth of infants and toddlers as well as older children. In other words, the challenge is not merely to "keep" children when their parents are at work but to help them develop as well.

According to studies reviewed by the Ford Foundation, "children placed in quality care outside the home develop as well as children in the full-time care of their mothers."

Staff qualifications and training are the most critical factors in determining the quality of child-care programs.

Early Childhood Education

One of the most important ways to improve family welfare and accommodate the increased employment of mothers is to provide adequate child care. These services are important not only to permit mothers to work but also because so much learning takes place during the earliest years of life.[65] Mounting evidence suggests that well-designed childhood-education programs can produce positive results. The best-known study documents the success of the Perry Preschool Project in Ypsilanti, Michigan, from 1962 to 1967.[66] The project enrolled five successive groups of children with low IQ scores and low socioeconomic status in either one- or two-year preschool programs. The program entailed morning classes with trained teaching teams for 7.5 months a year, supplemented by weekly 90-minute visits by teachers to the children's homes. A control group, paired with program participants according to IQ scores, received no such treatment.

When they entered elementary school, program children performed better in classrooms, were less likely to be retained a grade, and were less likely to be placed in special education than were similar students who did not participate in the preschool programs. More than two-thirds (67%) of participants graduated from high school, compared with 49% of the control group. Program participants also were more likely to undertake vocational or academic education after high school (38% and 21%, respectively). At age 19, participants were more likely to be working than were members of the control group (50% vs. 32%), were markedly more likely to be self-supporting (45% vs. 25%), were significantly less likely to be on welfare (18% vs. 32%), and were less likely to experience teen pregnancy or to be involved with the criminal-justice system as teenagers or adults. Earnings of the program participants were 24% higher than for the control group.

Many other studies, including those of the Head Start program, while generally less sophisticated and controlled, confirm the Perry Preschool results. All of these cases show that participation in preschool programs increases the rate of high school graduation.[67] In addition, these analyses show that preschool programs reduced the percentage of children who were retained a grade or more in school by 12% and placement of children in special education classes by 19%.

Quality preschool services are expensive, and one of the most important obstacles to their provision is the relatively high initial cost. The current cost of a Perry Preschool program would be around $6,000 per participant, which means that the provision of such services to every poor child would cost approximately $3.6 billion.[68] However, careful evaluation of the benefits of the Perry Preschool program to age 19 indicated that benefits outweighed costs by 7 to 1 for the one-year program and 3.6 to 1 for the two-year program.[69] If we decided to invest significantly in preschool services for disadvantaged children, ways could be found to finance the programs. For example, Harold Watts and Suzanne Donovan suggest using the surpluses in the Social Security Trust Fund to make these kinds of high-yield investments.[70] Otherwise, the Social Security Trust Fund will very likely be used simply to offset deficits in general revenues.

Federal Child-Care Programs

The federal government already supports child care, directly and indirectly, in several ways. The largest of these federal programs is the child and dependent care tax credit (CDCTC), which permits an income tax deduction of 30% of child-care costs of up to $2,400 for one child and $4,800 for two or more. Because a working family without enough income to pay taxes gets nothing from this program, most of the benefits go to higher-income families. In 1989, for example, 77% of the $3.6 billion in credits went to families with annual incomes of more than $30,000; 43% went to families making more than $50,000.

A second tax program, the earned income tax credit (EITC), is more beneficial to low-income families. The EITC has the added feature of providing an incentive for people to work and it is nonstigmatizing.[71] The EITC provides refundable tax credits to families with at least one worker who earns less than $20,270 (i.e., the government pays low-income people with no tax liability an amount equal to the credit). The maximum credit is $953 a year. A child-care bill proposed by the House of Representatives in 1990 would raise the limit for an eligible family with three children to $2,218. This proposal is estimated to cost $18.5 billion over five years. The House bill would pay part of the added cost of the EITC by reducing the CDCTC for families with incomes more than $70,000 and eliminating the credit entirely for those making more than $90,000. House sponsors of this bill felt that it was equitable because low-income groups pay a higher proportion of their income for child care. For example, a 1986 Census Bureau study found that families earning more than $45,000 a year paid 4% of their income on average for child care, whereas those earning a poverty level paid 22%.[72] As mentioned earlier, substantial evidence indicates that absence of day care is a major deterrent to employment of many women, especially low-income single women with children.[73]

Another source of federal funding for day care is the Title XX Social Services Block Grant program, which provides grants to the states for this and other purposes. The federal government appropriated $2.7 billion for Title XX in 1990; this was about half as much in inflation-adjusted terms as appropriated in 1977.

Finally, Head Start provides more than $1.2 billion in child-development services to about 450,000 children aged three to five years. Head Start programs primarily serve low-income communities through a variety of public and private organizations. Services include nutrition, medical, social, mental health, and educational assistance. Head Start stresses parental involvement and active, participatory learning processes. Most programs operate half-day classes during the school year.[74]

Head Start was a controversial project at first because early evaluations suggested that although the program produced significant gains for young people, most gains withered away by the third grade.[75] However, the program's main purpose was to compensate for the developmental inadequacies of poor families, enabling poor children to start school ready to learn, which it did. The withering away of many benefits suggests not failure of the program but rather the need to reform the schools to build on Head Start gains.[76] Moreover, subsequent evaluations have found that quality preschool programs not only produced lasting results, but also were very cost effective. Statistics from the House Select Committee on Children, Youth and Families reported in 1987 that $1 spent on preschool education could save $4.75 in social costs. The Perry Preschool experiment found even higher returns for a one-year program. However, the Perry Preschool program, which has produced the strongest evidence to date of the effectiveness of quality preschool programs, had higher per-pupil costs than Head Start and a lower ratio of pupils to professional staff.[77]

Statistics from the House Select Committee on Children, Youth and Families reported in 1987 that $1 spent on preschool education could save $4.75 in social costs.

Head Start's greatest weakness is that it does not pay enough to attract and retain highly qualified professionals.

Although Head Start is a successful program, it needs to be improved. For one thing, it reaches less than one-fourth of all poor three- to four-year-olds, fewer than half of whom are served by any public early childhood program. Head Start should also be extended to a full day for children of poor working mothers. Although slightly more than half (51%) of all Head Start mothers work outside the home, only 6% of Head Start children are enrolled full time.[78]

Perhaps Head Start's greatest weakness is that it does not pay enough to attract and retain highly qualified professionals. Not all Head Start staffers need to be highly qualified professionals, but the key to quality programs is having enough trained staff to help educate parents and nonprofessional staff in child development. Although Head Start has been able to employ many highly dedicated people, it is not likely to retain the caliber of professionals needed with beginning average annual salaries for teachers of only $12,074 in general and $15,403 for teachers with bachelor's degrees. Comparable public school teachers earn an average of $29,547 a year, and that is considered low pay relative to other professionals. One-fifth of Head Start's teachers do not have either a bachelor's degree in early childhood education or a competency-based child development associate certificate.[79]

As front-line practitioners in a demanding job, Head Start program operators have demonstrated an understandable impatience with, and resistance to, rigorous evaluation and research. However, as two experts associated with the Perry Preschool project also argue, "for Head Start to maintain and build on its successes over the long term, it must . . . have a strong agenda for research and development. While Head Start has reaped the harvest of research on the long-term effectiveness of similar non-Head Start programs, research on Head Start itself continues to be inadequate."[80] Unless Head Start has a stronger research component, they continue, "the value of our public investment in early-childhood development cannot be documented."[81]

They conclude,

> Our nation's policy makers have finally recognized the importance of programs for young children. If we do not take advantage of this opportunity, we may never have it again. . . . The mandate to increase Head Start enrollment must now be joined by a commitment to maintain and improve the quality of this most successful program.[82]

"For Head Start to maintain and build on its successes over the long term, it must have a strong agenda for research and development."

Although Congress and the Bush administration have not agreed on a child-care policy for the United States, support appears to be growing for such a program. Low-income families, who pay a large proportion of their income for child care, need special help, even though most families with incomes less than $15,000 use family-care arrangements involving no direct cash payments. Mothers whose incomes are at or just above the federal poverty level rarely pay cash for child care. When they do, according to Census Bureau data for 1987, they pay more than 20% of their income, compared with approximately 7% for all working women.[83] The Census Bureau also reported that the total cost of child care was $15.5 billion in 1987. In fiscal 1990, an estimated $7.2 billion was subsidized by the federal government through Head Start ($1.4 billion), poverty and block-grant programs ($1.5 billion), and tax credits ($4.4 billion).

In order to help develop a better factual and analytical base for the child-care debate, the Department of Health and Human Services commissioned a study by the National Research Council (NRC), an arm of the National Academy of Sciences. The NRC report, released in 1990 as Congress was debating this issue, recommended increased spending on child care to meet the needs of a rapidly changing work force. The NRC panel recommended spending between $5 billion to $10 billion on child care, creating national child-care standards, and requiring employers to provide up to one year's unpaid leave for new parents. John Palmer, the panel's chairman, reported that during the course of the NRC study, the panel became convinced that the nation's child-care system was inadequate to meet the needs of children, parents, and society as a whole. By 2000, the report predicted, nearly 80% of all children would have mothers in the work force. The rapidity with which mothers of small children have entered the work force has transformed the quality, affordability, and accessibility of child care from "a strictly private family matter into one with profound implications for the nation as a whole," according to Palmer.[84] The NRC panel was particularly concerned about the quality of child care for low-income groups. The report noted that in 1972, 80% of all federal child-care spending was targeted to low-income groups, compared with only 30% in the late 1980s.[85]

One of the major obstacles to a federal child-care program has been the reluctance of some political groups to provide tax credits to working parents. As Representative Patricia Schroeder, a strong child-care advocate, has observed:

> Conservatives . . . feel [tax credits] would be an incentive for women to work and would discriminate against women who chose to stay home. Actually, since the first tax code was passed in 1913, our tax policies have been geared to families in which the mother stays at home. The marriage penalty tax, Social Security discrimination, and limited child care deductions all penalize working women.[86]

However, she reports that economic trends have been sufficiently powerful to counterbalance the tax code's bias against working women. She observes: "If government tax policy had so much influence on the way we live our lives, most women would now be at home."[87] Schroeder favors child-care tax credits for working mothers because universal tax credits would be too expensive.

She notes, in addition, how important it is to encourage employers to provide day care for their employees' children. This has become a very important personnel problem because women of childbearing age are a permanent, integral component of the work force: 80% of women in the work force are of childbearing age, and 93% of them are likely to become pregnant. Of course, major obstacles exist to company-provided day care, especially cost, liability, and a shortage of technical assistance in establishing programs. However, as Schroeder observes,

> most managers don't realize they can offer some child-care benefits that are relatively inexpensive and not burdensome. They include courses to teach parents how to find and evaluate providers; child care resource and referral services to help parents find good child care; and salary reduction programs, under which specific amounts of money from employee paychecks are withheld, deposited into accounts to pay child care expenses, and subtracted from the employee's taxable income.[88]

Family Relations and Adolescence

Although early childhood learning experiences powerfully influence human capital development, it would be a mistake to assume that the effects of these influences cannot be changed later in life, especially during early adolescence, a time when young people confront choices that will affect the rest of their lives. Early adolescence is characterized by significant bodily growth and change—the most rapid physical growth of any period except infancy—and

The rapidity with which mothers of small children have entered the work force has transformed the quality, affordability, and accessibility of child care from a private matter into one with profound implications for the nation as a whole.

One of the major obstacles to a federal child-care program has been the reluctance of some political groups to provide tax credits to working parents.

considerable cognitive growth. Young adolescents generally experience an increased awareness of self and an enhanced capacity for intimate relations. Adolescence is therefore a period of considerable risk and opportunity. It is also a time when many young people start experimenting with drugs and therefore risk permanent addiction, as well as a period of increased sexual activity, concomitantly increasing the risks of sexually transmitted disease, pregnancy, and low birth-weight babies with substantial health problems. These risks are intensified by the deterioration of family and community relationships for many adolescents and by the fact that the period of adolescence has become much longer than it was in previous generations.[89]

Although the risks to adolescents are greater for some families than others, mounting evidence associates negative outcomes for adolescents with certain types of family behavior. What this implies, of course, is that negative outcomes may be avoided by appropriate behavior within families. It should be stressed, moreover, that certain behavioral factors influence adolescent behavior regardless of "social addresses" such as class, family structure, or ethnic background. According to Sanford Dornbusch, director of the Center for the Study of Families, Children and Youth at Stanford University, research has demonstrated that although these "social addresses" predict adolescent outcomes, "family characteristics are not the sole, nor the most powerful determinants of adolescent behavior. Processes within each family are, in fact, better predictors of achievement or failure."[90]

Dornbusch calls the combination of parenting behaviors that can produce positive outcomes "authoritative parenting." He asserts that "American adolescents thrive when parents 1) are warm, 2) establish and maintain clear standards, and 3) are willing to negotiate the enforcement of their rules."[91] When parents are warm and accepting, adolescents are more likely to be "responsible and socially skilled, have higher self-esteem, and do better academically," whereas when parents are "hostile, rejecting, or distant [adolescents] are more likely to develop psychological and behavioral problems."[92]

Authoritative parenting includes rules and monitoring as well as love.

> Adolescents care more about evaluations by their parents than by their peers, yet, paradoxically, they say they are more likely to do as their peers wish when peer and parent values are in conflict. The reason for this seemingly incompatible set of findings is that adolescents follow parental injunctions, but only when their parents are likely to find out if they deviate.[93]

As a consequence, authoritative parenting involves supervision and informed interest. "In general, parental submissiveness, whether motivated by an ideology of indulgence or by parental neglect, is associated with poor outcomes: delinquent behavior, precocious sexuality, drug and alcohol abuse, and poor grades."[94]

Finally, democratic negotiation is a constructive way to settle disagreements over rules. These negotiations are important learning processes because they involve joint parent–adolescent explorations of the reasons for the rules. Considering the adolescent's point of view can reinforce the young person's values and his or her ability to make good judgments.

Dornbusch concludes,

> within every ethnic group, social class, and family structure, children from authoritative families (in which parents combine firm standards with warmth and democratic discussion) are more self-reliant, report less

anxiety and depression, are less delinquent, and have higher levels of school performance. . . . By contrast, permissive parenting consistently produces poor adolescent outcomes.[95]

The point that Dornbusch and other family researchers make is not that family structure is unimportant, because there are strong associations between, say, single-parent households and negative outcomes for children. Their point is that these outcomes are not inevitable and can be overcome by parental actions and policies to counteract the negative behaviors that lead to undesirable outcomes. For example, single parents tend to grant autonomy to their children early in childhood, "allowing the youth to make his or her own decisions about friends, clothing, money, and staying out late."[96] This tendency is understandable, given the limited time and resources of single parents, usually mothers. However,

> across all social classes and ethnic groups, . . . granting autonomy early to male and female adolescents is associated with lower grades in school and numerous forms of deviance, including early dating, smoking, running away from home, truancy, contacts with police and arrests. . . . Such family behavior, in addition to the problems of poverty, contributes to many of the problems of youth in single parent households."[97]

Similarly, the problems created by divorce and stepparenting are not irreversible, even though children tend to rebel against stepparents and stepparents often wish to defer authority to the biological parent(s). These maladaptive behaviors can have negative outcomes, unless worked out jointly by all the parents involved and their children in a constructive manner.

Divorce can have both negative and positive effects on children, depending on the behavior of the parents. As noted earlier, it has been found that the single stress of divorce ordinarily does not create long-term psychological problems for children. However, serious emotional problems can result from divorce accompanied by multiple stresses such as parental conflict, the absence of the noncustodial parent, depressed financial resources, changes in the custodial parent's availability, health problems associated with the stress accompanying divorce, and chaotic households. As a consequence, children of divorced parents are three times as likely as those from nondivorced families to receive psychological or psychiatric treatment and are more likely to experience such problems as "aggressive, noncompliant, and delinquent behavior; decrements in presocial behavior; problems in academic achievement and school adjustment leading to high rates of school dropouts; and disruptions in peer relations and early sexual activity."[98]

Thus, it is the behavior of the parents and not the fact of divorce that creates problems for young people. "Researchers consistently find that children adapt better in a well-functioning single-parent family than in a conflict-ridden family of origin."[99] In addition, the negative effects of divorce and other family problems can be counteracted by such supporting systems as responsive friends and family members (especially grandparents). Other resources include "day care centers and schools that provide warm, structured, and predictable environments" and "responsive peers and school personnel [who] can validate the self-worth, competence, and personal control of older children from these households."[100]

Families and Schools

If our country's children are to develop to the fullest extent, parents and institutions with child-development responsibilities must become more closely

There are strong associations between single-parent households and negative outcomes for children. But these outcomes are not inevitable and can be overcome by parental actions and policies.

The single stress of divorce ordinarily does not create long-term psychological problems for children. However, serious emotional problems can result from divorce accompanied by multiple stresses.

connected. In turn, if educators are to perform their functions effectively, they must understand the changes that are taking place in the family and the effects of those changes on the family members they seek to serve. The effectiveness of service-delivery processes depends heavily on the rapport between servers and the served. Conflict and ineffectiveness usually come when servers and the served have such different frames of reference that they are unable to empathize or communicate with one another very well. In no area is this more critical than in the schools.

Schools, like many other institutions in our society, have a strong orientation toward "traditional" families and the mass-production economy. The basic organization of most American public schools has the same top-down, producer-driven orientation that characterized the mass-production companies discussed in chapter 2. The schools' main role has been to prepare students for their place in the goods-producing society. The assumption was that some students would become part of the elite and others would do routine jobs requiring fewer higher-order thinking skills. Schools therefore took their place among institutions that tended to perpetuate existing economic and social arrangements for most people.[101] In short, they molded their policies and structures to the needs of the economy and the characteristics of the families they served. The changes discussed in this volume, however, require corresponding changes in the schools to meet the shifting needs of families and the economy.

In the past, school systems were not completely homogeneous or rigid, of course, because education has been a major channel for upward mobility for immigrants and poor children who were willing to work hard against the odds. Indeed, this is one reason many minority and poor families have always valued education for their children. The main requirement for this upward mobility, however, appears to have been not just aspirations, but the families' willingness to work hard to inculcate the values demanded by major employers or institutions of higher education and to provide structured learning opportunities for their children. Learning is accomplished at least as much by the example set by parents, other influential adults, and peers as it is by formal learning opportunities afforded children. Child-development specialists also emphasize delayed gratification, disciplined concentration on tasks, social and communication skills, and fairness in dealing with other people as especially important values for children to learn if they are to succeed in life. What is required, therefore, is for schools, families, and other institutions to work together to see that children learn what they need to know to succeed in society. This will require stronger efforts to restructure schools and involve parents more in their children's education.

Traditional schools must, in short, be transformed if children are to acquire the education they need to deal with a rapidly changing world. Traditionalists argue that the schools' main function is not to substitute for families and other institutions, but to educate children. The trouble with that argument is that the traditional public schools' definition of education is drill, practice, and repetition until students are at least literate and numerate. They do not perceive their function as assuring that students actually acquire thinking skills. This latter function would require that schools understand and value students, diagnose their learning needs, and develop supportive learning systems to meet those needs.

Likewise, too many teachers and administrators, however well-meaning, may fail to understand and value their students' cultural backgrounds and values, due to class and race biases.[102] A learning environment depends heavily on trust between teachers and students, and such biases impede teachers in relating to students and

The basic organization of most American public schools has the same top-down, producer-driven orientation that characterized the mass-production companies. They molded their policies and structures to the needs of the economy and the characteristics of the families they served.

Traditional schools must be transformed if children are to acquire the education they need to deal with a rapidly changing world.

their parents. Too many educators show disrespect for parents with lower levels of education or very different life-styles from their own and may actually consider parental involvement in school affairs to be an undesirable intrusion, despite abundant evidence of the importance of parental involvement for student achievement.

The entire fault, of course, is not with the schools. Most of our basic institutions are predicated upon a system that served the nation reasonably well in a simpler era in which critical-thinking skills were less essential for most people. Americans have generally valued schooling for its economic and social value but have assigned lower status to teachers and intellectual activity than have the citizens of most other industrialized democracies.

In addition, abundant evidence suggests that too many parents pay very little attention to the moral, intellectual, and social development of their children. This neglect is due to a number of factors associated with changing families, especially the fact that working parents, particularly mothers, are strapped for time. Many poor and minority parents themselves have had bad experiences with schools. Less educated parents often are uncomfortable dealing with teachers and administrators. And most parents undoubtedly realize that many of the values that guided their lives must be modified to meet the requirements of a very different world, but they have not been able to think out the means to make these modifications.

For whatever reasons, too few parents pay attention to their children's intellectual development. Instead, they let television, peers, and entertainers instill values and "educate" their children, with disastrous consequences for children, families, and society. This parental neglect has been confirmed by surveys that show that American children do relatively little homework and rarely discuss schooling with their parents. For example, the 1989 National Educational Longitudinal Survey (NELS) of 24,600 eighth graders in 1,000 public and private schools by the United States Department of Education reported that nearly half of the respondents said they rarely discuss school with their parents. Similarly, this survey revealed that only about half of the eighth graders' parents had any contact with their children's schools.[103] In the NELS survey, students reported that they watched television 21.4 hours a week, but spent only 5.6 hours a week on homework and 1.8 hours on outside reading. Almost 63% of the students reported that their parents "rarely or never" limited the amount of television they watched. According to the executive director of the National Association of Elementary School Principals, the "family revolution is the greatest single cause of the decline in student achievement during the last 20 years. It's not better teachers, texts, or curricula that our children need most; it's better childhoods, and we will never see lasting school reform until we first see parent reform."[104]

School Restructuring

Because of its importance for all students, especially low-income and minority students, it is essential to discuss what restructuring means and what the role of families in effective school restructuring should be.

Restructuring means making fundamental changes in the rules, roles, and relationships in schools. As a report published by the National Center on Education and the Economy explains,

> Education, like private industry, can improve by restructuring operations following some very simple principles. First, go for quality and build it in the first time whenever possible. Second, reward success in producing quality.[105]

Too many parents pay very little attention to the moral, intellectual, and social development of their children. They let television, peers, and entertainers instill values and "educate" their children, with disastrous consequences.

The family revolution is the greatest single cause of the decline in student achievement during the last 20 years. It's not better teachers, texts, or curricula that our children need most; it's better childhoods.

> *Minorities would benefit greatly from restructured learning systems that value students by demonstrating sensitivity to their backgrounds, values, and ways of viewing the world.*

A restructured school would make student achievement the main criterion by which teachers, principals, and administrators are judged and rewarded. A restructured system would decentralize decisions about how to improve learning, making teachers and schools responsible for them. Policymakers would establish basic outcome objectives but would leave decisions about how to achieve those objectives to teachers, principals, child-development professionals, parents, and other interested parties at the school level. In addition to goals formulated by elected officials and policymakers, restructured schools would be guided by professional standards based on knowledge and skills developed through research and experience.

Thus, restructuring depends heavily on highly qualified teachers and administrators who are held accountable for student achievement but who have the ability to diagnose individual learning needs and the authority to prescribe learning procedures to remedy deficits.

No process is more important to providing quality education for all students than restructuring; schools must be radically changed if they are to improve. Restructuring is especially important for minority students, who constitute the fastest growing component of public school students. Minority concerns were ignored in the school reforms of the early 1980s, resulting in negative consequences for minority teachers and students. Simplistic and irrelevant tests still hinder many minority persons from entering teaching. Furthermore, teacher education and professional standards ignore the importance of minority cultures and backgrounds of both teachers and students. Thus, education of minority students has suffered and we have fewer and fewer minority teachers at a time when minorities constitute a growing proportion of school enrollments. For instance, it has been estimated that in the year 2000, minority students will account for nearly 40% of public school enrollments but only 5% of teachers will be from minority backgrounds.

Restructuring is, therefore, important to minority students for a number of additional reasons:

1. Although the traditional American school model does not serve many students well, it has been particularly damaging to the disadvantaged—minorities and white—whose home backgrounds have not prepared them as well as their more advantaged peers to function in an impersonal, bureaucratic school system.

2. The traditional school model has repelled many able teachers, but the rate of decline in teacher-education enrollments has been twice as great for non-whites as for whites. The model's negative features include stultifying, even degrading, work environments, low pay and professional status, and poor student outcomes. Restructuring promises to attract more and better teachers by creating a more professional environment, higher rewards for teachers, and better outcomes for students.

3. Minorities would benefit greatly from restructured learning systems that value students by demonstrating sensitivity to their backgrounds, values, and ways of viewing the world and by assuming responsibility for their learning.

4. Restructuring would result in fundamental systemic changes that would give schools and teachers greater flexibility and incentives to incorporate the lessons of hundreds of localized, *ad hoc* programs into their systems. Investigators have uncovered numerous individual success stories, but no exemplary school system.[106] Restructuring would make it possible to have successful systems.

> *The traditional, hierarchical education model is obsolete because it was designed to meet the skill requirements of an agricultural-industrial world.*

Restructuring is needed for a very basic reason: the traditional, hierarchical education model is obsolete and unsustainable. It is obsolete because it was designed to meet the basic skill requirements of an agricultural-industrial world.

The system still does an adequate job of turning out students who are literate, but it does not turn out many with the higher-order thinking skills needed to solve complex problems, to analyze abstract knowledge, to communicate with precision, to learn, and to work well with other people. As noted in chapter 2, all of these skills are required for our country's economic success.

The Comer Model

One of the best examples of how restructuring can improve student performance is suggested by James Comer's work in New Haven, Connecticut.[107] Beginning in 1968, Comer, a professor of child psychiatry at the Yale University Medical School, and his colleagues at the Yale Child Study Center developed a model that greatly improved the performance of two schools with the lowest achievement and worst attendance records of New Haven's 33 elementary schools. The combined enrollment of these schools was 99% black; 70% of the students were children of welfare recipients.

Fifteen years later, the socioeconomic makeup of the schools was unchanged, but the academic performance of the two schools singled out by Comer had surpassed the national average. They ranked third and fifth in composite fourth-grade test scores among New Haven schools, and both had superior attendance records. Comer reported that no serious behavior problem had occurred in either school for over a decade.

A follow-up study tracked 24 students through three years in a Comer school and compared them with a control group that had spent the same period in another New Haven school. The Comer-school students were more than a year ahead in reading and math. The success of the New Haven schools caused Comer's model to be adopted in more than 100 schools in nine school districts of eight states by 1990. By 1990, moreover, New Haven had extended the Comer model to all of that city's 42 schools and 18,000 students.

What accounted for these achievements? Comer's answer seems simple: these schools paid attention to child development and established a basic participatory school-management system in which the principals shared power with parents, teachers, and professional support staff. To a very significant degree, Comer's success came about because he created processes and structures that changed attitudes, incentive structures, and behavior. One of the most important attitudinal changes was the conviction instilled in teachers, students, parents, and school administrators that with proper attitudes and hard work these students could learn as much as anybody.

Comer and his colleagues adapted child-development and behavioral science research to the needs of New Haven schools. Comer's approach differed from other school reforms of the 1980s in that his management model involved all relevant groups, not just parents, principals, or teachers. His system is driven mainly by incentives to improve student achievement in reading, reasoning, attendance, behavior, learning ability, and knowledge development, informed by child-development and behavioral science concepts. It recognizes children's need for social and psychological development, not just academic work. This research demonstrates that children whose family and social development match mainstream values can adjust to schools' requirements much better than can children from poor families, who are less likely to have the social skills needed to cope with a traditional school environment. The mismatch between home and school environments impedes the latter children's learning. As Comer explains,

One of the most important attitudinal changes in New Haven was the conviction instilled in teachers, students, parents, and school administrators that with proper attitudes and hard work these students could learn as much as anybody.

lack of development or development that is at odds with the mainstream occurs disproportionately often among children from minority groups that have had the most traumatic experiences in this society: Native Americans, Hispanics and blacks. The religious, political, economic and social institutions that had organized and stabilized their communities have suffered severe discontinuity and destruction. Furthermore, these groups have been excluded from educational, economic, and political opportunity.[108]

In order to change this negative environment, Comer and his colleagues developed school structures and processes, discussed below, that promoted the students' psychological and social development, thereby promoting a better match between students and the schools. They also promoted positive interactions between minority parents and the schools.

Realizing that change had to come from within the school and could not be mandated from outside, Comer and his colleagues organized a governance and management team in each school. The teams had approximately 12 members each. They were led by the school principal and made up of elected parents and teachers, mental health specialists, and representatives from the nonprofessional support staff. Although these teams recognized the authority of the principals, the principals could not make decisions without considering the concerns of other members of the team. After some initial reluctance, the principals came to see the value of the participatory process.

Because most schools no longer draw most of their students from the neighborhoods around them, a school governance and management team (SGMT) had to create a new community within the school. Comer and his colleagues stressed the importance of cooperation and mutual learning among all members of the SGMT. Parental involvement is particularly important. Comer schools have three sequential levels of parental participation. First, structured, broad-based activities involve a large number of parents. Second, the School Development Program (SDP), as Comer's model is called, calls for approximately one parent for each professional staff person to work in the school as tutors, classroom assistants, or aides. Third, a few highly active parents are members of the SGMT.

The main emphasis of the SGMT is to facilitate cooperation in meeting the learning needs of children. Joint activities can reduce the natural friction between parents and teachers and between teachers, principals, and other school professionals. Joint programs overcome the traditional fragmentation within schools and between schools and families.

Comer discovered that

> a reasonable consensus is needed to accomplish the schools' mission. This consensus can't be mandated as it was in the past—it doesn't exist in our schools or our communities. A mechanism must be created through which school building leadership can create desirable relationships and develop a consensus consistent with school system goals that will allow staff and parents to support the development of students—and to involve students in their own self-development and learning.[109]

The SGMT's success is due in large measure to the early decision to concentrate on problem solving, not blame fixing, and to make decisions by consensus rather than by formal votes. This decision-making process gives each member a sense of participation and ownership of the process and avoids the tendency to polarize members into "winners" and "losers" groups. Consensus building eases communication between parents and school staff, facilitates joint discussions to solve students' problems, and gives teachers and principals expert professional help in dealing with student behavior problems they are not trained to address. This consensus mechanism has the added advantage of giving schools the flexibility to correct problems and improve the system as it evolves.

This self-correcting developmental process made it possible to model the SDP and to discover that the key ingredients for success were the governance team, the mental health group, and parental involvement. Most important, Comer states,

> With each intervention the [school] staff became increasingly sensitive to the concerns of developing children and to the fact that behavior problems result mainly from unmet needs rather than from willful badness—and that actions can be taken to meet these needs.[110]

Organizing Families and Community Organizations to Support Schools

The Texas Industrial Areas Foundation (TIAF) provides another example of improving schools through parental involvement. Whereas Comer focused directly on improving the schools by changing the management system and developing greater parental involvement, TIAF focuses on families and community institutions, especially churches, as learning systems and empowering processes. The foundation is an extension of the Industrial Areas Foundation (IAF) movement initiated by Saul Alinsky in Chicago during the 1940s. The main objective of TIAF is to create "new democratic institutions to empower families and congregations to defend their integrity and to participate meaningfully in public life."[111] In 1990, IAF had some 20 affiliated organizations, consisting of 600 congregations and nearly one million families, from a broad range of faiths and ethnic backgrounds. The IAF organizations do not engage in traditional party politics; they "are radically nonpartisan, endorsing neither candidates nor political parties."[112] However, the TIAF does engage in voter education efforts; it establishes positions on issues that come "out of the experiences of the families" and seeks to "hold public officials and corporate leaders accountable to commitments to these platforms."[113]

The IAF approach is based on the need for institutions to mediate the relationships among individuals, families, and the larger society. Mediating institutions protect vulnerable families from more powerful groups and form support networks to provide access to jobs, political power, education, means of acculturation, and other basic needs. In the early stages of industrialization, these mediating functions were performed by such social institutions as the parish, neighborhood, extended family, local school, political machine, union, and fraternal or social association. With suburbanization, the decentralization of economic activity, and the decline of basic mass production industries, many of these mediating institutions no longer exist, especially in urban areas where many low-income and minority families are concentrated. Little other than television has replaced these mediating institutions. As a consequence,

> the organizations of the IAF are mediating institutions through which families create a space to learn about power and leadership and to act on what they learn . . . they act to counter the pressures on families and to re-shape other institutions in their relationships to families.[114]

The oldest IAF organization in Texas is Communities Organized for Public Service (COPS), established in San Antonio in 1974. The COPS organization consists of 26 Catholic parishes located in Mexican neighborhoods in San Antonio. In the words of its organizer, Ernie Cortes, director of TIAF,

The IAF approach is based on the need for institutions to mediate the relationships among individuals, families, and the larger society, protecting vulnerable families and forming support networks.

[COPS] was founded to empower low-income people. . . . Through the hard work of thousands of IAF-trained leaders, COPS won over $750 million in new streets, drainage, parks, libraries, and other improvements, reversing a long history of disinvestment in the inner city.[115]

Ernie Cortes sees mediating institutions like COPS as being needed to strengthen families in their learning and value-forming processes.

> The family forms—or fails to form—persons able to relate to each other in public life. Families teach the first lessons of relationships among persons, some of which are central not only to private life but to public life as well. Within the family one learns to act upon others and to be acted upon. It is within the family where we learn to identify ourselves with others—or fail to learn to love. It is in the family where we learn to give and take with others—or fail to learn to be reciprocal. It is in the family where we learn to trust others as we depend on them—or learn to distrust them. . . . These lessons of reciprocity, trust, discipline and self-restraint are important to the forming of relationships in public life, in which one must play one's roles and hold others accountable to their roles.[116]

If the family does not function as an effective learning and value-forming institution, it will be vulnerable to the teachings of the state and the market. Although important, these institutions alone do not provide the means for sustaining just and viable communities.

If the family does not function as an effective learning and value-forming institution, it will be vulnerable to the teachings of the state and the market, the "principal institutions of contemporary social life."[117] Although very important, these institutions alone do not provide the means for treating or sustaining just and viable communities. Modern political and economic life are dominated by ideas that may be contrary to the family's basic values and interests. "Unless the family is strong enough to challenge such powerful messages and teach children a different way of making decisions, the advertiser and not the family will shape the family's wants."[118]

TIAF and the Schools

An illustration of how TIAF works to improve schools is afforded by the experiences of one of its 12 Texas organizations, Allied Communities of Tarrant (ACT) in Fort Worth. Founded in 1982, ACT consists of 14,000 families from 22 diverse ethnic and religious congregations. Like COPS in San Antonio, ACT's initial objective was to direct public investments to the inner city.

In 1986, ACT developed a plan to improve a largely dysfunctional, predominantly African American middle school. The school's students ranked last among 20 middle schools in the district on most performance measures. Half of the students had failed the state's writing skills test, half were failing at least one subject, and behavior problems were so bad that the police were called to the school two or three times every day. Parental involvement was so poor that parent–teacher meetings were typically attended by only one or two parents.

Working closely with the school's principal, ACT leaders developed a plan to revitalize the school by strengthening the relationships among parents, teachers, and the school. The principal built a leadership team within the school's staff and ACT developed leadership among the parents. Churches sought to strengthen parent–school–student relations through "recognition days,"

> in which the congregation as a whole would applaud children for progress at school. Each congregation takes care to recognize every child for some form of progress, no matter how far it has to stretch, even if a child has only raised his or her grade from an F to a D or has started attending classes more regularly.[119]

The second part of ACT's work is to attempt to contact the parents of every child, whether or not they belong to an ACT congregation or to any congregation at all.

> The building of relationships in individual meetings is slow, hard work, but there is no shortcut or substitute. The one-on-one meeting is a process of give-and-take. It is the means by which people begin to recognize and understand their own interests. It is how they articulate their vision of themselves and their hopes for their families. It is how they build reciprocal relationships with others.[120]

Allied Communities of Tarrant held more than 600 meetings with parents during an 18-month period. Parental concerns were collected through a standardized survey. Parents became much more closely involved with the school; they attended training sessions on how to support their children's study habits and began to meet more often with their children's teachers.

Ernie Cortes explains how these processes strengthened families, churches, and schools:

> The web of relationships forming each institution took on new, more interesting and vital significance for the families. The congregations acquired a new significance in their ability to respond to the needs of families. Relationships with administration and teachers, which were once at best benign and at worst hostile, became collaborative. . . . The most visible sign of change was the school's transformation into a successful institution. The children's performance on standardized tests rose from 20th of the district's middle schools to third. The percentage of students passing the state writing skills test increased from 50 to 89 percent. The percentage of children failing at least one subject decreased from 50 to 6 percent. Police calls fell off to virtually none. Now it is not unusual for 200 or more to attend parent assemblies at the school to learn about drug awareness, study habits, or other education-related themes. Parents also staff an after school enrichment program. . . . Leaders in other churches and schools have begun to duplicate this effort in another middle school and three elementary schools who feed to them.
>
> In the second middle school, parents identified the need for substantial physical renovation of the building. They drew up a $1.8 million plan and negotiated it with the school board. The board approved the plan and doubled the capital spending originally allocated to the school.[121]

These successes, as important as they are, "are only the outward signs of the organization's real achievement—the development of churches into institutions of public life which shape and support their families in both their public and private lives."[122] These new processes strengthened family relationships as well as school performance. Parents not only learned how to be better parents, they also learned how to act. "They became empowered. They do not merely celebrate their values and their hopes as fantasies in the privacy of home or pew, but acquire the power to make them a real part of the public life of Fort Worth."[123]

Texas Industrial Areas Foundation has become more deeply involved in the education reform process through an independent organization, the Texas Interfaith Education Fund (TIEF). The fund's vision is to create a "community of learners" on school campuses. In this community of learners,

> both students and educators are committed to learning the skills of problem-solving, teaching of self and others, and collaboration. Such a commitment would be lived out on school campuses where all stakeholders—parents, teachers, administrators, and community leaders—are empow-

Allied Communities of Tarrant's real achievement was the development of churches into institutions of public life that shape and support families in both their public and private lives.

ered to bring their fullest talents, creativity, and energy to bear on achieving high levels of learning for all children.[124]

Between 1986 and 1990, three TIAF organizations installed the TIAF model in seven disadvantaged neighborhood schools. Their experiences made it possible for TIEF to develop three "organizing concepts" for its efforts: (1) working with local community institutions such as churches and neighborhood associations that already mediate between families and other institutions; (2) building relationships among parents, educators, and community leaders through contacts with individual parents that build on parents' self-interest in the education of their children and their "own personal development and sense of efficacy"; and (3) leadership development for parents, which provides knowledge of how schools operate and skills necessary for working effectively with public institutions and instills the self-esteem and self-confidence that come from opportunities where parents are able to "experience themselves as effective and powerful persons."[125]

Using this model, TIEF has developed education projects in Phoenix, Arizona, and in the following places in Texas: Houston, the Rio Grande Valley, San Antonio, Austin, El Paso, and Fort Bend County.

In addition, TIAF is exploring with Jim Comer the possibliity of using his model in the schools with which the foundation works to supplement its organizing support outside the schools. Ernie Cortes and his associates believe community-led organizations have a better chance of sustaining school restructuring than outside experts or organizations. Given the preliminary successes of both the TIAF and Comer models, this appears to be a very promising approach to improving schools through greater parental and community involvement and better school management. Experience suggests, however, that no one best way exists to restructure schools, though it is doubtful that any restructuring will be successful without strong parental involvement, highly qualified teachers, and a management system that focuses on high standards and provides strong incentives to schools to achieve those standards.

School-Linked Services

The needs of students also can be served by school-linked comprehensive social welfare, health, and other systems. Under present administrative arrangements, the delivery of health and counseling services is, as it is with traditional mass-production schools, based on the bureaucratic assumption that one best way exists to deliver services to clients. These systems are too often more concerned about professional boundaries and values and the ease of delivering services than in effectively meeting human needs. Such bureaucratic structures are grossly inadequate for the complex problems confronting today's young people, especially disadvantaged students.

School-linked comprehensive service systems can overcome these problems, more effectively meet needs, and thereby improve student achievement. These school-based systems take various forms, but to be effective they seem to require several basic features, including shared governance among the schools and service-delivery systems, a flexible menu of services, collaborative funding, and minimization of referrals to service agencies in order to concentrate on developing sustained relationships with students and their families. This model also provides the flexibility for staff to move across professional turf lines in order to meet their clients' needs.

With few exceptions, school-based service-delivery systems have been developed too recently to permit the kind of review afforded by Comer's School

Development Program. However, the anecdotal evidence with respect to the impact of these systems on academic achievement, delinquent behavior, and the prevention of problem behaviors is generally positive.

Parents as Teachers

An emerging body of evidence indicates that educating parents to be better caregivers can have positive results for their children. Two state efforts show promising results. Missouri has developed a program in all of its 543 school districts to serve more than 30% of parents with young children. Local school districts employ child-development specialists to visit the parents of young children in their homes, starting soon after birth and continuing until the children start school. The schools also provide group activities in their facilities to help parents become better connected to the schools early in their children's lives. A careful evaluation after one year showed that in comparison with a control group of other three-year-olds, the program participants were more advanced in language skills, were better problem solvers, and had developed other skills predictive of higher achievement when these children entered school.[126]

Arkansas has developed a program modeled on Israel's Home Instruction Program for Preschool Youngsters, which also is school-based. This demonstration project, at 10 sites, provides mothers or other family members with materials designed to promote the language and math skills of four- and five-year-olds. Mothers use the materials for 30 minutes a day during the course of two years. Paraprofessionals visit participating homes each week to distribute and review materials. Groups of mothers or other care providers meet with educators every other week to discuss materials and research findings related to child development. Early evaluations suggest that this program is having positive results.

In addition to Arkansas and Missouri, a number of other states have developed family support programs to strengthen education. These states include Connecticut, Maryland, Kentucky, Minnesota, Iowa, Oregon, Vermont, and Washington. Most of the activity in these states originated spontaneously in response to local community needs. Although the programs vary considerably, their experience has been synthesized by the Harvard Family Research Project (HFRP), which reports the following shared "ideology of service delivery":

> 1) based on evidence that demonstrates the influence of the family environment on children's behavior and cognitive development, they take an "ecological" approach to human development, working with families rather than exclusively with children;
>
> 2) they provide opportunities for parents to learn about children's social, psychological, and cognitive development;
>
> 3) they provide formal and informal support to families;
>
> 4) they emphasize family strengths rather than assuming family deficits;
>
> 5) they emphasize prevention and family maintenance rather than remediation; and
>
> 6) they consider the healthy development of children to be the shared responsibility of the family and the community.[127]

Heather Weiss, HFRP director, emphasizes that these local programs generally were initiated with limited resources and were less "projects" than processes impelling local communities to encourage families to support education. The states generally encourage a variety of types of local organizations to provide

School-linked comprehensive service systems more effectively meet needs and thereby improve student achievement. This model also provides the flexibility for staff to move across professional turf lines in order to meet their clients' needs.

services within the framework of general legislative guidelines. The states also encourage the cooperation, collaboration, and networking of education agencies at the local level. This cooperation includes multiple sources of funding.

This chapter has raised a number of family policy issues. It has shown that changes in family structures create serious risks for family members, especially women and children. These risks must be public as well as private concerns, because the family is important to society as a human resource development institution and because many family problems create economic and social problems for everybody. Fortunately, the evidence suggests that family relationships can reduce negative outcomes of changing family structure, especially for children. In addition, evidence suggests that properly structured family policies can improve outcomes for families and for society. Some suggestions about how developmental family policies might be structured were developed in chapter 5, which outlines the family policies of some other countries. My family policy recommendations for the United States are presented in chapter 7, which also summarizes this book's main conclusions.

Notes

1. Charles Murray, *Losing Ground* (New York: Basic Books, 1984).

2. U.S. Congress, House Ways and Means Committee, *Background Material on Programs under the Jurisdiction of the Committee on the Ways and Means* (Washington, DC: House Ways and Means Committee, 1987).

3. David T. Ellwood and Mary Jo Bane, "The Impact of AFDC on Family Structure and Living Arrangements," in Ronald G. Ehrenberg, ed., *Research in Labor Economics* (Greenwich, CT: JAI Press, 1985).

4. Greg J. Duncan and Saul D. Hoffman, "Economic Consequences of Marital Instability," in David Martin and Timothy Smeeding, eds., *Horizontal Equity, Uncertainty, and Economic Well-Being* (Chicago: University of Chicago Press, 1985).

5. Ibid.

6. U.S. Bureau of the Census, *Child Support and Alimony: 1985*, Current Population Reports, Series P-23, No. 125, August 1987.

7. Andrew J. Cherlin, *Marriage, Divorce, Remarriage* (Cambridge, MA: Harvard University Press, 1981); Nicholas Zill and Carolyn C. Rogers, "Recent Trends in the Well-Being of Children in the United States and Their Implications for Public Policy," in Andrew J. Cherlin, ed., *The Changing American Family and Public Policy* (Washington, DC: The Urban Institute Press, 1988), pp. 31–116.

8. Peter Uhlenberg and David Eggebeen, "The Declining Well-Being of American Adolescents," *Public Interest* 82 (Winter 1986), pp. 25–38.

9. Ibid., p. 34.

10. Ibid., p. 38.

11. Frank Furstenberg and Gretchen Contran, "Family Change and Adolescent Well-Being: A Reexamination of U.S. Trends," in *The Changing American Family*, pp. 117–156.

12. Ibid., p. 126.

13. Ibid., p. 127.

14. Ibid., p. 127, references omitted.

15. Ibid., p. 130.

16. Ibid., p. 129.

17. Ibid.

18. Ibid.

19. Edgar G. Epps, "Foreword," in Reginald M. Clark, *Family Life and School Achievement: Why Poor Black Children Succeed or Fail* (Chicago: University of Chicago Press,

1983), p. xi.

20. Ibid.

21. James P. Comer, "Is 'Parenting' Essential to Good Teaching?" *Families and Schools* (January 1988), pp. 34–40.

22. Epps, "Foreword," p. xii.

23. Ibid.

24. E. Mavis Hetherington, "The Impact of Divorce and Maternal Employment on Families and Children" (Paper presented at meeting on "Our Children's Future," Captiva Island, Florida, April 20–22, 1990), p. 11.

25. Ibid., p. 9.

26. Ibid., pp. 12–13.

27. Ronald C. Kessler and James A. McRae, Jr., "The Effects of Wives' Employment on the Mental Health of Married Men and Women," *American Sociological Review* 47, No. 2 (April 1982), pp. 216–227.

28. Sylvia Ann Hewlett, *A Lesser Life: The Myth of Women's Liberation in America* (New York: William Morrow, 1986).

29. Frank F. Furstenberg, Jr., "Good Dads–Bad Dads: Two Faces of Fatherhood," in *The Changing American Family*, pp. 193–218.

30. Ellen Galensky, "Child Care and Productivity" (Unpublished paper, New York, Bank Street College, 1988.)

31. "Family Oriented Policies Become Competitiveness Advantage," *Challenges* [Council on Competitiveness] 2, No. 7 (May 1990), pp. 1, 4.

32. Ibid., p. 1.

33. Ibid.

34. Ibid.

35. Ibid.

36. Mary Jo Bane and Paul Jargowsky, "The Links between Government Policy and Family Structure: What Matters and What Doesn't," in *The Changing American Family*, pp. 219–261.

37. Ibid., p. 233.

38. National Research Council, *Risking the Future* (Washington, DC: National Academy Press, 1987).

39. Gordon Berlin and Andrew Sum, *Toward a More Perfect Union* (New York: Ford Foundation, 1988).

40. Frank Furstenberg, Jr., J. Brooks-Gunn, and S. Philip Morgan, *Adolescent Mothers in Later Life* (New York: Cambridge University Press, 1987).

41. Paul Demeny, "Pronatalist Policies in Low Fertility Countries: Patterns, Performance and Prospects," *Population and Development Review* 12 (supplement, 1986), p. 350.

42. Michael S. Teitelbaum and Jay M. Winter, *The Fear of Population Decline* (Orlando, FL: Academic Press, 1985).

43. Gary S. Becker, *A Treatise on the Family* (Cambridge, MA: Harvard University Press, 1981); Gary S. Becker, "A Theory of Marriage," in Theodore W. Schultz, ed., *Economics of the Family* (Chicago: University of Chicago Press, 1974).

44. Richard A. Easterlin, *Birth and Fortune: The Impact of Numbers on Personal Welfare* (New York: Basic Books, 1980).

45. William Julius Wilson, *The Truly Disadvantaged* (Chicago: University of Chicago Press, 1987).

46. William P. Butz and Michael P. Ward, "The Emergence of Countercyclical U.S. Fertility," *American Economic Review* 69, No. 3 (June 1979), p. 318.

47. Ibid., p. 321.

48. Cherlin, *The Changing American Family*, p. 18.

49. Pat Wong, "Child Support and Welfare Reform: Past, Present, and Future," *Public Affairs Comment* 35, No. 4 (September 1989), p. 4.

50. Ibid., p. 6.

51. Ibid., p. 8.

52. "The Family Leave Veto," *Washington Post*, July 4, 1990, p. A-18.

53. National Center on Education and the Economy, *America's Choice: High Skills or Low Wages,* Report of the Commission on Skills of the American Workforce (Rochester, NY: National Center on Education and the Economy, 1990).

54. Roberta Spalter-Roth and Heidi Hartmann, "Science and Politics: The Dual Vision of Feminist Policy Research, The Example of Family and Medical Leave," *Proceedings*, First Annual Women's Policy Research Conference, Institute for Women's Policy Research, Washington, DC, May 19, 1989, p. 110.

55. Cathy Trost, "Survey Fortifies Parental Leave Backers," *Wall Street Journal*, August 9, 1990, p. 1.

56. Shelby Miller, *Early Childhood Services: A National Challenge* (New York: Ford Foundation, 1989), p. 2.

57. David Hamburg, "Early Interventions to Prevent Lifelong Damage: Lessons from Current Research," testimony before the Senate Committee on Labor and Human Resources and the House Committee on Education and Labor, September 9, 1987, p. 9.

58. Ibid., pp. 6–7.

59. Ibid., p. 16.

60. Ibid., p. 17.

61. Ibid., p. 18.

62. Miller, *Early Childhood Services*, p. 3.

63. Ibid., p. 11.

64. Ibid.

65. For further information, see K. Allison Clarke-Stewart and Greta Fein, "Early Childhood Programs," in Paul H. Mussen, ed., *Handbook of Child Psychology* (New York: John Wiley, 1983).

66. John R. Berruetta-Clement, Lawrence J. Schweinhart, W. Steven Barnett, Ann S. Epstein, and David Weikart, *Changed Lives: The Effect of the Perry Pre-School Program on Youths through Age 19* (Ypsilanti, MI: High/Scope Press, 1984).

67. Sandra Condry, "History and Background of Preschool Intervention Programs and the Consortium for Longitudinal Studies," *As the Twig Is Bent: Lasting Effects of Preschool Programs* (Hillsdale, NJ: Lawrence Erlbaum, 1983); Jacqueline M. Royce, Richard B. Darlington, and Harry W. Murray, "Pooled Analysis: Findings Across Studies," *As the Twig Is Bent.*

68. Harold W. Watts and Suzanne Donovan, "What Can Child Care Do for Human Capital?" (Unpublished paper, Public Policy Research Center, Columbia University, New York, New York, July 1, 1988), p. 21.

69. Steven Barnett, "The Perry Preschool Program and Its Long-Term Effects: A Benefit-Cost Analysis," *High/Scope Early Childhood Policy Papers,* No. 2, Ypsilanti, Michigan, 1985.

70. Watts and Donovan, "What Can Child Care Do for Human Capital?" p. 23.

71. C. Eugene Steuerle, "Policy Watch: Tax Credits for Low-Income Workers with Children," *Journal of Economic Perspective* 4, No. 3 (Summer 1990), pp. 201–212.

72. Steven A. Holmes, "Day Care Bill Marks a Turn toward Help for the Poor," *New York Times*, April 8, 1990, p. E-4.

73. Population Reference Bureau, *Juggling Jobs and Babies: America's Child Care Challenge* (Washington, DC: Population Reference Bureau, February 1987).

74. General Accounting Office, *Head Start: Information on Sponsoring Organizations and Center Facilities*, GAO/HRD-89-123F7, July 1989.

75. Lois-Ellen Dotta, "A Report of the Follow-Through Experiment," in A. Rivlin and P. M. Timpane, eds., *Planned Variations in Education: Should We Give Up or Try Harder?* (Washington, DC: Brookings, 1975); Ruth Hubbell McKey, Larry Condelli, Harriet Ganson, Barbara Barrett, Catherine McConkey, and Margaret Plantz, *The Impact of Head Start on Children, Families, and Communities* (Washington, DC: U.S. Government Printing Office, 1985).

76. Action Council on Minority Education, *Education That Works: An Action Plan for*

the Education of Minorities (Cambridge, MA: Massachusetts Institute of Technology, 1990).

77. Lawrence J. Schweinhart and David P. Weikart, "What Do We Know So Far? A Review of the Head Start Synthesis Project," *Young Children* 42, No. 2 (January 1986), pp. 49–55.

78. Lawrence J. Schweinhart and David P. Weikart, "A Fresh Start for Head Start?" *New York Times*, May 13, 1990, p. E19.

79. Ibid.

80. Ibid.

81. Ibid.

82. Ibid.

83. Felicity Barringer, "Census Report Shows a Rise in Child Care and Its Costs," *New York Times*, August 16, 1990, p. 1.

84. Frank Swoboda, "Panel Urges More Child-Care Funding," *New York Times*, March 15, 1990, p. 1.

85. Ibid.

86. Patricia Schroeder, "From Star Wars to Child Care," *New Perspectives Quarterly* 7, No. 1 (Winter 1990), p. 10.

87. Ibid.

88. Ibid., p. 11.

89. See Carnegie Council on Adolescent Development, *Turning Points: Preparing American Youth for the 21st Century* (New York: Carnegie Council on Adolescent Development, 1989), p. 21.

90. Sanford Dornbusch, "Parenting in an Age of Prolonged Adolescence" (Paper presented at meeting on "Our Children's Future," Captiva Island, Florida, April 20–22, 1990), p. 2.

91. Ibid.

92. Ibid.

93. Ibid., p. 3.

94. Ibid.

95. Ibid., pp. 3–4.

96. Ibid., p. 5.

97. Ibid.

98. Hetherington, "The Impact of Divorce and Maternal Employment on Families and Children," p. 9.

99. Ibid.

100. Ibid., p. 10.

101. For a discussion of this point, see Raymond Callahan, *Education and the Cult of Efficiency* (Chicago: University of Chicago Press, 1962).

102. Action Council for Minority Education, *Education That Works*.

103. Kenneth H. Bacon, "Many Educators View Involved Parents as Key to Children's Success in School," *Wall Street Journal*, July 30, 1990, p. B2.

104. Ibid.

105. National Center on Education and the Economy, *To Secure Our Future* (Washington, DC: National Center on Education and the Economy, 1989), p. 6.

106. Action Council on Minority Education, *Education That Works*.

107. James Comer, *School Power* (New York: Free Press, 1980); James Comer, "Educating Poor Minority Children," *Scientific American* 259, No. 5 (November 1989), pp. 42–47; James Comer, "Is 'Parenting' Essential to Good Teaching?" *Families and Schools* (January 1988), pp. 34–40.

108. Comer, "Educating Poor Minority Children," p. 45.

109. Comer, "Is 'Parenting' Essential to Good Teaching?" p. 38.

110. Comer, "Educating Poor Minority Children," p. 47.

111. Ernie Cortes, "Reflections on the Catholic Tradition of Family Rights" (Unpublished paper, 1990, copy in possession of Ray Marshall, Lyndon B. Johnson School of Public Affairs, University of Texas at Austin, Austin, Texas), p. 3.

112. Ibid., p. 4.

113. Ibid.

114. Ibid., p. 5.

115. Ibid., p. 3.

116. Ibid., p. 9.

117. Ibid., p. 14.

118. Ibid., p. 15.

119. Ibid., p. 9.

120. Ibid., p. 12.

121. Ibid., p. 13.

122. Ibid.

123. Ibid., p. 14.

124. Texas Interfaith Education Fund, "Report to Rockefeller Foundation" Unpublished paper, 1990, copy in possession of Ray Marshall, Lyndon B. Johnson School of Public Affairs, University of Texas at Austin, Austin, Texas), p. 2.

125. Ibid.

126. Miller, *Early Childhood Services*, p. 15.

127. Harvard Family Research Project, *Innovative States, Emerging Family Support and Education Programs* (Cambridge, MA: Harvard University Graduate School of Education, 1989), p. ii.

7

Summary and Recommendations

Strong interrelationships have always existed between families and economic institutions. Many of our basic conceptions of family, for example, are rooted in economic arrangements. When agriculture replaced hunting and gathering as the basic means of sustaining people, the extended family became both the basic producing unit and the main form of human social organization. With industrialization, families became less self-sufficient and more dependent on markets for consumer goods and services as well as for the incomes to pay for those goods and services. In the early division of labor within the family, men were the main wage earners, although women and children also worked to supplement family income. As industrialization proceeded, however, high levels of productivity growth made it increasingly possible for one wage earner to support a family, especially when government policies provided for universal public education, helped prevent depressions, and supported family members who were not expected to work.

Our present conception of the traditional family is rooted in the economic era when the mass-production system, reinforced by public safety nets and Keynesian macroeconomic policies, produced what was probably the longest period of equitably shared economic prosperity in history. However, neither family nor economic relationships were ever as stable as idealized memories of American life, say, in the 1950s imply—both were always in a state of flux.

During the past 20 years, family relationships have undergone considerable changes. The principal developments include increased employment of women outside the home; technological innovation, especially in information, communications, and transportation; internationalization of the economy; and changes in prevailing values and attitudes. It is difficult to specify cause-and-effect relationships among these developments, as sources of change were highly interrelated. Moreover, the epochal economic changes discussed in chapter 2 have fundamentally altered our basic social and economic institutions. We have moved from an economy in which economic success depended heavily on natural resources and economies of scale to one that is more competitive and knowledge-intensive. In the economy of the 1990s and beyond, success depends mainly on the quality of human resources, and the quality of human resources depends heavily on what happens in families.

International competition and technological change also ushered in a very different kind of economy, in which improvements in productivity and incomes required higher skill levels. The slowdown in productivity growth and intensified competition consequently reduced the growth of family incomes during the 1970s and '80s, making it much more difficult for families to maintain their living standards with the income of one wage earner. Most women thus went to work because of economic necessity, not just because of a desire for career development, although that, too, was an important reason for working. In order to sustain the living standards to which their parents had accustomed them, many baby boomers postponed marriage and had fewer children. Married women went to work in increasing numbers and returned to jobs sooner after their children were born. As competition intensified and production became more knowledge-intensive, real wages not only declined but became more unequal. About the only workers whose earnings were higher in 1990 than they had been 20 years earlier were workers with college educations. High school graduates' and dropouts' real wages declined, as did those of young workers, minorities, and men.

The "New" American Family

The economic and labor-market changes described above were associated with some dramatic changes in families and households, including:

1. *A decline in the proportion of family households, especially those classified as "traditional,"* i.e., married families with children. These families have also become smaller. Simultaneously, nonfamily and single-person households have proliferated. The immediate causes of these changes have been delayed marriage, increased divorce rates, more widowhood, and births to unmarried women. Besides the economic transformations mentioned earlier, changing attitudes about marriage, families, cohabitation, and nonmarital sexual activity have been important factors altering the composition of families and households.

2. *Fertility rates have declined because women are having fewer children and at older ages.* The total fertility rate has been below the replacement rate since 1972.

3. It is important to note, however, that *despite their decline, a substantial majority of Americans live in family households and the rates of change in living arrangements appear to have stabilized during the 1980s.* Families are nevertheless more heterogeneous and less stable than they were in the 1950s and '60s.

Today there are more single-parent families. In addition, the proportion of mothers who are unmarried when their children are born has increased from slightly more than 5% of all births in 1960 to almost 25% in 1988. The increased proportion of out-of-wedlock births is due to the steep decline in childbearing rates by married women, however, not to a sharp increase in the rate of births to unmarried mothers.

Single parents maintain almost a fourth of families with children; this is double the proportion of such families in 1970 and almost triple the proportion in 1950. These households have special human-resource-development problems because their high incidence of poverty and little parental time for children often cause poor environments for the intellectual and physical development of children. Moreover, the clear danger is that these conditions will be self-perpetuating. In 1985, 20% of white children and 60% of black children lived in one-parent families. Perhaps half of all white children and three-fourths of all black children will spend at least some of their childhood in a one-parent family. To compound the dilemma, children in households maintained by single women are almost five times as likely to be poor as children in two-parent families, and they are much less likely to finish school or achieve academically.

Families at Risk

These economic and social changes have created serious financial, moral, and intellectual hazards for American families. Declining real wages, the need for mothers to work longer hours, job insecurity, and rising costs of living (especially for housing and education) reduce living standards, diminish expectations, and create stressful situations for families. Stress, in turn, leads to mental and physical problems. Although the risks are much greater for low-income and single-parent households, most families with children are at risk for at least some problems. The burden of dual responsibility for work and parenting is particularly serious for working mothers, who do just about as much housework and child rearing as their peers who do not work outside the home.

Economic pressures therefore cause parents to be increasingly fearful about their ability to provide adequately for their families. A mood that had been rare for American families, at least since the 1930s, is for most parents to believe that things are going to be worse for their children than it was for them. This pessimistic cast is beginning to manifest itself: According to a September 1990 *Washington Post*–ABC poll, for example, 89% of respondents "said that 10 years from now it will be more difficult for young people to afford college; 75 percent said it will be harder to find a good job; 87 percent saw worse prospects for buying a house."[1]

Geographic mobility has reduced the impact of many neighborhood institutions that formerly supported families. Suburbanization of higher-income groups has eroded the base of support for churches and other community organizations in many urban areas. This development has had especially pernicious effects on minority and low-income communities, where these institutions had provided role models for children and had mediated between vulnerable families and larger social institutions. Of course, the erosion of a sense of community is not restricted to low-income or minority families. The dispersal of the extended family, greater geographic mobility, smaller family sizes, and the increased labor-force participation of women have all reduced the amount of time that women and other family members have to participate in the community organizations that once helped parents develop their children and themselves. The erosion of community organizations, in turn, has left children more vulnerable to a variety of hazards. The increased physical threats to children include drug and alcohol addiction, violence, crime, teen pregnancy, and sexually transmitted diseases. Moral and intellectual hazards are created by the media, popular culture, and peer pressures. Needless to say, all of these influences can be either positive or negative, but "messages" from these sources that glorify drugs, alcohol, promiscuous sexual activity, violence, irresponsible personal behavior, and excessive materialism pose grave risks for children.

Both the physical and moral hazards are exacerbated by the limited time working parents have with their children and will cause problems for the nation as well as for families. This point was made by one of the nation's most perceptive child psychiatrists, Robert Coles of Harvard University, who predicts that

> the values children are learning today will be felt collectively when this generation reaches adulthood. . . . "Some of the frenzied need of children

Economic pressures cause parents to be increasingly fearful about their ability to provide adequately for their families.

The erosion of community organizations has left children more vulnerable to a variety of hazards, including drug and alcohol addiction, violence, crime, teen pregnancy, and sexually transmitted diseases.

to have possessions isn't only a function of the ones they see on T.V. It's a function of their hunger for what they aren't getting—their parents' time."[2]

Parents face the added difficulty of not knowing what to do or say in the little time they do have for their children. Part of this uncertainty is caused by our rapidly changing society, in which shifting community values and attitudes have made learning from one's own parents at best a problematic guide to parenting, even when one's own childhood experiences were largely positive. Some experts believe this will be a particularly serious problem for the very large baby-boom generation, which has postponed parenting longer than any generation in recent history. Social historian Barbara Whitehead, for example, believes the baby boomers will "cross a great cultural divide" when they "step into parenthood." She reasons as follows:

> If the classic tension in American life has been between individualism and community, they have, up until now, been living quite comfortably within a culture that stresses materialism and individualism. In this respect, the cycle of their lives has differed sharply from the pattern of their parents' lives. The father of the typical baby boomer quite likely spent his early adulthood eating K-rations in a barracks somewhere—hardly an environment that placed a premium on expressing a distinctive material identity. Many of the current generation of new parents, however, spent their early adulthood building careers, acquiring possessions and expressing their identity through the marketplace.
>
> As they become parents, however, something changes. They discover that the values that guided them as adults aren't very useful in raising children. The same culture that supported them as individuals, they now are realizing, is indifferent or even hostile to them as parents and to their children.
>
> For raising children isn't an individual act. It is a social and communal enterprise, involving kin, neighbors, other parents, friends, and many other unrelated adults. Typically, hermits don't raise kids; villagers do.[3]

How does a family gain direction in this environment? I don't believe any one best answer exists. Each family has to develop its own guidance. I am, however, convinced that most of the answers are to be found by families learning together. Public policy can help support and stabilize families, but public policy is limited in what it can do because much of the learning that takes place in families involves moral and religious matters that governments should stay away from, especially in our multicultural democracy. This is not to argue that public schools and other public institutions should avoid value education. I believe they should teach such democratic values as respect for others, self-restraint, the importance of service to community and country, and responsibility for one's own behavior. But democratic governments should not teach the religious underpinnings of these and other values.

Other institutions can help with some of the learning that children have missed in families. But, as Urie Bronfenbrenner has observed, these other routes "are far less efficient and far more expensive, both in time and money."[4]

Thus, the main responsibility for the health of families rests with the adults in each family, who have joint responsibility for themselves and for their children. It is particularly important for men to understand the pressures that working women face in trying to accommodate their dual roles as workers and mothers. Moreover, mounting scientific evidence suggests that the presence of two adults greatly improves the effectiveness of the family as an institution of child development. Employers, schools, and community and religious organizations also can help families strengthen themselves and their children, as we discussed in chapter 6. However, public policies can also do much to help strengthen families. The experience of other industrialized countries, discussed in chapter 5, suggests that supportive policies, especially for the most vulnerable families, can be high-yield personal and social investments.

Policies to Strengthen Families

Assumptions

My policy recommendations are based on several assumptions. The first is that family policies should be made explicit and given very high priority by policymakers at every level. Otherwise, policies can, and often do, inadvertently damage families and children. And unless families are the specific focus of policy, these issues are likely to occupy a low position on policy agendas.

Second, although the social changes documented in this book put many family members, especially women and children, at risk of problems, these hazards can be reduced by constructive parental behavior reinforced by well-structured public policies. I do not accept the fatalistic conclusions of those who believe that government interventions necessarily have had, or will have, unintended negative consequences for families or the country. Further, this assumption implies the need for a *developmental* approach to family policy, which assumes that public and private expenditures to make family members self-supporting can be high-yield *investments*, not just budget *costs*.

The third main assumption is that to be most effective, family policies should have broad public support based on principles of justice, efficiency, and self-interest. Justice implies a bias toward helping the most vulnerable families and family members. Efficiency requires that policies be based on clear, explicit goals, objectives, and strategies grounded in the best factual and analytical evidence available. Efficiency also requires good program administration, a matter discussed at greater length below. Ordinarily it is more efficient to prevent negative outcomes than to merely respond to them after they occur. This is one of the reasons education, health, nutrition, and other human resource development activities, especially for women and children, ordinarily yield such high returns. One of the highest yielding activities, for example, would be the prevention of unwanted pregnancies to teenagers. This can be accomplished through programs like the Summer Training and Education Project discussed in chapter 6, which reduced negative behavioral outcomes and summer learning loss through a program for disadvantaged youth that combined summer employment with education in personal behavior and basic skills. Another high-yield activity would be to prevent teen pregnancies by providing free family-planning services at or near schools or other accessible places. International comparisons suggest that the lack of such services is a major reason for the high incidence of births to teenage mothers in the United States relative to many other industrialized countries.

To some degree, of course, the requirements of justice, efficiency, and self-interest as well as broad public support will present policymakers with unavoidable conflicts. For example, broad public support might entail program benefits that are universally available and do not stigmatize participants. Budget restrictions, however, might require that programs be targeted to particular groups, which leads to income or means tests that could, in turn, lead to inequities and stigmatize the programs. As noted in chapter 5, in order to avoid this conflict, some countries have used income and not means tests and others have achieved equity by making programs universal and paying for them with progressive taxes.

We need a developmental approach to family policy, which assumes that public and private expenditures to make family members self-supporting can be high-yield investments, not just budget costs.

To be most effective, family policies should have broad public support based on principles of justice, efficiency, and self-interest.

Because poverty is a major impediment to children's learning and development, public policy should give high priority to helping poor children and their parents.

Public policy can help economically vulnerable women and children by guaranteeing them adequate minimum levels of material support.

Policy Priorities

My list of the most important problems family policies should address is as follows: (1) helping poor and disadvantaged children; (2) providing single-parent households with child support and development services; (3) helping parents with their dual roles as workers and child developers; and (4) integrating family-support systems with other economic and social policies. These problems are, of course, highly interrelated, and proposed solutions must take into account the relationships among them.

Poor Children. As we have seen, poverty among children has not only increased, but children are now worse off than is any other age group in our population. Because poverty is a major impediment to children's learning and development, public policy should give high priority to helping poor children and their parents. Activities that should receive high priority include helping families with job training, counseling, education, housing, and health care. Strengthening the Women, Infants, and Children (WIC) program should receive high priority. The links among health, nutrition, and cognitive development are sufficiently strong to require little debate about the importance of such programs. Nevertheless, only about 40% of eligible women currently participate in WIC.

The reduction of poverty among children also requires more attention to parental education. The education of parents, especially mothers, is probably the best single way to break the cycle of poverty. In addition, quality preschool programs such as Head Start should be strengthened and expanded to all eligible children. Our objective should be to make quality preschool programs available to all children. As noted in chapters 5 and 6, empirical research and international experience show early childhood care to be critical to the cognitive and social development of children.

Single-Parent Families and Child Support. Women and children are the part of our population most vulnerable to deprivation, neglect, and abuse. Public policy can help them by guaranteeing adequate minimum levels of material support to overcome the worst effects of poverty. The measures discussed earlier to help poor children will, of course, help single mothers, who are disproportionately poor. Similarly, measures to help single parents prepare for and find better jobs, discussed below, will do much to improve their economic welfare. In addition, some specific initiatives can help single-parent families. One of these, the mandatory child-support programs used in other countries and being experimented with in Wisconsin, guarantee child support from noncustodial parents, regardless of the custodial parent's ability to collect from the other parent. Because separated or divorced parents often live in different states, and because the poorest states often have scarce resources, it makes sense for child-support payments to become a federal responsibility. Also, as suggested in the previous section, adequate health and nutrition are absolutely essential for all mothers and children. It is disgraceful that the United States, still the wealthiest country on earth, ranks 19th in the world in infant mortality and has by far the largest percentage of impoverished children of any industrialized democracy.

Work and Parenting. Quality child care is another service that should be available to all parents, especially those from low-income families. Because no one best way to deliver child care exists, we should continue to provide tax benefits and encourage companies to establish work-based systems, wherever appropriate.

The main goals of a child-care system in the United States should be quality, accessibility, and affordability for low- and moderate-income families. Evidence suggests that services are gradually improving, but that much remains to be done. A National Research Council (NRC) panel concluded in 1990, for example, that

> [e]xisting child care services in the United States are inadequate to meet the current and future needs of children, parents, and society as a whole. . . . Of greatest concern is the large number of children who are presently cared for in settings that do not protect their health and safety and do not provide appropriate developmental stimulation. Poor quality care, more than any single type of arrangement, threatens children's development, especially children from poor and minority families.[5]

The NRC panel made five recommendations to improve the nation's child-care system:

1. Federal and state governments should expand subsidies to support quality child care for low-income families.

2. Governments at every level should strengthen child-care-infrastructure components such as resource and referral services, caregiver training and wages, child-care volunteer programs, the organization of family day-care systems, and planning and coordinating processes.

3. Head Start and other compensatory preschool programs should be expanded for income-eligible three- and four-year-olds who are at risk of early school failure.

4. A federal initiative should be launched to develop standards for child care.

5. The federal government should mandate unpaid leave with job protection for employed parents of infants up to one year of age.

With respect to the last point, the panel report noted,

> Our conclusion, based on a review of the available research and the panel's professional judgment, is that, in the long run, policies should provide paid leave with partial income replacement for up to 6 months, with job-related health benefits and job guarantees during the year.[6]

My reading of the evidence causes me to agree with the NRC panel's conclusion and recommendations. The evidence nevertheless suggests some additional considerations. First, as noted earlier, any child-care system should recognize the great diversity of child-care arrangements in the United States. This implies giving high priority to choice for parents. However, choice is not likely to be very meaningful without affordability, which means subsidizing child care for low- and moderate-income parents. These subsidies could take a variety of forms, but should be designed to encourage the development of efficient, high-quality systems. Such systems, in turn, require the development of a child-care infrastructure in each community as well as the training of child-care professionals. Finally, one of the best ways to maximize individual choice, efficiency, and quality is to develop broad consensus for child-care standards. These standards should be national, with appropriate flexibility to accommodate local differences. The NRC panel believes, and I agree, that we now have sufficient evidence about quality child-care arrangements to provide the basis for developing such standards. The incentive for caregivers to meet the standards would be to make those standards a condition for receiving subsidies and for being licensed.

The provision of child care and child support would help parents with their dual roles, but more needs to be done, including:

1. *Strengthen parental involvement with schools* along the lines of the Comer and Texas Industrial Areas Foundation (TIAF) models and of such state activities as those in Missouri, Arkansas, and elsewhere, discussed in chapter 6. Parental involvement is essential if schools are to be restructured to better provide the

---

The main goals of a child-care system in the United States should be quality, accessibility, and affordability for low- and moderate-income families.

Any child-care system should recognize the great diversity of child-care arrangements in the United States. This implies giving high priority to choice for parents. However, choice is not very meaningful without affordability.

higher-order thinking skills required to maintain and improve personal incomes and the competitiveness of American industry. These activities also strengthen the parents' role both in parenting and as educators of their own children.

2. *Churches, schools, and other institutions can help compensate for the erosion of extended family and community-support systems.* The value of this function is suggested by the experiences of TIAF in creating "mediating" institutions to empower parents. These organizations can work with the schools to provide counseling and nontraditional educational opportunities. Similar institutions should be created in other places. Government agencies should fund evaluation of these activities and disseminate information about them.

3. *Employers should help parents meet their dual family and employment obligations* in a variety of ways: by providing child care and flexible working arrangements, by supporting company-based schooling, especially in the early grades, and by providing parental child-care referral and information services. There are already many examples of exemplary company-based dependent-care programs all over the United States. Government initiatives can evaluate and disseminate information about these programs as well as strengthen tax or other incentives to further their adoption. As noted earlier, some workplace policies, for example, parental leave, should be mandated by federal law. Clearly the benefits of such a measure far outweigh the costs.

Integrating Family and Other Policies. Governments at every level should make a conscious effort to integrate family policies with other social and economic initiatives. Naturally, it is hard to imagine a public policy that does not affect families. However, American economic and social policies are so fragmented and narrowly focused that little thought is given to their implications for families, especially those that are most vulnerable.

As noted in chapters 3 and 4, American economic policies have permitted and even encouraged companies to compete by reducing wages rather than by improving productivity and quality. This has contributed not only to declining real wages but has widened already-yawning wage and income gaps. These economic developments have had particularly nasty consequences for young families, single-parent families, minorities, and families headed by persons with little education. The effects of these groups' worsening economic condition on national well-being are all the more serious because these groups are the fastest-growing components of our population and work force.

Furthermore, not only does the United States lack a strategy for being a high-wage country, but the high real interest rates caused by our macroeconomic policies have greatly increased the cost of housing at the same time that real wages are declining. These policies have contributed to increases in homelessness and poverty. As documented in chapter 4, many poor families now spend half or more of their income for housing. Similarly, the absence of a coherent national health policy causes many American families to have grossly inadequate health care, in spite of the fact that as a nation we spend more on our medical care than does any other country. An adequate health care system could greatly improve the condition of most moderate- and low-income American families.

No other area is more important to the economic future of America and its families than the development of work-force skills. The competitiveness of American industry depends heavily on improving the education and training of the great majority of workers who do not go to college. About the only American families who are better off now than they were 20 years ago are those with college-educated members. This is so because many of our colleges and universities are still world-class educational institutions. The main problem is with our public schools, which are surely not world class, and with the education and training of frontline workers, less than 10% of whom receive work-related education and training. Unlike almost every other industrialized country, the United States has no standards for secondary-school graduates. Other countries also have well-organized systems of professional and technical training for most of their frontline workers. The development of such a system in the United States would do much to strengthen the competitiveness of the American economy, halt the erosion of real wages, and reverse the polarization of wages and incomes for American families. Restoring productivity growth would, in addition, provide the resources for more effective family and other human resource development policies. A skill-development system would also enable more families to support themselves through work, thus maximizing the impact of public assistance resources on family well-being.

To achieve these objectives, we need to develop a national consensus that the United States should be a high-wage country with equal opportunity for all who are willing and able to work. The alternative is lower and more unequal real wages and considerable trouble for low- and middle-income families and ultimately for all Americans. In addition, I recommend adoption of the following specific measures:[7]

1. Establish national standards, pegged to the best in the world, for students who complete high school. Such standards would provide incentives for non–college-bound students to strive for high achievement in school; provide a better means to evaluate the schools, thus facilitating school restructuring; provide employers with better information about the knowledge and skills of high school graduates; and provide parents with better information about what their children should know.

2. Provide youth centers as alternative learning systems for young people who do not meet the standards specified above in regular schools by, say, age 16. They could transfer from public schools to the youth centers and take their funding with them. This would provide greater incentives for the high schools to help young people meet these standards and would encourage innovative approaches to learning by both the schools and the youth centers.

3. Provide a system of professional and technical certification and associate degrees for the non–college-bound. Currently some exemplary apprenticeship and community college programs exist. But, as noted earlier, less than 10% of non–college-bound young people receive any job training at all. The policy objective should be to extend these programs to more occupations and/or to most young people who do not go to college immediately after high school. Standards for these occupations would be set by employers, workers, educators, training specialists, and public officials. Child-care workers should be one of the occupations certified by this process. The system should be financed by providing "GI Bill"-type benefits of four years of education and training for all workers after they meet the standards for high school graduation and for adults older than 18 who have not met the standards. This training ordinarily would combine work and academic studies, as is now done with apprenticeship training.

4. Employers should be provided an incentive to devote at least 1% of payroll to the training of frontline workers. This could be done with a refundable tax—i.e., employers who did not devote 1% of payroll costs to training would pay that amount into a public fund to be used for training.

5. Establish a system of employment and training boards at the federal, state, and local levels to provide oversight and management to the nation's employ-

Unlike almost every other industrialized country, the United States has no standards for secondary-school graduates. Other countries also have well-organized systems training for most of their frontline workers. The development of such a system in the United States would strengthen the competitiveness of the American economy.

We need to develop a national consensus that the United States should be a high-wage country with equal opportunity for all who are willing and able to work.

ment and training system. These boards would be made up of education and training specialists, employers, workers, and community leaders. Education and training services could be provided by a great variety of organizations. The local employment and training boards could see that services were geared to the unique needs of each community but would not themselves deliver such services. These employment and training boards could combine many existing councils, boards, and commissions and would have general oversight of job training. Programs should be designed to make it possible for single parents and others to acquire the knowledge and skills needed for higher-paying jobs. The local employment and training boards could, in addition, coordinate child care and other programs to help young people and parents prepare for work. An infrastructure of employment and training boards to provide guidance, evaluation, and professional trainers and educators is more important than specific categorical programs.

In conclusion, although specific family policies are needed to help adults cope with their dual roles as parents and workers, these policies alone will not be sufficient to improve the conditions of American families. Measures to strengthen the competitiveness of the American economy and increase the thinking skills of family members also are required. I said at the outset of this section that to have broad public support, family policies should appeal to the self-interest of voters and taxpayers. It would be hard to imagine a set of policies that would have broader benefits or that are more important for the nation's future.

Notes

1. Barbara Vobejda and Paul Taylor, "Suddenly a Pessimistic America," *Washington Post*, November 6, 1990, p. A1.

2. Ibid., p. A9.

3. Barbara Dafoe Whitehead, "The Family in an Unfriendly Culture," *Family Affairs* 3, No. 1-2 (Spring/Summer 1990), p. 5.

4. Urie Bronfenbrenner, "Discovering What Families Do," in David Blankenhorn, Steven Bayme, and Jean Bethke Elshtain, eds., *Rebuilding the Nest* (Milwaukee, WI: Family Service America, 1990), p. 33.

5. The National Research Council, *Who Cares for America's Children* (Washington, DC: National Research Council, 1990), p. xii.

6. Ibid., p. xvii.

7. These recommendations are similar to those of the Commission on Skills of the American Workforce, which I co-chaired. See National Center on Education and the Economy, *America's Choice: High Skills or Low Wages*, Report of the Commission on Skills of the American Workforce (Rochester, NY: National Center on Education and the Economy, 1990).

Appendix A

Tables 2.1 to 5.6

TABLE 2.1

Civilian Labor Force and Participation Rates by Sex, Age, Race, and Hispanic Origin
For 1976, 1988, and Moderate Growth Projection to 2000

Group	Participation rate (in percent) 1976	1988	2000	Level (in thousands) 1976	1988	2000	Change (in thousands) 1976–88	1988–2000	Change (in percent) 1976–88	1988–2000	Annual growth rate (in percent) 1976–88	1988–2000
Total, 16 and older	61.6	65.9	69.0	96,158	121,669	141,134	25,511	19,465	26.5	16.0	2.0	1.2
Men, 16 and older	77.5	76.2	75.9	57,174	66,927	74,324	9,753	7,397	17.1	11.1	1.3	0.9
16 to 19	59.3	56.9	59.0	4,886	4,159	4,422	-727	263	-14.9	6.3	-1.3	0.5
20 to 24	85.1	85.0	86.5	7,866	7,594	6,930	-272	-664	-3.5	-8.7	-0.3	-0.8
25 to 34	95.2	94.3	94.1	14,784	19,742	16,572	4,958	-3,170	33.5	-16.1	2.4	-1.4
35 to 44	95.4	94.5	94.3	10,500	16,074	20,188	5,574	4,114	53.1	25.6	3.6	1.9
45 to 54	91.6	90.9	90.5	10,293	10,566	16,395	273	5,829	2.7	55.2	0.2	3.7
55 to 64	74.3	67.0	68.1	7,020	6,831	7,796	-189	965	-2.7	14.1	-0.2	1.1
65 and older	20.2	16.5	14.7	1,826	1,960	2,021	134	61	7.3	3.1	0.6	0.3
Women, 16 and older	47.3	56.6	62.6	38,983	54,742	66,810	15,759	12,068	40.4	22.0	2.9	1.7
16 to 19	49.8	53.6	59.6	4,170	3,872	4,399	-298	527	-7.1	13.6	-0.6	1.1
20 to 24	65.0	72.7	77.9	6,418	6,910	6,705	492	-205	37.7	-3.0	0.6	-0.3
25 to 34	57.3	72.7	82.4	9,419	15,761	15,105	6,342	-656	67.3	-4.2	4.4	-0.4
35 to 44	57.8	75.2	84.9	6,817	13,361	18,584	6,544	5,223	96.0	39.1	5.8	2.8
45 to 54	55.0	69.0	76.5	6,689	8,537	14,423	1,848	5,886	27.6	68.9	2.1	4.5
55 to 64	41.0	43.5	49.0	4,402	4,977	6,140	575	1,163	13.1	23.4	1.0	1.8
65 and older	8.2	7.9	7.6	1,069	1,324	1,454	255	130	23.9	9.8	1.8	0.8
Whites, 16 and older	61.8	66.2	69.5	84,767	104,756	118,981	19,989	14,225	23.6	13.6	1.8	1.1
Men	78.4	76.9	76.6	51,033	58,317	63,288	7,284	4,971	14.3	8.5	1.1	0.7
Women	46.9	56.4	62.9	33,735	46,439	55,693	12,704	9,254	37.7	19.9	2.7	1.5
Blacks, 16 and older	58.9	63.8	66.5	9,565	13,205	16,465	3,640	3,260	38.1	24.7	2.7	1.9
Men	69.7	71.0	71.4	5,105	6,596	8,007	1,491	1,411	29.2	21.4	2.2	1.6
Women	50.0	58.0	62.5	4,460	6,609	8,458	2,149	1,849	48.2	28.0	3.3	2.1
Asian and other, 16 and older[a]	62.8	65.0	65.5	1,826	3,709	5,688	1,883	1,979	103.1	53.4	6.1	3.6
Men	74.9	74.4	74.6	1,036	2,015	3,029	979	1,014	94.5	50.3	5.7	3.5
Women	51.6	56.5	57.5	790	1,694	2,659	904	965	114.4	57.0	6.6	3.8
Hispanic-origin, 16 and older[b]	60.7	67.4	69.9	4,279	8,982	14,321	4,703	5,339	109.9	59.4	6.4	4.0
Men	79.6	81.9	80.3	2,625	5,409	8,284	2,784	2,875	106.1	53.2	6.2	3.6
Women	44.1	53.2	59.4	1,654	3,573	6,037	1,919	2,464	116.0	69.0	6.6	4.5

Source: Howard N. Fullerton, Jr., "New Labor Force Projections, Spanning 1988–2000," *Monthly Labor Review* 112 (November 1989), p. 8.

[a] The "Asian and other" group includes American Indians, Alaskan natives, Asians, and Pacific islanders. The historic data are derived by subtracting "Black" from the "Black and other" group; projections are made directly.

[b] Persons of Hispanic origin may be of any race. The 1980 decennial census indicates that persons of Hispanic origin identified their racial classification approximately as follows: White, 93%; Black, 5%; Asian and other, 2%.

TABLE 2.2

Civilian Noninstitutional Population by Sex, Age, Race, and Hispanic Origin, 1976, 1988, and Moderate Growth Projection to 2000

Group	Level (in thousands) 1976	Level (in thousands) 1988	Level (in thousands) 2000	Change (in thousands) 1976–88	Change (in thousands) 1988–2000	Annual growth rate (in percent) 1976–88	Annual growth rate (in percent) 1988–2000
Total, 16 and older	156,150	184,613	204,613	28,463	20,000	1.4	0.9
16 to 24	35,722	32,960	31,515	-2,762	-1,445	-0.7	-0.4
25 to 54	78,158	101,398	116,229	23,240	14,831	2.2	1.1
55 and older	42,271	50,253	58,869	7,982	8,616	1.5	1.3
Men, 16 and older	73,759	87,857	97,879	14,098	10,022	1.5	0.9
16 to 24	17,481	16,233	15,509	-1,248	-724	-0.6	-0.4
25 to 54	37,780	49,570	57,145	11,790	7,575	2.3	1.2
55 and older	18,499	22,052	25,225	3,553	3,173	1.5	1.1
Women, 16 and older	82,390	96,756	106,734	14,366	9,978	1.3	0.8
16 to 24	18,241	16,727	16,006	-1,514	-721	-0.7	-0.4
25 to 54	40,378	51,828	59,084	11,450	7,256	2.1	1.1
55 and older	23,772	28,201	31,644	4,429	3,443	1.4	1.0
White, 16 and older	137,106	158,194	171,171	21,088	12,977	1.2	0.7
Black, 16 and older	16,216	20,692	24,754	4,476	4,062	2.1	1.5
Asian and other, 16 and older[a]	2,910	5,725	8,688	2,815	2,963	5.8	3.5
Hispanic, 16 and older[b]	7,051	13,325	20,490	6,274	7,165	5.4	3.7

Source: Howard N. Fullerton, Jr., "New Labor Force Projections, Spanning 1988–2000," *Monthly Labor Review* 112 (November 1989), p. 6.

[a] The "Asian and other" group includes American Indians, Alaskan natives, Asians, and Pacific islanders. The historic data are derived by subtracting Black from the Black and other group; projections are made directly.

[b] Persons of Hispanic origin may be of any race. The 1980 decennial census indicates that persons of Hispanic origin identified their racial classification approximately as follows: White, 93%; Black, 5%; Asian and other, 2%.

TABLE 2.3

Civilian Labor Force by Sex, Age, Race, and Hispanic Origin, 1976, 1988, and Moderate Growth Projection to 2000

Group	Level (in thousands) 1976	Level (in thousands) 1988	Level (in thousands) 2000	Change (in thousands) 1976–88	Change (in thousands) 1988–2000	Change (in percent) 1976–88	Change (in percent) 1988–2000	Distribution (in percent) 1976	Distribution (in percent) 1988	Distribution (in percent) 2000	Annual growth rate (in percent) 1976–88	Annual growth rate (in percent) 1988–2000
Total, 16 and older	96,158	121,669	141,134	25,511	19,465	26.5	16.0	100.0	100.0	100.0	2.0	1.2
16 to 24	23,339	22,535	22,456	-804	-79	-3.4	-0.4	24.3	18.5	15.9	-0.3	0.0
25 to 54	58,502	84,041	101,267	25,539	17,226	43.7	20.5	60.8	69.1	71.8	3.1	1.6
55 and older	14,319	15,094	17,411	775	2,317	5.4	15.4	14.9	12.4	12.3	0.4	1.2
Men, 16 and older	57,174	66,927	74,324	9,753	7,397	17.1	11.1	59.5	55.0	52.7	1.3	0.9
Women, 16 and older	38,983	54,742	66,810	15,759	12,068	40.4	22.0	40.5	45.0	47.3	2.9	1.7
White, 16 and older	84,768	104,756	118,981	19,988	14,225	23.6	13.6	88.2	86.1	84.3	1.8	1.1
Black, 16 and older	9,549	13,205	16,465	3,656	3,260	38.3	24.7	10.0	10.9	11.7	2.7	1.9
Asian and other, 16 and older[a]	1,827	3,708	5,688	1,881	1,980	103.0	53.4	1.9	3.0	4.0	6.1	3.6
Hispanic, 16 and older[b]	4,279	8,980	14,321	4,701	5,341	109.9	59.5	4.4	7.4	10.1	6.4	4.0

Source: Howard N. Fullerton, Jr., "New Labor Force Projections, Spanning 1988–2000," *Monthly Labor Review* 112 (November 1989), p. 4.

[a] The "Asian and other" group includes American Indians, Alaskan natives, Asians, and Pacific islanders. The historic data are derived by subtracting "Black" from the "Black and other" group; projections are made directly.

[b] Persons of Hispanic origin may be of any race. The 1980 decennial census indicates that persons of Hispanic origin identified their racial classification approximately as follows: White, 93%; Black, 5%; Asian and other, 2%.

TABLE 3.1

United States Households, by Type, Selected Years, 1950 to 1989

Type of household	Households			Percent increase	
	1950	1970	1989	1950–70	1970–89
Total	43,554	63,401	92,830	46.0	46.0
Family:					
Married couples	34,075	44,728	52,100	31.0	16.0
Female householder, no spouse present	3,594	5,500	10,890	53.0	98.0
Male householder, no spouse present	1,169	1,228	2,847	5.0	131.8
Nonfamily:					
Single person	3,954	10,851	22,708	174.4	109.3
Multiple persons	762	1,094	4,286	44.0	291.8
Unmarried couples	na	523	2,588	na	394.8

Source: James R. Wetzel, "American Families: 75 Years of Change," *Monthly Labor Review* 113 (March 1990), p. 7.

TABLE 3.2

**Family and Nonfamily Households by Race and Hispanic Origin,
1960–1988, Selected Years: Levels, Percent Distribution, and Average Annual Rates of Growth**

A: Household type (levels in thousands)	Year	Total	White	Black	Hispanic origin
All households	1960	52,610	47,503	5,107	na
	1970	63,401	56,602	6,223	2,303
	1980	80,776	70,766	8,586	3,684
	1988	91,066	78,469	10,186	5,698
Family households	1960	44,856	40,714	4,142	na
	1970	51,456	46,166	4,856	2,004
	1980	59,550	52,243	6,184	3,029
	1988	65,132	56,044	7,177	4,588
Married couple	1960	39,260	36,180	3,080	na
	1970	44,728	41,029	3,317	1,615
	1980	49,112	44,751	3,433	2,282
	1988	51,809	46,644	3,682	3,204
Other family, male householder	1960	1,174	na	na	na
	1970	1,228	1,038	181	82
	1980	1,733	1,441	256	138
	1988	2,715	2,165	421	312
Other family, female householder	1960	4,422	na	na	na
	1970	5,500	4,099	1,358	307
	1980	8,705	6,052	2,495	610
	1988	10,608	7,235	3,074	1,072
Nonfamily households	1960	7,754	6,789	965	na
	1970	11,945	10,436	1,367	299
	1980	21,226	18,522	2,402	654
	1988	25,934	22,426	3,009	1,109
Male householder	1960	2,624	na	na	na
	1970	4,063	3,406	564	150
	1980	8,807	7,499	1,146	365
	1988	11,310	9,592	1,429	612
Female householder	1960	5,130	na	na	na
	1970	7,882	7,030	803	148
	1980	12,419	11,023	1,256	289
	1988	14,624	12,834	1,580	497

Source: See notes at end of table.

TABLE 3.2, cont'd.

Family and Nonfamily Households by Race and Hispanic Origin, 1960–1988, Selected Years: Levels, Percent Distribution, and Average Annual Rates of Growth

B: Household type (percentage distribution by race and Hispanic origin)	Year	Total	White	Black	Hispanic origin
All households	1960	100.0	90.3	9.7	na
	1970	100.0	89.3	9.8	3.6
	1980	100.0	87.6	10.6	4.6
	1988	100.0	86.2	11.2	6.3
Family households	1960	100.0	90.8	9.2	na
	1970	100.0	89.7	9.4	3.9
	1980	100.0	87.7	10.4	5.1
	1988	100.0	86.0	11.0	7.0
Married couple	1960	100.0	92.2	7.8	na
	1970	100.0	91.7	7.4	3.6
	1980	100.0	91.1	7.0	4.6
	1988	100.0	90.0	7.1	6.2
Other family, male householder	1960	100.0	na	na	na
	1970	100.0	84.5	14.7	6.7
	1980	100.0	83.2	14.8	8.0
	1988	100.0	79.7	15.5	11.5
Other family, female householder	1960	100.0	na	na	na
	1970	100.0	74.5	24.7	5.6
	1980	100.0	69.5	28.7	7.0
	1988	100.0	68.2	29.0	10.1
Nonfamily households	1960	100.0	na	na	na
	1970	100.0	87.4	11.4	2.5
	1980	100.0	87.3	11.3	3.1
	1988	100.0	86.5	11.6	4.3
Male householder	1960	100.0	na	na	na
	1970	100.0	83.8	13.9	3.7
	1980	100.0	85.1	13.0	4.1
	1988	100.0	84.8	12.6	5.4
Female householder	1960	100.0	na	na	na
	1970	100.0	89.2	10.2	1.9
	1980	100.0	88.8	10.1	2.3
	1988	100.0	87.8	10.8	3.4

Source: See notes at end of table.

TABLE 3.2, cont'd.

Family and Nonfamily Households by Race and Hispanic Origin, 1960–1988, Selected Years: Levels, Percent Distribution, and Average Annual Rates of Growth

C: Household type (percentage distribution of race and Hispanic origin by type of household)	Year	Total	White	Black	Hispanic origin
All households	1960	100.0	100.0	100.0	na
	1970	100.0	100.0	100.0	100.0
	1980	100.0	100.0	100.0	100.0
	1988	100.0	100.0	100.0	100.0
Family households	1960	85.0	85.7	81.1	na
	1970	81.2	81.6	78.0	87.0
	1980	73.7	73.8	72.0	82.2
	1988	71.5	71.4	70.5	80.5
Married couple	1960	74.3	76.2	60.3	na
	1970	70.5	72.5	53.3	70.1
	1980	60.8	63.2	40.0	61.9
	1988	56.9	59.4	36.1	56.2
Other family, male householder	1960	2.3	na	na	na
	1970	1.9	1.8	2.9	3.6
	1980	2.1	2.0	3.0	3.7
	1988	3.0	2.8	4.1	5.5
Other family, female householder	1960	8.4	na	na	na
	1970	8.7	7.2	21.8	13.3
	1980	10.8	8.6	29.1	16.6
	1988	11.6	9.2	30.2	18.8
Nonfamily households	1960	15.0	14.3	18.9	na
	1970	18.8	18.4	22.0	13.0
	1980	26.3	26.2	28.0	17.8
	1988	28.5	28.6	29.5	19.5
Male householder	1960	5.1	na	na	na
	1970	6.4	6.0	9.1	6.5
	1980	10.9	10.6	13.3	9.9
	1988	12.4	12.2	14.0	10.7
Female householder	1960	9.8	na	na	na
	1970	12.4	12.4	12.9	6.4
	1980	15.4	15.6	14.6	7.8
	1988	16.1	16.4	15.5	8.7

Source: See notes at end of table.

TABLE 3.2, cont'd.

Family and Nonfamily Households by Race and Hispanic Origin, 1960–1988, Selected Years: Levels, Percent Distribution, and Average Annual Rates of Growth

D: Household type (annual average percentage rates of change)	Year	Total	White	Black	Hispanic origin
All households	1960–70	1.8	1.8	2.0	na
	1970–80	2.5	2.3	3.3	4.8
	1980–88	1.5	1.3	2.2	5.6
Family households	1960–70	1.4	1.3	1.6	na
	1970–80	1.5	1.2	2.4	4.2
	1980–88	1.1	0.9	1.9	5.3
Married couple	1960–70	1.3	1.3	0.7	na
	1970–80	0.9	0.9	0.3	3.5
	1980–88	0.7	0.5	0.9	4.3
Other family, male householder	1960–70	0.0	na	na	na
	1970–80	3.5	3.3	3.5	5.3
	1980–88	5.8	5.2	6.4	10.7
Other family, female householder	1960–70	2.2	na	na	na
	1970–80	4.7	4.0	6.3	7.1
	1980–88	2.5	2.3	2.6	7.3
Nonfamily households	1960–70	4.2	4.4	3.5	na
	1970–80	5.9	5.9	5.8	8.1
	1980–88	2.5	2.4	2.9	6.8
Male householder	1960–70	4.1	na	na	na
	1970–80	8.0	8.2	7.3	9.3
	1980–88	3.2	3.1	2.8	6.7
Female householder	1960–70	4.3	na	na	na
	1970–80	0.0	0.0	0.0	0.1
	1980–88	0.0	0.0	0.0	0.1

Sources: Total households, by type of household, 1960, 1970, 1980, and 1988: U.S. Bureau of the Census, Current Population Reports, Series P-10, No. 441 (Washington, DC: United States Government Printing Office, 1989), Table 5, pp. 6–9.

Race and Hispanic origin of householder, by type of household, 1970, 1980, 1988: Ibid., Table 4, p. 5; and U.S. Bureau of the Census, *Statistical Abstract of the United States: 1990,* 110th ed. (Washington, DC: United States Government Printing Office, 1990), No. 57, p. 46.

Race and Hispanic origin of household, by type of household, 1960: U.S. Bureau of the Census, Current Population Reports, Series P-20, No. 218 (Washington, DC: United States Government Printing Office, 1971), Table a, p. l.

Notes:
1. Two different percentage distributions of the data are presented in this table. The former presents a distribution of the different household categories by race and Hispanic origin. The latter presents a distribution of the different race and Hispanic-origin categories by type of household. The final section of the table presents annual average percentage rates of change for the various cells for three different periods: 1960–70, 1970–80, and 1980–88.

2. The 1960 Current Population Survey (CPS) reported some of its estimates classified by the "color" of the household head. Two classifications of color were generally reported: "White" and "Negro and Other Races." The estimates presented here for "Blacks" in 1960 therefore include the category "Other Races." Further, these estimates are available only for the largest components of the "household type" category. All of these comments also apply to the 1970 CPS, with two exceptions. First, the "Negro and Other Races" category is intermittently disaggregated in the 1970 CPS into "Blacks" and "Other Races." Second, the estimates by racial classification were available for all, not just the largest, household types.

3. Neither the 1960 nor the 1970 CPS attempted to count the Hispanic-origin population. For 1960, no estimates at all are available. For 1970, estimates are taken from the 1970 Census of Population.

4. At irregular intervals, the Census Bureau publishes some revisions of its earlier published estimates. This typically occurs for one of two reasons: The numbers are revised on the basis of population controls from the most recent decennial census or a new processing or classification procedure is implemented. In general, changes in the estimates due to the latter reason have been minimal. With respect to the former, however, changes may be quite large. For example, the total count of households for March 1980 according to the original CPS was 79,108,000. The total count based on population controls from the 1980 census was 80,776,000, a difference of almost 1.7 million households. Unfortunately, only the most highly aggregated revised figures (to my knowledge) are republished. This table presents the most recently revised series for all years except 1960, for which the original series is presented. Where appropriate, the other tables in this book that are based upon the CPS present the unrevised estimates for 1960, 1970, and 1980, in order to achieve consistency among more disaggregated characteristics and household types. This was necessary because, as noted, only the most highly aggregated categories of revised estimates are published.

TABLE 4.1

Labor-Force Participitation Rates of Women and Men, 16 Years and Older, Annual Averages, Selected Years, 1950–1988, January–June 1990, and Middle Series Projections to 2000 (in percentages, seasonally adjusted)

	Participation rate	
Year	Women	Men
1950	33.9	86.7
1952	34.7	86.9
1954	34.6	86.1
1956	36.9	86.0
1958	37.1	84.8
1960	37.7	83.9
1962	37.9	82.6
1964	38.7	81.6
1966	40.3	81.1
1968	41.6	80.8
1970	43.3	80.3
1972	43.9	76.5
1974	45.7	79.2
1976	47.3	78.0
1978	50.0	78.3
1980	51.5	77.8
1982	52.6	77.0
1984	53.6	76.8
1986	55.3	76.7
1988	56.6	76.6
1990	57.7	76.7
2000[a]	62.6	75.9

Sources: 1950-86: U.S. Department of Labor, Bureau of Labor Statistics, *Revised Seasonally Adjusted Labor Force Statistics, 1978-87* (Washington, DC: United States Government Printing Office, March 1988), Table A-3, pp. 14–15.

1988: U.S. Department of Labor, Bureau of Labor Statistics, *Monthly Labor Review* 113 (January 1990), Table 4, p. 84.

1990: *The Employment Situation: May 1990*, USDL 90-279 (Washington, DC: United States Department of Labor, 1990), Table A-1.

2000: U.S. Department of Labor, Bureau of Labor Statistics, *Monthly Labor Review* 112 (November 1989), Table 2, p. 5.

[a] Projected

TABLE 4.2

Labor-Force Participation Rates of Women 20 Years and Older by Year of Birth and Age, Annual Averages, Selected Years, 1955–89 (in percentages)

Year of birth	1955 Age	%	1960 Age	%	1965 Age	%	1970 Age	%
1966–70								
1961–65								
1956–60								
1951–55								
1946–50							20–24	57.7
1941–45					20–24	49.9	25–29	45.2
1936–40			20–24	46.1	25–29	38.9	30–34	44.7
1931–35	20–24	45.9	25–29	35.6	30–34	38.2	35–39	49.2
1926–30	25–29	35.3	30–34	36.3	35–39	43.6	40–44	52.8
1921–25	30–34	34.7	35–39	40.8	40–44	48.5	45–49	55.0
1916–20	35–39	39.2	40–44	46.3	45–49	51.7	50–54	53.8
1911–15	40–44	44.1	45–49	50.7	50–54	50.1	55–59	49.0
1906–10	45–49	45.9	50–54	48.7	55–59	47.1	60–64	36.1
1901–05	50–54	41.5	55–59	42.2	60–64	34.0	65–69	17.3
1896–1901	55–59	35.6	60–64	31.4	65–69	17.4	70 and older	5.7
1895 or before	60–64	29.0	65–69	17.6	70 and older	6.1		
	65–69	17.8	70 and older	6.8				
	70 and older	6.4						

Year of birth	1975 Age	%	1980 Age	%	1985 Age	%	1989 Age	%
1966–70							20–24	72.4
1961–65					20–24	71.8	25–29	73.9
1956–60			20–24	68.9	25–29	71.4	30–34	73.1
1951–55	20–24	64.1	25–29	66.7	30–34	70.3	35–39	75.0
1946–50	25–29	57.3	30–34	64.1	35–39	71.7	40–44	77.2
1941–45	30–34	51.9	35–39	64.9	40–44	71.9	45–49	74.3
1936–40	35–39	55.0	40–44	66.1	45–49	67.8	50–54	65.9
1931–35	40–44	56.7	45–49	62.1	50–54	60.8	55–59	54.8
1926–30	45–49	55.9	50–54	57.8	55–59	50.3	60–64	35.5
1921–25	50–54	53.3	55–59	48.5	60–64	33.4	65–69	16.4
1916–20	55–59	47.9	60–64	33.2	65–69	13.5	70 and older	4.6
1911–15	60–64	33.2	65–69	15.1	70 and older	4.3		
1906–10	65–69	14.5	70 and older	4.5				
1901–05	70 and older	4.8						
1896–1901								
1895 or before								

Sources: 1955–60: U.S. Department of Labor, Bureau of Labor Statistics, *Perspectives on Working Women: A Databook* (Washington, DC: United States Government Printing Office, October 1980), Bulletin 2080.

1965–85: U.S. Department of Labor, Bureau of Labor Statistics, *Labor Force Statistics Derived from the Current Population Survey, 1948-87* (Washington, DC: United States Government Printing Office, August 1980), Bulletin 2080, Table B-4, pp. 580–84.

1989: U.S. Department of Labor, Bureau of Labor Statistics, *Employment and Earnings* 37 (January 1990), Table 3, p. 162.

TABLE 4.3

Women in the Civilian Labor Force, Annual Averages, Selected Years, 1956–89 (numbers in thousands)

Year	Women in labor force	Men in labor force	Total in labor force	Women as a % of total labor force
1956	21,461	45,091	66,552	32.2
1960	23,240	46,388	69,628	33.4
1965	26,200	48,255	74,455	35.2
1970	31,543	51,228	82,771	38.1
1975	37,475	56,299	93,775	40.0
1980	45,487	61,453	106,940	42.5
1985	51,050	64,411	115,461	44.2
1989	56,030	67,840	123,869	45.2

Source: U.S. Department of Labor, Bureau of Labor Statistics, *Employment and Earnings* 37 (January 1990), Table 1, pp. 160–61.

TABLE 4.4

Mean Money Earnings of Year-round, Full-time Workers, 18 Years and Older, by Educational Attainment and Sex, 1987 (in current dollars)

School attainment in years	\multicolumn{7}{c}{Sex and age — Males}						
	Total	18–24 years old	25–34 years old	35–44 years old	45–54 years old	55–64 years old	65 years and older
All persons	29,855	15,088	25,597	34,083	36,361	32,664	29,892
Elementary							
Total	17,726	11,043	14,244	18,234	20,308	18,764	17,777
Less than 8 years	16,863	10,653	13,951	17,720	19,236	17,696	na
8 years	18,946	na	15,104	19,189	21,484	19,909	16,344
Secondary							
Total	24,110	14,289	22,031	26,626	28,963	27,914	24,883
1–3 years	21,327	12,297	18,724	21,882	27,155	24,681	19,392
4 years	24,745	14,732	22,675	27,442	29,450	29,143	27,010
College							
Total	37,132	17,523	29,881	40,459	46,598	43,430	38,684
1–3 years	29,253	15,692	25,053	32,385	37,772	34,145	29,383
4 years	38,117	22,255	31,596	40,787	48,148	46,467	35,815
5 or more years	47,903	na	37,397	49,882	54,298	50,606	49,214

School attainment in years	\multicolumn{7}{c}{Sex and age — Females}						
	Total	18–24 years old	25–34 years old	35–44 years old	45–54 years old	55–64 years old	65 years and older
Total	18,846	13,088	18,811	20,775	20,032	18,579	16,237
Elementary							
Total	11,292	8,420	10,019	11,568	12,140	12,149	na
Less than 8 years	10,163	na	8,864	9,901	11,628	10,918	na
8 years	12,655	na	na	na	12,824	13,025	na
Secondary							
Total	15,805	12,002	15,460	16,641	17,168	16,865	15,752
1–3 years	13,136	10,301	12,780	12,881	14,270	13,778	na
4 years	16,223	12,180	15,769	17,193	17,739	17,739	16,321
College							
Total	22,780	14,967	21,987	25,119	25,013	23,622	19,293
1–3 years	19,336	13,591	18,832	21,944	21,060	18,960	16,573
4 years	23,506	17,584	23,307	24,829	26,301	23,027	na
5 or more years	30,255	na	27,454	31,713	31,060	34,072	na

Source: U.S. Department of Commerce, Bureau of the Census, *Statistical Abstract of the United States: 1990*, 110th ed. (Washington, DC: United States Government Printing Office, 1990), No. 737, p. 455.

TABLE 4.5

Education Levels of Population, 1970–1988, by Age and Sex

Age and sex	Percent of labor force with					
	Less than 4 years of high school			4 years or more of college		
	1970	1980	1988	1970	1980	1988
16–24 years	31.1	27.8	28.2	6.2	5.5	6.8
Women	26.5	24.1	24.2	7.5	6.3	7.9
Men	35.0	30.9	31.9	5.1	4.9	5.8
25–64 years	36.1	20.6	14.7	14.1	22.0	25.7
Women	33.5	20.1	12.4	11.2	18.7	23.1
Men	37.5	22.2	16.5	15.7	24.3	27.8

Sources: 16–24 yrs. old, 1970–80: U.S. Department of Labor, Bureau of Labor Statistics, *Employment and Earnings* 37 (January 1990), Table 3, p. 162; Table 6, pp. 167–68.

16–24 yrs. old, 1989: U.S. Department of Labor, Bureau of Labor Statistics, *Labor Force Statistics from the Current Population Survey, 1948-87* (Washington, DC: United States Government Printing Office, 1988), Bulletin 2307, Table B-3, p. 567; Table B-4, pp. 569–603; Table C-19, pp. 818–23; Table C-20, pp. 824–33.

25–64 yrs. old, 1970–80: Ibid., Table C-22, p. 844.

25–64 yrs. old, 1988: U.S. Department of Labor, Bureau of Labor Statistics, *Employment and Earnings* 37 (January 1990), Table 3, pp. 162–64; Table 6, pp. 167–68.

TABLE 4.6

Occupational Distribution of Employed Women, Annual Averages, Selected Years, 1975–1989 (in percentages, except as noted)

Women, 16 years and older, as a percent of total employed women, 16 and older

	1972	1975	1980	1985	1989
Total employed (in thousands)	31,257	33,989	42,117	47,259	53,027
Managerial and professional specialty	17.0	18.4	20.4	23.4	25.9
Executive, administrative, and managerial	4.6	5.2	7.2	9.2	11.1
Professional specialty	12.4	13.2	13.2	14.2	14.8
Technical, sales, and administrative support	45.0	45.6	46.0	45.5	44.2
Technicians and related support	2.4	2.7	3.0	3.3	3.3
Sales occupations	11.1	11.3	11.6	12.9	13.1
Administrative support, including clerical	31.5	31.6	31.4	29.4	27.8
Service occupations	21.2	20.8	18.9	18.5	17.7
Private household	4.5	3.4	2.5	na	1.6
Protective service	0.2	0.3	0.4	na	0.6
Service, except private household and protective	16.4	17.1	16.1	na	15.6
Precision production, craft, and repair	1.6	1.7	1.9	2.4	2.2
Operators, fabricators, and laborers	13.4	12.0	11.4	9.1	8.9
Machine operators, assemblers, and inspectors	10.6	9.2	8.5	6.7	6.4
Transportation and material moving occupations	0.5	0.6	0.7	0.8	0.8
Handlers, equipment cleaners, helpers, and laborers	2.3	2.2	2.2	1.6	1.7
Farming, forestry, and fishing	1.9	1.6	1.4	1.2	1.1

Women, 16 years and older, as a percent of all employed persons in occupation category

	1972	1975	1980	1985	1989
Total employed	38.0	39.6	42.4	44.1	45.2
Managerial and professional specialty	33.0	34.8	39.1	50.4	45.2
Executive, administrative, and managerial	19.7	21.9	29.7	35.6	39.5
Professional specialty	44.0	45.3	47.1	49.1	50.3
Technical, sales, and administrative support	59.5	61.3	63.9	36.9	64.9
Technicians and related support	38.4	41.5	43.9	47.2	48.1
Sales occupations	40.5	41.9	45.2	48.1	49.3
Administrative support, including clerical	75.0	77.2	79.6	80.2	80.0
Service occupations	61.1	61.0	60.9	60.6	60.1
Private household	97.6	97.5	97.6	na	103.3
Protective service	6.5	7.1	10.3	na	15.9
Service, except private household and protective	62.6	64.4	64.4	na	65.3
Precision production, craft, and repair	4.8	5.5	6.4	8.4	8.4
Operators, fabricators, and laborers	24.1	24.4	26.7	38.9	26.1
Machine operators, assemblers, and inspectors	38.6	38.7	40.4	40.3	41.3
Transportation and material moving occupations	3.5	4.8	6.9	8.3	8.6
Handlers, equipment cleaners, helpers, and laborers	15.4	16.9	20.0	16.8	18.3
Farming, forestry, and fishing	15.4	14.0	16.0	15.9	17.1

Source: 1972–85: U.S. Department of Labor, Bureau of Labor Statistics, *Labor Force Statistics from the Current Population Survey, 1948-87* (Washington, DC: United States Government Printing Office, 1988), Bulletin 2307, Table B-14, p. 664; Table B-15, p. 668.

Source: 1989: U.S. Department of Labor, Bureau of Labor Statistics, *Employment and Earnings* 37 (January 1990), Table 21, p. 182.

TABLE 4.7

Women's Median Earnings as a Percent of Men's for All Year-round, Full-time Workers

Year	Women's earnings as a percent of men's
1955	63.9
1956	63.3
1957	63.8
1958	63.0
1959	61.3
1960	60.8
1961	59.4
1962	59.5
1963	59.6
1964	59.6
1965	60.0
1966	58.0
1967	57.8
1968	58.2
1969	60.5
1970	59.4
1971	59.5
1972	57.9
1973	56.6
1974	58.6
1975	58.8
1976	60.2
1977	58.9
1978	59.4
1979	59.7
1980	60.2
1981	59.2
1982	61.7
1983	63.6
1984	63.7
1985	64.6
1986	64.3
1987	65.2
1988	66.0

Sources: 1955–66: U.S. Department of Labor, Bureau of Labor Statistics, *Perspectives on Working Women: A Databook* (Washington, DC: U.S. Government Printing Office, 1980), Bulletin 2080.
1967–88: U.S. Department of Commerce, Bureau of the Census, Current Population Reports, Series P–60, No. 167 (Washington, DC: U.S. Government Printing Office, 1988), Table 51, p. 76.

Notes:
1. Estimates for 1955–79 are for persons 14 years old and older; those for 1980–88 are for persons 15 years old and older.
2. Data for 1955–66 are for wage and salary workers only and exclude self-employed persons.

TABLE 4.8

Families by Employment Status of Members, Race, and Hispanic Origin, Quarterly Averages, Not Seasonally Adjusted

Characteristic	Number of families (1st quarter, in thousands) 1989	Number of families (1st quarter, in thousands) 1990	Percent distribution (1st quarter) 1989	Percent distribution (1st quarter) 1990
Total				
Total families	64,899	65,279	100.0	100.0
With no members in the labor force	10,881	10,861	16.8	16.6
With at least one member in the labor force	54,018	54,418	83.2	83.4
No member employed	1,483	1,470	2.3	2.3
Some member employed	52,535	52,948	80.9	81.1
No one unemployed	48,951	49,326	75.4	75.6
One or more employed full time	45,259	46,224	69.7	70.8
Some member unemployed	3,584	3,622	5.5	5.5
One or more employed full time	3,113	3,235	4.8	5.0
White				
Total families	55,693	55,889	100.0	100.0
With no members in the labor force	9,170	9,096	16.5	16.3
With at least one member in the labor force	46,523	46,793	83.5	83.7
No member employed	966	1,004	1.7	1.8
Some member employed	45,557	45,789	81.8	81.9
No one unemployed	42,717	42,908	76.7	76.8
One or more employed full time	39,623	40,315	71.1	72.1
Some member unemployed	2,840	2,881	5.1	5.2
One or more employed full time	2,479	2,577	4.5	4.6
Black				
Total families	7,289	7,366	100.0	100.0
With no members in the labor force	1,442	1,504	19.8	20.4
With at least one member in the labor force	5,846	5,862	80.2	79.6
No member employed	471	425	6.5	5.8
Some member employed	5,376	5,437	73.8	73.8
No one unemployed	4,750	4,824	65.2	65.5
One or more employed full time	4,240	4,408	58.2	59.8
Some member unemployed	626	613	8.6	8.3
One or more employed full time	532	544	7.3	7.4
Hispanic origin				
Total families	4,718	4,839	100.0	100.0
With no members in the labor force	703	706	14.9	14.6
With at least one member in the labor force	4,015	4,133	85.1	85.4
No member employed	147	173	3.1	3.6
Some member employed	3,868	3,960	82.0	81.8
No one unemployed	3,501	3,583	74.2	74.0
One or more employed full time	3,234	3,374	68.5	69.7
Some member unemployed	367	377	7.8	7.8
One or more employed full time	315	340	6.7	7.0

Source: Bureau of Labor Statistics, "Employment and Earnings Characteristics of Families," USDL News Release 90-202 (Washington, DC: U.S. Department of Labor, 27 April 1990).

Note: Detail for the above race and Hispanic-origin groups will not sum to totals because data for the "other races" group are not presented and Hispanics are included in both the white and black population groups.

TABLE 4.9

Families by Employment Status of Members and Type of Family, Quarterly Averages, Not Seasonally Adjusted

Characteristic	Number of families (1st quarter, in thousands) 1989	Number of families (1st quarter, in thousands) 1990	Percent distribution (1st quarter) 1989	Percent distribution (1st quarter) 1990
Married-couple families	51,023	51,413	100.0	100.0
With no members in the labor force	7,834	7,886	15.4	15.3
With at least one member in the labor force	43,190	43,526	84.6	84.7
No member employed	664	677	1.3	1.3
Some member employed	42,526	42,849	83.3	83.3
Husband only	11,105	10,956	21.8	21.3
Wife only	2,572	2,651	5.0	5.2
Husband and wife	25,225	25,550	49.4	49.7
Husband and wife only	20,206	20,857	39.6	40.6
Other combinations	3,624	3,692	7.1	7.2
Families maintained by women	10,992	10,984	100.0	100.0
With no members in the labor force	2,709	2,648	24.6	24.1
With at least one member in the labor force	8,283	8,336	75.4	75.9
No member employed	671	656	6.1	6.0
Some member employed	7,612	7,680	69.3	69.9
Householder employed	6,283	6,313	57.2	57.5
Householder only	3,993	4,107	36.3	37.4
Householder and other(s)	2,290	2,207	20.8	20.1
Other combinations	1,329	1,367	12.1	12.4
Families maintained by men	2,883	2,883	100.0	100.0
With no members in the labor force	338	327	11.7	11.3
With at least one member in the labor force	2,545	2,556	88.3	88.7
No member employed	149	137	5.2	4.8
Some member employed	2,397	2,419	83.1	83.9
Householder employed	2,059	2,078	71.4	72.1
Householder only	1,076	1,153	37.3	40.0
Householder and other(s)	983	925	34.1	32.1
Other combinations	338	340	11.7	11.8

Source: Bureau of Labor Statistics, "Employment and Earnings Characteristics of Families," USDL News Release 90–202 (Washington, DC: U.S. Department of Labor, 27 April 1990).

TABLE 4.10

Employment Status of Persons in Families by Family Relationship, Race, and Hispanic Origin, Quarterly Averages, Not Seasonally Adjusted

Characteristic	1st quarter 1989, numbers in thousands, except as indicated					1st quarter 1990, numbers in thousands, except as indicated				
	Civilian noninstitutional population	Civilian labor force participation rate	Unemployed			Civilian noninstitutional population	Civilian labor force participation rate	Unemployed		
			Level	Percent of labor force	Percent with employed family member(s)			Level	Percent of labor force	Percent with employed family member(s)
Total										
In families	148,679	66.0	5,526	5.6	69.0	149,232	66.3	5,650	5.7	69.9
In married-couple families	122,542	66.6	3,724	4.6	78.5	123,131	67.0	3,892	4.7	79.1
Husbands	51,023	78.1	1,369	3.4	64.6	51,413	77.9	1,465	3.7	66.1
Wives	51,023	57.7	1,018	3.5	83.5	51,413	58.2	1,101	3.7	83.0
Other family member(s)	20,496	60.6	1,337	10.8	89.1	20,305	61.4	1,326	10.6	90.1
In families maintained by women	20,318	61.0	1,427	11.5	47.9	20,335	61.2	1,381	11.1	47.5
Householder	10,992	62.2	559	8.2	17.2	10,984	62.4	542	7.9	14.4
Other family member(s)	9,326	59.6	868	15.6	67.7	9,351	59.8	839	15.0	68.9
In families maintained by men	5,817	70.0	375	9.2	54.1	5,768	70.0	377	9.3	57.0
Householder	2,883	77.1	165	7.4	33.0	2,883	77.0	143	6.4	32.1
Other family member(s)	2,934	62.9	210	11.4	70.7	3,885	62.9	234	9.6	72.3
White										
In families	127,496	66.4	4,078	4.8	72.6	127,715	66.8	4,262	5.0	72.7
In married-couple families	109,365	66.7	3,078	4.2	78.5	109,731	67.0	3,231	4.4	79.4
Husbands	45,980	78.1	1,155	3.2	64.1	46,240	77.9	1,231	3.4	65.8
Wives	45,926	57.0	841	3.2	83.9	46,246	57.5	917	3.4	83.4
Other family member(s)	17,459	62.1	1,082	10.0	89.6	17,265	63.1	1,083	9.9	91.4
In families maintained by women	13,654	63.1	755	8.8	52.7	13,441	63.5	740	8.7	48.5
Householder	7,448	63.6	297	6.3	21.0	7,361	63.5	279	6.0	18.3
Other family member(s)	6,206	62.5	458	11.8	73.4	6,080	63.6	461	11.9	66.8
In families maintained by men	4,477	70.5	245	7.8	59.6	4,543	72.1	290	8.9	60.0
Householder	2,235	77.7	108	6.2	39.4	2,267	79.3	105	5.8	35.4
Other family member(s)	2,242	63.3	137	9.7	75.3	2,276	64.9	185	12.5	74.2
Black										
In families	16,201	63.2	1,269	12.4	57.4	16,349	62.6	1,200	11.7	59.4
In married-couple families	9,026	67.0	510	8.4	79.6	9,141	66.9	514	8.4	77.4
Husbands	3,525	76.4	162	6.0	68.2	3,594	75.9	175	6.4	66.4
Wives	3,449	65.3	141	6.3	82.2	3,507	65.6	138	6.0	80.5
Other family member(s)	2,052	53.5	207	18.9	66.8	2,040	53.2	201	18.5	83.9
In families maintained by women	6,119	56.8	644	18.5	42.5	6,281	56.6	615	17.3	46.5
Householder	3,247	59.6	249	12.9	13.1	3,301	60.4	254	12.7	10.6
Other family member(s)	2,872	53.7	395	25.6	61.1	2,980	52.4	361	23.1	71.7
In families maintained by men	1,056	68.9	114	15.7	42.1	927	60.3	70	12.5	44.3
Householder	534	76.0	51	12.6	a	491	67.3	30	9.1	a
Other family member(s)	522	61.8	63	19.5	60.7	436	52.5	40	17.5	a
Hispanic origin										
In families	11,249	65.2	583	7.9	69.8	11,703	64.5	619	8.2	67.4
In married-couple families	8,369	65.9	400	7.3	74.0	8,829	65.6	419	7.2	75.7
Husbands	3,222	85.7	132	4.8	53.8		83.2	147	5.3	54.0
Wives	3,382	52.8	121	6.8	80.8	3,485	52.8	125	6.8	83.6
Other family member(s)	1,765	54.9	147	15.2	86.3	1,986	58.4	147	12.7	90.2
In families maintained by women	2,098	58.0	146	12.0	59.6	2,091	54.1	138	12.2	39.1
Householder	1,141	56.1	58	9.1	a	1,132	52.2	61	10.3	11.7
Other family member(s)	957	60.2	88	15.3	80.2	959	56.3	77	14.3	61.6
In families maintained by men	782	76.0	37	6.2	a	783	79.7	62	9.9	74.2
Householder	356	83.6	13	4.4	a	350	87.7	22	7.2	a
Other family member(s)	426	69.5	24	8.1	a	438	73.2	40	12.5	a

Source: Bureau of Labor Statistics, "Employment and Earnings Characteristics of Families," USDL News Release 90-202 (Washington, DC: U.S. Department of Labor, 27 April 1990).

[a] Data not shown where base is less than 60,000.

Note: Detail for the above race and Hispanic-origin groups will not sum to totals because data for the "other races" group are not presented and Hispanics are included in both the white and black population groups.

TABLE 4.11

Families with Wage and Salary Earners by Race, Type of Family, and Median Usual Weekly Wage and Salary Earnings, Quarterly Averages, Not Seasonally Adjusted

Characteristic	Number of families (1st quarter, in thousands) 1989	1990	Percent distribution (1st quarter) 1989	1990	Median weekly earnings (1st quarter, in dollars) 1989	1990
Total						
Families with wage or salary earners	43,317	43,657	100.0	100.0	$605	$644
One earner	18,642	18,643	43.0	42.7	367	387
Two or more earners	24,676	25,013	57.0	57.3	794	841
Married-couple families	33,877	34,060	100.0	100.0	678	723
One earner	12,419	12,264	36.7	36.0	420	453
Husband	9,283	9,165	27.4	27.0	494	525
Wife	2,443	2,392	7.2	7.0	265	267
Other family member	693	707	2.0	2.1	225	269
Two or more earners	21,458	21,796	63.3	64.0	824	873
Husband and wife only	15,545	15,798	45.9	46.4	790	836
Husband, wife, and other family member(s)	3,498	3,551	10.3	10.4	1,097	1,131
Husband and other family member(s)	1,699	1,728	5.0	5.1	768	816
Wife and other family member(s)	560	533	1.7	1.6	499	596
Other family member(s) only	156	187	0.5	0.5	589	593
Families maintained by women	7,362	7,512	100.0	100.0	344	358
One earner	5,016	5,103	68.1	67.9	272	284
Householder	3,969	4,051	53.9	53.9	278	292
Other family member	1,046	1,052	14.2	14.0	242	254
Two or more earners	2,347	2,408	31.9	32.1	567	614
Families maintained by men	2,078	2,085	100.0	100.0	482	512
One earner	1,207	1,276	58.1	61.2	347	380
Householder	964	1,017	46.4	48.8	396	407
Other family member	243	259	11.7	12.4	247	257
Two or more earners	870	809	41.9	38.8	672	769
White						
Families with wage or salary earners	36,968	37,060	100.0	100.0	626	672
One earner	15,557	15,351	42.1	41.4	389	412
Two or more earners	21,411	21,710	58.0	58.6	803	856
Married-couple families	30,167	30,201	100.0	100.0	687	736
One earner	11,111	10,943	36.8	36.2	436	474
Husband	8,434	8,326	28.0	28.0	503	547
Wife	2,088	2,004	6.9	6.6	270	273
Two or more earners	19,056	19,257	63.2	63.8	831	883
Husband and wife only	13,831	13,997	45.8	46.3	795	846
Families maintained by women	5,200	5,202	100.0	100.0	355	385
One earner	3,496	3,425	67.2	65.8	283	296
Two or more earners	1,703	1,777	32.8	34.2	572	617
Families maintained by men	1,601	1,658	100.0	100.0	490	527
One earner	950	982	59.3	59.2	370	391
Two or more earners	652	676	40.7	40.8	670	787
Black						
Families with wage or salary earners	5,027	5,161	100.0	100.0	438	439
One earner	2,530	2,730	50.3	52.9	267	283
Two or more earners	2,497	2,431	49.7	47.1	685	715
Married-couple families	2,624	2,721	100.0	100.0	572	590
One earner	890	938	33.9	34.5	297	303
Husband	560	552	21.3	20.3	347	340
Wife	280	311	10.7	11.4	223	238
Two or more earners	1,734	1,782	66.1	65.5	740	764
Husband and wife only	1,257	1,265	47.9	46.5	727	738
Families maintained by women	2,011	2,099	100.0	100.0	308	308
One earner	1,420	1,546	70.6	73.7	238	263
Two or more earners	591	553	29.4	26.3	551	590
Families maintained by men	392	341	100.0	100.0	454	419
One earner	220	245	56.1	71.8	301	340
Two or more earners	172	95	43.9	27.9	775	a

Source: Bureau of Labor Statistics, "Employment and Earnings Characteristics of Families," USDL News Release 90-202 (Washington, DC: U.S. Department of Labor, 27 April 1990).

[a] Data not shown where base is less than 60,000.

TABLE 4.12

All Households and Family Households, by Total Money Income in 1988, Levels and Percent Distributions

Income level in 1988 by race and Hispanic origin	All households %	All households Level	Family households Total %	Family households Total Level	Married couple %	Married couple Level	Other family, male head %	Other family, male head Level	Other family, female head %	Other family, female head Level
All households	100.0	92,830	100.0	65,837	100.0	52,100	100.0	2,847	100.0	10,890
White	85.9	79,734	85.8	56,492	90.0	46,877	79.9	2,274	67.4	7,342
Black	11.4	10,561	11.3	7,409	7.1	3,722	16.3	464	29.6	3,223
Hispanic origin	6.4	5,910	7.3	4,823	6.5	3,398	11.0	314	10.2	1,112
$0,000–$9,999	100.0	15,743	100.0	6,844	100.0	2,950	100.0	183	100.0	3,580
White	74.7	11,766	67.6	4,627	82.2	2,426	74.3	136	55.2	1,976
Black	22.6	3,561	28.7	1,964	13.4	395	22.4	41	41.6	1,491
Hispanic origin	8.8	1,391	13.8	943	13.6	400	8.7	16	14.1	504
$10,000–$19,999	100.0	18,642	100.0	11,661	100.0	8,190	100.0	618	100.0	2,852
White	83.9	15,632	81.8	9,540	87.8	7,190	71.4	441	67.0	1,910
Black	13.4	2,498	15.2	1,767	9.1	745	26.1	161	30.2	861
Hispanic origin	8.1	1,516	10.7	1,249	10.6	872	15.5	96	9.9	281
$20,000–$29,999	100.0	16,075	100.0	11,523	100.0	9,052	100.0	565	100.0	1,906
White	87.1	14,005	86.8	9,997	89.8	8,129	77.7	439	75.0	1,429
Black	10.5	1,689	10.7	1,236	7.7	693	17.3	98	23.3	445
Hispanic origin	7.0	1,121	8.1	928	8.0	727	9.6	54	7.8	148
$30,000–$39,999	100.0	13,398	100.0	10,536	100.0	8,934	100.0	473	100.0	1,129
White	89.3	11,962	88.9	9,370	90.5	8,081	87.1	412	77.7	877
Black	8.0	1,074	8.4	884	7.0	624	9.3	44	19.2	217
Hispanic origin	5.6	748	6.2	656	5.7	510	13.7	65	7.3	82
$40,000–$49,999	100.0	9,638	100.0	8,126	100.0	7,117	100.0	380	100.0	629
White	90.1	8,685	89.9	7,308	91.3	6,495	80.0	304	80.8	508
Black	7.2	695	7.4	603	6.4	453	15.0	57	14.8	93
Hispanic origin	5.1	490	5.6	459	5.4	386	7.4	28	7.0	44
$50,000–$59,999	100.0	6,811	100.0	5,956	100.0	5,421	100.0	203	100.0	332
White	91.5	6,232	91.4	5,442	91.9	4,984	93.6	190	80.4	267
Black	6.5	440	6.8	405	6.3	341	4.4	9	16.3	54
Hispanic origin	3.7	249	3.9	233	3.6	197	5.4	11	7.5	25
$60,000–$69,999	100.0	4,243	100.0	3,795	100.0	3,518	100.0	98	100.0	178
White	90.0	3,820	90.1	3,418	91.1	3,206	89.8	88	70.2	125
Black	6.3	266	6.3	239	5.7	199	3.1	3	20.8	37
Hispanic origin	3.3	142	3.4	129	3.2	113	5.1	5	6.2	11
$70,000–$79,999	100.0	2,622	100.0	2,368	100.0	2,188	100.0	69	100.0	111
White	91.8	2,406	91.2	2,160	91.5	2,002	88.4	61	86.5	96
Black	4.5	118	4.7	112	4.6	100	7.2	5	6.3	7
Hispanic origin	3.1	81	3.1	73	2.8	62	8.7	6	4.5	5
$80,000–$89,999	100.0	1,595	100.0	1,413	100.0	1,326	100.0	40	100.0	47
White	92.7	1,478	92.2	1,303	92.6	1,228	82.5	33	89.4	42
Black	4.1	66	4.3	61	3.8	51	15.0	6	6.4	3
Hispanic origin	2.9	47	3.2	45	3.2	43	5.0	2	2.1	1
$90,000–$99,999	100.0	1,113	100.0	1,020	100.0	939	100.0	27	100.0	54
White	91.0	1,013	91.3	931	91.2	856	100.0	27	90.7	49
Black	4.5	50	3.9	40	3.7	35	0.0	0	9.3	5
Hispanic origin	4.2	47	4.2	43	3.1	29	22.2	6	14.8	8
$100,000 and over	100.0	2,948	100.0	2,594	100.0	2,463	100.0	59	100.0	72
White	92.7	2,734	92.3	2,395	92.5	2,278	91.5	54	86.1	62
Black	3.5	103	3.7	97	3.5	85	3.4	2	13.9	10
Hispanic origin	2.6	77	2.6	67	2.4	60	3.4	2	5.6	4

TABLE 4.12, cont'd.

All Households and Family Households, by Total Money Income in 1988, Levels and Percent Distributions

Income level in 1988 by race and Hispanic origin	All households %	All households Level	Family households Total %	Family households Total Level	Married couple %	Married couple Level	Other family, male head %	Other family, male head Level	Other family, female head %	Other family, female head Level
All households	100.0	92,830	100.0	65,837	100.0	52,100	100.0	2,847	100.0	10,890
White	100.0	79,734	100.0	56,492	100.0	46,877	100.0	2,274	100.0	7,342
Black	100.0	10,561	100.0	7,409	100.0	3,722	100.0	464	100.0	3,223
Hispanic origin	100.0	5,910	100.0	4,823	100.0	3,398	100.0	314	100.0	1,112
$0,000–$9,999	17.0	15,743	10.4	6,844	5.7	2,950	6.4	183	32.9	3,580
White	14.8	11,766	8.2	4,627	5.2	2,426	6.0	136	26.9	1,976
Black	33.7	3,561	26.5	1,964	10.6	395	8.8	41	46.3	1,491
Hispanic origin	23.5	1,391	19.6	943	11.8	400	5.1	16	45.3	504
$10,000–$19,999	20.1	18,642	17.7	11,661	15.7	8,190	21.7	618	26.2	2,852
White	19.6	15,632	16.9	9,540	15.3	7,190	19.4	441	26.0	1,910
Black	23.7	2,498	23.8	1,767	20.0	745	34.7	161	26.7	861
Hispanic origin	25.7	1,516	25.9	1,249	25.7	872	30.6	96	25.3	281
$20,000–$29,999	17.3	16,075	17.5	11,523	17.4	9,052	19.8	565	17.5	1,906
White	17.6	14,005	17.7	9,997	17.3	8,129	19.3	439	19.5	1,429
Black	16.0	1,689	16.7	1,236	18.6	693	21.1	98	13.8	445
Hispanic origin	19.0	1,121	19.2	928	21.4	727	17.2	54	13.3	148
$30,000–$39,999	14.4	13,398	16.0	10,536	17.1	8,934	16.6	473	10.4	1,129
White	15.0	11,962	16.6	9,370	17.2	8,081	18.1	412	11.9	877
Black	10.2	1,074	11.9	884	16.8	624	9.5	44	6.7	217
Hispanic origin	12.7	748	13.6	656	15.0	510	20.7	65	7.4	82
$40,000–$49,999	10.4	9,638	12.3	8,126	13.7	7,117	13.3	380	5.8	629
White	10.9	8,685	12.9	7,308	13.9	6,495	13.4	304	6.9	508
Black	6.6	695	8.1	603	12.2	453	12.3	57	2.9	93
Hispanic origin	8.3	490	9.5	459	11.4	386	8.9	28	4.0	44
$50,000–$59,999	7.3	6,811	9.0	5,956	10.4	5,421	7.1	203	3.0	332
White	7.8	6,232	9.6	5,442	10.6	4,984	8.4	190	3.6	267
Black	4.2	440	5.5	405	9.2	341	1.9	9	1.7	54
Hispanic origin	4.2	249	4.8	233	5.8	197	3.5	11	2.2	25
$60,000–$69,999	4.6	4,243	5.8	3,795	6.8	3,518	3.4	98	1.6	178
White	4.8	3,820	6.1	3,418	6.8	3,206	3.9	88	1.7	125
Black	2.5	266	3.2	239	5.3	199	0.6	3	1.1	37
Hispanic origin	2.4	142	2.7	129	3.3	113	1.6	5	1.0	11
$70,000–$79,999	2.8	2,622	3.6	2,368	4.2	2,188	2.4	69	1.0	111
White	3.0	2,406	3.8	2,160	4.3	2,002	2.7	61	1.3	96
Black	1.1	118	1.5	112	2.7	100	1.1	5	0.2	7
Hispanic origin	1.4	81	1.5	73	1.8	62	1.9	6	0.4	5
$80,000–$89,999	1.7	1,595	2.1	1,413	2.5	1,326	1.4	40	0.4	47
White	1.9	1,478	2.3	1,303	2.6	1,228	1.5	33	0.6	42
Black	0.6	66	0.8	61	1.4	51	1.3	6	0.1	3
Hispanic origin	0.8	47	0.9	45	1.3	43	0.6	2	0.1	1
$90,000–$99,999	1.2	1,113	1.5	1,020	1.8	939	0.9	27	0.5	54
White	1.3	1,013	1.6	931	1.8	856	1.2	27	0.7	49
Black	0.5	50	0.5	40	0.9	35	0.0	0	0.2	5
Hispanic origin	0.8	47	0.9	43	0.9	29	1.9	6	0.7	8
$100,000 and over	3.2	2,948	3.9	2,594	4.7	2,463	2.1	59	0.7	72
White	3.4	2,734	4.2	2,395	4.9	2,278	2.4	54	0.8	62
Black	1.0	103	1.3	97	2.3	85	0.4	2	0.3	10
Hispanic origin	1.3	77	1.4	67	1.8	60	0.6	2	0.4	4

TABLE 4.12, cont'd.

All Households and Family Households, by Total Money Income in 1988, Summary Statistics

Income level in 1988 by race and Hispanic origin	All households	Total	Married couple	Other family, male head	Other family, female head
Median income (in dollars)					
All races	27,225	32,491	36,436	28,642	16,051
White	28,781	34,222	36,883	30,689	18,685
Black	16,407	19,823	30,424	19,501	10,995
Hispanic origin	20,359	22,157	25,769	23,656	11,321
Mean income (in dollars)					
All races	34,017	38,913	42,875	34,291	21,167
White	35,468	40,603	43,471	36,430	23,582
Black	22,477	25,689	34,758	23,560	15,524
Hispanic origin	25,993	27,819	31,361	27,880	16,982
Income per household member					
All races	12,976	12,176	13,265	11,359	6,900
White	13,751	12,933	13,650	12,394	8,095
Black	7,978	7,351	9,699	7,159	4,538
Hispanic origin	7,703	7,275	7,924	7,806	4,869
Gini ratio of income inequality					
All races	0.425	0.391	0.362	0.388	0.450
White	0.415	0.378	0.359	0.384	0.430
Black	0.466	0.443	0.365	0.374	0.467
Hispanic origin	0.434	0.419	0.386	0.366	0.487

Households (in thousands, except as indicated)

Source: U.S. Bureau of the Census, Current Population Reports, Series P-60, No. 166 (Washington, DC: U.S. Government Printing Office, 1989), Table 3, pp. 25–26.

Notes:

1. Two different distributions of the data are presented in Table 4.12. The first page presents a distribution by race or Hispanic-origin category for each income interval. The second page presents a distribution by income interval for each race or Hispanic-origin category. The final page presents several summary statistics for each household type.

2. The Gini coefficient is a common measure of inequality in the distribution of income among the population, broken up into income classes. A value of 0 indicates perfect equality, a value of 1 indicates perfect inequality.

TABLE 4.13

Earnings Growth in Families with Children by Family Type and Earner, 1973–79 and 1979–87

Numbers in percentages						
	\multicolumn{6}{c}{Families without children}					
Earner	Married couple		Single mother		Single father	
	1973–79	1979–87	1973–79	1979–87	1973–79	1979–87
Annual earnings growth						
All earners	6.0	2.2	31.1	-7.7	-15.5	-11.5
Adult men	-0.3	-5.0	na	na	na	-10.9
Adult women	42.6	32.3	31.4	-7.8	-15.6	na
Weekly earnings growth						
All earners	-2.9	-5.1	5.4	-0.4	-11.7	-2.1
Adult men	-0.4	-3.6	na	na	-11.8	-2.5
Adult women	7.7	8.4	5.4	-1.0	na	na
Change in annual weeks employed						
All earners	7.5	6.9	21.7	-9.3	-5.9	-10.9
Adult men	-1.0	-1.7	na	na	-6.4	-7.2
Adult women	30.1	23.6	22.3	-9.2	na	na
Change in annual weeks employed (number of weeks)						
All earners	5.1	5.0	5.6	-2.9	-2.9	-5.0
Adult men	-0.5	-0.8	na	na	-3.0	-3.1
Adult women	5.2	5.3	5.6	-2.8	na	na

Reprinted with permission from Lawrence Mishel and David Frankel, *The State of Working America* (Washington, DC: Economic Policy Institute, 1990), p. 204.

TABLE 4.14

Earnings Growth in Families without Children by Family Type and Earner, 1973–79 and 1979–87

Numbers in percentages						
	\multicolumn{6}{c}{Families without children}					
Earner	Married couple		Single mother		Single father	
	1973-79	1979-87	1973-79	1979-87	1973-79	1979-87
Annual earnings growth						
All earners	6.4	5.1	-0.6	1.7	0.1	5.8
Adult men	3.0	0.2	-0.6	1.7	na	na
Adult women	11.6	10.2	na	na	0.1	5.8
Weekly earnings growth						
All earners	0.6	2.3	-3.1	0.6	-0.5	5.2
Adult men	0.6	-0.2	na	na	-0.5	5.2
Adult women	5.7	10.3	-3.1	0.6	na	na
Change in annual weeks employed						
All earners	4.8	2.5	-0.1	0.7	1.5	1.0
Adult men	2.0	1.3	-0.1	0.7	na	na
Adult women	6.8	-1.3	na	na	1.5	1.0
Change in annual weeks employed (number of weeks)						
All earners	4.1	2.3	0.0	0.3	0.7	0.5
Adult men	0.9	0.6	0.0	0.3	na	na
Adult women	2.4	-0.5	na	na	0.7	0.5

Reprinted with permission from Lawrence Mishel and David Frankel, *The State of Working America* (Washington, DC: Economic Policy Institute, 1990), p. 206.

TABLE 5.1

Total Fertility Rates in 10 Countries, Selected Years, 1921–88

Country	1921	1941	1951	1961	1971	1981	1988
United States	3.3	2.3	3.2	3.6	2.3	1.8	1.9
Canada	4.0	2.8	3.5	3.8	2.2	1.7	1.7
Japan	5.3	4.5	3.2	1.9	2.1	1.7	1.6
Denmark	3.1	2.2	2.5	2.5	2.0	1.4	1.6
France	2.6	1.8	2.8	2.8	2.5	2.0	1.8
Germany	na	na	2.1	2.5	1.9	1.4	1.4
Italy	na	2.7	2.3	2.4	2.4	1.6	1.3
Netherlands	3.5[a]	2.6	3.0	3.2	2.4	1.6	1.5
Sweden	2.7	1.9	2.2	2.2	2.0	1.6	2.0
United Kingdom	2.7	1.7	2.1	2.8	2.4	1.8	1.8

Source: Constance Sorrentino, "The Changing Family in International Perspective," *Monthly Labor Review* 113, (March 1990), p. 42.

[a] 1921–25 average

Note: The total fertility rate is defined as the average number of children that would be born per woman if all women lived to the end of their childbearing years and at each year of age they experienced the birth rates ocurring in the specified year.

TABLE 5.2

Distribution of Population by Age in 10 Countries, 1950–90

Country	1950	1960	1970	1980	1990[a]
United States					
Birth to 14 years	26.9	31.1	28.3	22.5	21.8
15 to 64 years	64.9	59.7	61.9	66.2	66.0
65 years and older	8.1	9.2	9.8	11.3	12.2
Canada					
Birth to 14 years	29.7	33.6	30.3	23.0	20.8
15 to 64 years	62.6	59.0	61.7	67.5	67.9
65 years and older	7.6	7.5	8.0	9.5	11.4
Japan					
Birth to 14 years	35.3	30.2	23.9	23.6	18.3
15 to 64 years	59.5	64.1	69.0	67.4	70.3
65 years and older	5.2	5.7	7.1	9.0	11.4
Denmark					
Birth to 14 years	26.3	25.2	23.3	20.9	16.8
15 to 64 years	64.5	64.2	64.4	64.7	67.9
65 years and older	9.1	10.6	12.3	14.4	15.3
France					
Birth to 14 years	22.7	26.4	24.8	22.4	20.3
15 to 64 years	65.9	62.0	62.3	63.7	65.9
65 years and older	11.3	11.6	12.9	13.9	13.8
Germany					
Birth to 14 years	23.5	21.3	23.2	18.2	15.1
15 to 64 years	67.1	67.8	63.6	66.3	69.4
65 years and older	9.3	10.8	13.2	15.5	15.5
Italy					
Birth to 14 years	26.4	23.4	22.9	20.5	17.8
15 to 64 years	65.5	67.6	66.5	66.7	68.4
65 years and older	8.0	9.0	10.5	12.9	13.8
Netherlands					
Birth to 14 years	29.3	30.0	27.3	22.3	18.1
15 to 64 years	62.9	61.0	62.6	66.2	69.2
65 years and older	7.7	9.0	10.2	11.5	12.7
Sweden					
Birth to 14 years	23.4	22.4	20.9	19.6	17.2
15 to 64 years	66.3	65.9	65.5	64.1	65.0
65 years and older	10.2	11.8	13.7	16.3	17.7
United Kingdom					
Birth to 14 years	22.3	23.4	24.1	21.0	19.1
15 to 64 years	66.9	66.4	62.9	64.1	65.8
65 years and older	10.7	11.7	13.0	14.9	15.1

Source: Constance Sorrentino, "The Changing Family in International Perspective," *Monthly Labor Review* 113 (March 1990), p. 43.

[a] Projected

TABLE 5.3

Average Number of Members per Household, 10 Countries, Selected Years, 1960–88

Country	1960	1970	1977	1985–88[a]
United States	3.3	3.1	2.9	2.6
Canada	3.9	3.5	2.9[b]	2.8
Japan	4.1	3.4	3.3[c]	3.1
Denmark	2.9	2.7	na	2.3
France	3.1	2.9	2.8	2.6
Germany	2.9	2.7	2.5	2.3
Italy	3.6	3.4	3.1	2.8
Netherlands	3.6	3.2	2.9	2.5
Sweden	2.8	2.6	2.4[c]	2.2
United Kingdom[d]	3.1	2.9	2.7	2.6

Source: Constance Sorrentino, "The Changing Family in International Perspective," *Monthly Labor Review* 113 (March 1990), p. 46.

[a] 1988 for the United States, Denmark, and France; 1987 for Germany, Italy, and the Netherlands; 1986 for Canada and the United Kingdom; 1985 for Japan and Sweden.
[b] 1981
[c] 1975
[d] Great Britain only (excludes Northern Ireland).

TABLE 5.4

Marriage and Divorce Rates in 10 Countries, Selected Years, 1960–86

Marriage rates
(per 1,000 population, ages 15 to 64)

Country	1960	1970	1980	1986
United States	14.1	17.0	15.9[a]	15.1
Canada	12.4	14.3	11.8	10.2
Japan	14.5	14.4	9.8	8.6
Denmark	12.2	11.5	7.9	9.0
France	11.3	12.4	9.7	7.3
Germany	13.9	11.5	8.9	8.7
Italy	11.7	11.3	8.7	7.5
Netherlands	12.7	15.2	9.6	8.7
Sweden	10.2	8.2	7.1	7.2
United Kingdom	11.5	13.5	11.6	10.6

Divorce rates
(per 1,000 married women)

Country	1960	1970	1980	1986
United States	9.2	14.9	22.6	21.2
Canada	1.8	6.3	10.9	12.9
Japan	3.6	3.9	4.8	5.4
Denmark	5.9	7.6	11.2	12.8
France	2.9	3.3	6.3	8.5
Germany	3.6	5.1	6.1	8.3
Italy	na	1.3	0.8	1.1
Netherlands	2.2	3.3	7.5	8.7
Sweden	5.0	6.8	11.4	11.7
United Kingdom	2.0	4.7	12.0	12.9

Source: Constance Sorrentino, "The Changing Family in International Perspective," *Monthly Labor Review* 113 (March 1990), p. 46.

[a] Beginning in 1980, includes unlicensed marriages registered in California.

TABLE 5.5

Average Number of Members per Household, 10 Countries, Selected Years, 1960–1988

Country	1960	1970	1980	1986	Percent change, 1960–86 All live births	Percent change, 1960–86 Births to unmarried women
United States	5.3	10.7	18.4	23.4	-12	292
Canada	4.3	9.6	11.3	16.9	-22	209
Japan	1.2	0.9	0.8	1.0	-14	-26
Denmark	7.8	11.0	33.2	43.9	-27	308
France	6.1	6.8	11.4	21.9	-5	243
Germany	6.3	5.5	7.6	9.6	-55	-2
Italy	2.4	2.2	4.3	5.6	-39	41
Netherlands	1.3	2.1	4.1	8.8	-23	403
Sweden	11.3	18.4	39.7	48.4	0	329
United Kingdom[a]	5.2	8.0	11.5	21.0	-18	231

Source: Constance Sorrentino, "The Changing Family in International Perspective," *Monthly Labor Review* 113 (March 1990), p. 45.

[a] Great Britain only (excludes Northern Ireland).

TABLE 5.6

Percent Distribution of Households by Type, 9 Countries, Selected Years, 1960–86

Country	Married-couple households[a] Total	With children[b]	Without children[b]	Single-parent households[b]	One-person households	Other households[c]
United States						
1960	74.3	44.2	30.1	4.4	13.1	8.2
1970	70.5	4.0	30.3	5.0	17.1	7.4
1980	60.8	30.9	29.9	7.5	22.7	9.0
1987	57.6	27.5	30.0	8.1	23.6	10.7
1988	56.9	27.0	29.9	8.0	24.0	11.1
Canada						
1961	78.0[d]	50.8[d]	26.7[d]	3.8[d]	9.3	8.9[d]
1971	74.0	46.5	27.5	4.5	13.4	8.1
1981	66.8	36.3	30.5	5.3	20.3	7.6
1986	64.5	32.3	32.2	5.6	21.5	8.4
Japan						
1960	65.3	49.4	15.9	3.1	17.2	14.4
1970	64.3	44.6	19.7	2.3	20.3	13.1
1980	68.4	42.9	25.6	2.2	19.8	9.6
1985	67.4	39.2	28.2	2.5	20.8	9.3
Denmark[e]						
1976	44.5	23.5	21.0	4.9	na	na
1983	43.7	22.6	21.1	5.4	na	na
1988	41.0	19.9	21.1	5.1	na	na
France						
1968	70.1	43.6	26.5	4.2	20.3	5.4
1975	68.8	42.1	26.8	4.1	22.1	5.0
1982	67.0	39.7	27.2	4.3	24.6	4.1
1988	63.4	36.2	27.3	5.1	27.1	4.4
Germany						
1971	66.7	44.3	22.4	10.8	20.6	1.9
1970	64.8	41.7	23.1	6.2	26.5	2.5
1980	60.5	37.0	23.5	6.6	30.2	2.7
1988	54.3	31.4	22.9	6.7	34.9	4.1
Netherlands						
1961	77.6	55.4	22.3	5.7	11.9	4.8
1971	74.1	51.8	22.3	5.1	17.1	3.7
1981	66.5	43.7	22.9	6.1	21.4	6.0
1985	60.0	38.5	21.5	6.7	27.8	5.5
Sweden						
1960	66.4	35.7	30.6	3.5	20.2	9.9
1970	64.3	30.2	34.1	3.2	25.3	7.2
1980	57.9	24.8	33.1	3.1	32.8	6.2
1985	54.8	21.7	33.1	3.2	36.1	5.9
United Kingdom[f]						
1961	73.7	37.8	36.0	2.3	11.9	12.1
1971	69.7	34.4	35.2	2.8	18.1	9.4
1981	64.3	30.5	33.7	4.7	21.8	9.2
1987	64.0	28.0	36.0	4.0	25.0	7.0

Source: Constance Sorrentino, "The Changing Family in International Perspective," *Monthly Labor Review* 113 (March 1990), p. 47.

[a] May include unmarried cohabiting couples. Such couples are explicitly included under married couples in Canada (beginning in 1981) and France. For Sweden, beginning in 1980, all cohabitants are included as married couples, and the figures for 1970 have been adjusted to include all cohabitants. The 1960 data have not been adjusted, but the number of unmarried cohabitants was insignificant in 1960. For Denmark, from 1983 onward, persons reported separately as living in consensual unions with joint children have been classified as married couples. There was no separate reporting of such persons in 1976. In other countries, some unmarried cohabitants are included as married couples, while some are classified under "other households," depending on responses to surveys and censuses.

[b] Children are defined as unmarried children living at home according to the following age limits: Under 18 years old in the United States, Canada, Japan, Denmark, and the United Kingdom, except that the United Kingdom includes 16- and 17-year-olds only if they are in full-time education; under 25 years old in France; under 16 years old in Sweden; and children of all ages in Germany and the Netherlands.

[c] Includes both family and nonfamily households not elsewhere classified. These households comprise, for example, siblings residing together, other households composed of relatives, and households made up of roommates. Some unmarried cohabiting couples may also be included in the "other" group (see note a above).

[d] Estimated by the Bureau of Labor Statistics, based on ratios of adjusted to unadjusted series in 1971. For more details, see source.

[e] From family-based statistics. However, one person living alone constitutes a family in Denmark. In this respect, the Danish data are closer to household statistics.

[f] Great Britain only (excludes Northern Ireland).

Appendix B
Related Family Service America Research Projects

Family Service America (FSA) recently conducted two national studies, the Adolescent Family Project and American Families in Trouble, that indicate many American families have minimal financial and social resources for coping with the problems confronting them. Results from the studies suggest that a greater investment in and commitment to helping economically vulnerable families are essential if human service organizations are to meet the needs of these families.

The Adolescent Family Project found that poor families with pregnant and parenting teens have multiple problems and need multifaceted services, often for the whole family. Nonetheless, program funding falls short of meeting their needs. Similarly, the American Families in Trouble study found that families coming to FSA agencies have changed drastically over the past 20 years. Single parents and single elderly people constitute an increasing number of clients and, in general, families seeking assistance have become poorer and more vulnerable. Since 1970, special programs have been developed by member agencies to assist families experiencing family violence and abuse, substance abuse, single parenting difficulties, work-related problems, health problems, and AIDS, all of which have increased drastically in the past two decades. The average number of problems families in this study brought to FSA agencies was three, indicating that comprehensive care from human service agencies is essential to meet the needs of these vulnerable families.

Adolescent Family Project

The Adolescent Family Project, funded in part by the Prudential Foundation, examined five pregnant and parenting teen programs across the nation for more than two years. The five family service agencies were Families First, Atlanta, Georgia; Child and Family Service, Honolulu, Hawaii; Family Service Association of Nassau County, Hempstead, New York; Child and Family Services of Knox County, Knoxville, Tennessee; and Family Service of Milwaukee, Milwaukee, Wisconsin. The main purpose of the project was to determine whether family involvement in the programs, which usually included the teen's mother and/or the father of the baby, resulted in more positive outcomes. The goals of the teen-parent programs were to promote family stability by helping the teen mother to keep the baby and herself healthy, develop good parenting skills, stay in school or get a job, find adequate child care, maintain a stable living environment, develop good interpersonal relationships with other family members, and to delay a second pregnancy.

Preliminary reports of the study indicate that family involvement in these programs was very difficult to achieve. A large proportion of the mothers of the parenting teens were not available because the mothers were single and working. Relations between the teen and her mother and/or boyfriend were strained and sometimes abusive. For this and other reasons, many teens moved out of their homes and sometimes away from the area. In addition, some family members simply did not want to be involved in agency programs; others lacked transportation to attend meetings. On the other hand, parenting adolescents with supportive families who were involved in the programs appeared to have better outcomes. These teenagers were more likely to stay in school, delay a second pregnancy, live at home in a more stable environment, and have better family relations.

The Adolescent Family Project study also found that many teenage parents served came from dysfunctional families in which several family members needed services in order to meet their own needs. These families required a great deal of time and resources from the agencies and often their needs went beyond the scope of the teen-parent programs. The majority of these families were poor. More than 90% of the families received one or more types of public assistance, including aid from the Women, Infants and Children program, Medicaid, Aid to Families with Dependent Children, and food stamps. One in four families indicated that their family income was inadequate to pay for food, housing, and other basic needs. Program staff thus spent a large proportion of their time assisting these families in obtaining housing, government assistance, and other resources.

Funding for the programs to help parenting teens and their families was unstable. During the course of the study, one program's funds were cut entirely, and another's were greatly reduced. The majority of the funds for these programs came from federal and state governments. Other funders included the United Way and foundations. Several funders restricted the scope of family involvement by limiting funds only to the teens, requiring such large case loads that the staff members were inhibited from working with whole families, or by setting priorities that placed working with families low on the list. For example, one agency was funded mainly by the health department, whose chief interest was that the teens keep their medical appointments. However, according to the social workers who staffed the program, the teen clients failed to keep their appointments because of problems within the family. In turn, the social workers had such large case loads that they were unable to give each of the teen's families sufficient assistance.

The Adolescent Family Project concluded that (1) supportive family involvement benefits the teen and her baby; (2) many families with pregnant and parenting teens have multiple problems and need multiple services; (3) family service agencies are in a good position to coordinate multiple community services; (4) working with families takes a great deal of resources and a strong commitment on the part of agencies, communities, and funders; and (5) funding for these programs is volatile and sometimes restrictive of working with families.

American Families in Trouble

The American Families in Trouble study, funded in part by Shell Oil Company Foundation, van Amerigen Foundation, and Walter Schroeder Foundation, was conducted by FSA in order to understand better the needs of American families. Currently, as Ray Marshall has amply documented in this volume, American families are experiencing tremendous pressures and strains due to social changes, economic recession, unemployment, and other difficulties. The American Families in Trouble study assessed the needs and problems of more than 16,000 families who visited a group of family service agencies between April 30 and May 5, 1990. Eighty-two of FSA's 290 member agencies participated in this study.

The majority of the 16,446 families seeking help had multiple problems and often needed several kinds of services. The average number of serious problems families experienced was three. For instance, many families with marital problems also had parenting and school problems. Families that had members who abused drugs and alcohol were more likely also to report family violence. Elderly clients had health problems, trouble with basic management of their homes, and inadequate income.

In comparison with a similar but smaller study conducted by FSA in 1970, the American Families in Trouble survey found considerable differences in family structure and reported problems. In 1970, 73.5% of the families using family service agencies were headed by married couples, 23% by single female parents, and 3.1% by single male parents. In 1990, only 36.6% of the families were headed by married couples, whereas 42.2% were headed by single females and 12.4% by single males. Single female parents headed a large portion of the lower-income families seen by agencies in 1990. Single elderly female and male clients were also apt to be poor and vulnerable—75% of single elderly females and 64% of single elderly males in this study reported incomes of less than $10,000. Median family income for all families increased from $7,500 in 1970 to $15,000 in 1990, but in real dollars, family income has decreased. According to the annual average Consumer Price Index, a family earning $7,500 in 1970 would need to earn $18,000 in 1990 to have stayed even with inflation, indicating that the 1990 families in trouble were poorer than their counterparts in 1970.

Since 1970, several problems that plague families have increased, especially substance abuse, abuse and violence, single parenting, work-related problems, health problems, and AIDS. Family service agencies have responded by adding more diverse services and special programs. With help from the United Way and other contributors, FSA member agencies were able to lower fees for poor families. According to the 1990 study, 57% of the families served paid sliding or subsidized fees, 22% paid no fees, and 22% had third-party insurance. This illustrates Family Service America's traditional commitment to serve lower-income families and vulnerable families in general.